Student Assessment in Higher Education

A handbook for Assessing Performance

Allen H Miller • Bradford W Imrie • Kevin Cox

KOGAN
PAGE

YOURS TO HAVE AND TO HOLD
BUT NOT TO COPY

First published in 1998

Kogan Page Limited
120 Pentonville Road
London N1 9JN

British Library Cataloguing in Publication Data

A CIP record for this book is available from the British Library.

ISBN 0 7494 2797 3

Typeset by Jean Cussons Typesetting, Diss, Norfolk
Printed and bound in Great Britain by Biddles Ltd, Guildford and King's Lynn

Contents

For a list of all the ways technology has failed to improve the quality of life, please press three.

(Alice Kahn)

Introduction	*1*
Part 1: The place of assessment in higher education	**7**
1. Purposes of higher education	**9**
Introduction	9
Higher education in its social context	11
Academic functions of higher education	15
Professional/vocational functions	16
Cultural functions	19
2. Functions of assessment	**23**
Measures of potential or achievement?	23
Measuring levels of achievement – criterion vs norm referencing	24
Diagnostic assessment tests	30
Formative assessment tests	32
Summative assessment tests	33
Continuous assessment	34
Assessment as an aid to learning	35
Recording students' achievements	36
(Indirect) measures of teaching quality	38
3. Cognitive educational objectives, learning outcomes and levels of testing	**41**
Approaches to learning	41
Educational objectives	45
Bloom's cognitive objectives	47
Other cognitive taxonomies	54
Concluding comments on cognitive objectives	61

CONTENTS

4. **Measuring the outcomes of non-cognitive
   educational objectives**   **65**
   Affective objectives   65
   Psychomotor objectives   69
   Relationships between the domains of objectives   71
   Relating objectives to assessment procedures   74

5. **Stages of intellectual and ethical development**   **77**
   Dualism   77
   Multiplicity   79
   Relativism   80
   Commitment   81

Part 2: Some assessment methods   *85*

6. **Timing of assessment tasks**   **87**
   Difficulties with continuous assessment   88
   Advantages of continuous assessment   89
   Difficulties with final assessment   90
   Advantages of final assessment   91
   Timing of assignments and progress tests   92
   Decisions to be made concerning 'in-course'
     assessment   93

7. **Essays**   **95**
   Types of essays   96
   Setting essay questions   104
   Essay marking   108
   Some examples of essay topics   116
   Published criteria for grading   120
   Some concluding comments   121

8. **Theses**   **125**
   Arguments for and against a thesis in postgraduate
     studies   125
   Choice of a topic for investigation   126
   Decisions about research procedures   128
   Quality control   128
   Evaluating a literature survey   134
   Judging research skills – qualitative vs quantitative
     research   136
   Originality in a doctoral thesis   138
   Composition of the assessment panel   138
   Publication of thesis research   140

CONTENTS

9.   Objective tests   **141**
   Multiple-choice   144
   True-false   146
   Completion   147
   Multiple grid system   148
   Multiple completion   148
   Matching   149
   Relationship analysis   150
   Definitions and diagrams   151
   Compare and contrast   151
   Reviewing objective items   152
   Marking objective tests   153
   Computer-managed assessment   155

10. Assessing group projects   **159**
   Co-operative learning   159
   Team work or syndicates   160
   Examples of group projects   161
   Project assessment   164
   The comparative worth of individual contributions   165
   Self-assessment   167
   Peer assessment   169

11. Practical skills and field work   **175**
   Importance of practical experience in professional studies   175
   Assessing routine laboratory and studio work   177
   Resources and facilities   181
   Problem-based learning   182
   Interactions with clients   185
   Criteria for grading professional experience   186
   Judging creative performance   191

12. Designing a final examination   **193**
   Relation to objectives   193
   Time allowed for the final examination   194
   Facilities and resources   195
   Amount of choice allowed to students   197
   'Open-book' and similar examinations   199
   Pre-published examinations   199

Part 3: Examining assessment   *203*

13. Reporting on assessment   **205**
   The purposes   206
   Institutional memory and style   206

Student feedback   209
Class administration   209
A case study   210
Graphical representations   214
Adjusting marks   215
Assessor feedback   220
Implementing systems on an institution-wide basis   221
Computation and data entry facilities   222
Institutional integration   223
Problems of authority and access   224

14. Evaluation of assessment procedures   225
Introduction   225
Effects of assessment on learning styles and strategies   225
Cue-consciousness   230
Double marking of students' work   231
External pressures on assessment procedures   231
Validity   233
Reliability   235
The importance of evaluating assessment procedures   237

15. Academic (dis)honesty   241
Introduction   241
Plagiarism defined   242
Issues and implications   243
Regulations   245
Guidelines   246
Context   247
Code of ethics   248
Student development and perception   248
Quality assurance   250
Some definitions   251

16. Current and future developments   253
Introduction   253
Teaching and learning quality process review (TLQPR)   254
Computer-based examination/assessment   255
Expert system project assessment (THESYS)   258
Student portfolios and student development   259
Ethics   262
Quality assurance and assessment expertise   262

References   *265*

Index   *281*

Introduction

Allen Miller

> If I had to reduce all of educational psychology to just one principle, I would say this: The most important single factor influencing learning is what the learner already knows. Ascertain this and teach accordingly.
>
> (Ausubel, 1968)

My original intention in writing this book was to provide a useful reference for university teachers who were unfamiliar with the relevant research and literature in higher education and were not satisfied with the assessment procedures they were using for setting and marking assignments, examinations and theses. Accordingly I commenced a survey of recent literature on assessment and evaluation, concentrating on those features which were most likely to be relevant to the tasks associated with assessment in universities and colleges. The Centre for Educational Development (CEDAM) in the Australian National University (ANU) kindly offered me an Honorary Visiting Fellowship (following my retirement as Director of the Centre) during the book's gestation period. This post provided many opportunities for discussing the project with colleagues in the ANU and better access to library and computing facilities (including e-mail and the Internet), which greatly facilitated my reviews of the literature and subsequent contacts with my co-authors. I am grateful to the Vice-Chancellor of the ANU, Professor Deane Terrell, and the Director of CEDAM, Ms Margot Pearson, for their continued support in this project.

The journal, *Assessment and Evaluation in Higher Education*, published by Carfax in cooperation with the University of Bath, provides an excellent coverage of recent research on the subject. Any investigation of assessment practices cannot afford to ignore related research on how students learn and also broader aspects of higher education, such as provision of resources. Journals such as *Higher Education* and *Studies in Higher Education*, and publications of the Society for Research into Higher Education (SRHE) and the Higher Education Research and Development Society of Australasia (HERDSA) provided numerous case studies and reports of research on teaching and learning.

In July 1997, the National Committee of Inquiry into Higher Education, chaired by Sir Ron Dearing, produced a comprehensive report on the state of higher education in the United Kingdom (Dearing, 1997). The report, entitled *Higher Education in the Learning Society*, contains 93 recommendations, most of which relate to the future of higher education in the United Kingdom and, indirectly, to other countries with links to the UK. Wherever relevant we shall refer to those findings and recommendations which apply to the subject matter of this book and have implications for higher education around the world.

Fortunately this very large report is accessible on the World Wide Web through a number of sites, of which one is <www.leeds.ac.uk/educol/ncihe/>. Other sites are readily listed using a search engine such as Yahoo and the key words 'higher education' and 'Dearing Report'.

Concurrent with this review of the literature I began to collect examples of examination questions and assignments from different subject areas, which would illustrate the more theoretical principles which formed the basis of this book. The latter task was even more time consuming than the analysis of the literature, so I was delighted when Brad Imrie, of City University of Hong Kong, provided me with a large amount of illustrative material which he and his colleagues had gathered, some of which had been used in earlier publications (eg Imrie, 1984; Clift and Imrie, 1981; Hall and Imrie, 1994). I was very pleased when Brad Imrie accepted my invitation to become a joint author of the present work and am grateful to Professors Hall and Clift for permission to quote their work. Brad Imrie wrote Chapter 15 and much of Chapter 16; he generously provided material for Chapters 1, 3 and 9 and has made constructive criticisms of the other chapters. At a later stage Kevin Cox, also from City University of Hong Kong, agreed to write Chapter 13, in which he draws on his own research into assessment and describes recent developments in his university. Professor Cox has also made helpful contributions to other chapters, especially Chapter 16.

Another person to whom I am most indebted is Professor Alec Ross, formerly Pro-Vice-Chancellor of the University of Lancaster and Director of the School of Educational Research in that university. Professor Ross graciously gave me permission to use any relevant material from the *Teaching in Higher Education Series*, which included three booklets on assessment (Cockburn and Ross, 1977a, b; Mathews, 1977). We have made use of this material from the University of Lancaster in Chapters 3, 7 and 9.

The book is designed to provide university teachers with an overview of the many approaches to setting, marking and reviewing coursework, assignments, tests and examinations used in programs leading to an award in higher education, whether it be a certificate, a diploma, a first degree or a higher degree. An equally important aim is to demonstrate the strong influence that assessment has on the way students approach their learning tasks.

The authors would encourage all concerned with assessment to examine urgently how assessment is actually used in practice. Experience and the literature indicate that:

- more emphasis should be placed on using formative assessment for improving learning (see also Dearing, 1997 Rec. 8)
- more focus is required on the type of skills required in employment (see also Dearing, 1997 Recs. 18 and 19)
- some academic staff need to develop more competencies in the techniques and procedures of marking and grading
- in general, more professionalism and accountability are required
- greater emphasis needs to given to the development of transcripts and progress files as an indication of students' performance at university, with the present honours classification (where it is used) becoming increasingly redundant (Dearing, 1997 Section 9.52)
- ethics in assessment should be promoted (Murray *et al.*, 1996)
- the Principles of Student Assessment (HEQC, 1996) are commended with the caveat that institutional policy depends on competent implementation rather than compliance.

The word *assessment* is used throughout this book to describe the above activities. Some educationists do not distinguish between assessment and evaluation. We have chosen to use the term *evaluation* in the broader sense of 'a systematic examination of all aspects of a course, the selection and ordering of content, the choice of teaching and assessment methods, and the destination of its graduates' (Miller, 1984, p. 1). Thus *assessment* is seen as the means by which students' progress and achievement are measured, recorded and communicated to students and relevant university authorities.

Assessment is undertaken for many reasons, the more important of which are:

- to provide systematic indications of the quality of students' learning for both teachers and students
- to maintain standards in professional education and in higher education generally
- to motivate students throughout their studies.

It is interesting to note that dictionary definitions of assessment rarely, if ever, refer to its educational usage. The *Concise Oxford English Dictionary* (eg Sykes, 1982) defines 'assess' as 'estimate value of (esp. property for taxation)'. Nevertheless, it is a word that has come into increasing usage in the English-speaking world over the last two or three decades in relation to the measurement of educational achievements or other skills. Page and Thomas (1979), for example, define assessment in terms of various types of tests:

> the process by which one attempts to measure the quality and quantity of learning and teaching using various assessment techniques, eg assignments, projects, continuous assessment, objective-type tests, final examinations and standardised tests. (p. 26)

Other words which are constantly used throughout this book are 'university', 'teacher', 'course' and 'unit', each of which might require some clarification.

The word 'university' as used here includes all diploma and degree-granting institutions of higher education, including colleges associated with particular professions (eg agricultural, theological, mining), institutes of technology and polytechnics. Our reason for using 'university' as a generic term is that many former state colleges, teachers' colleges, polytechnics, institutes of technology and colleges of advanced education have either achieved university status through improved teaching and research or have been granted such status by government decree.

University teachers have different titles in different countries, not only to indicate their rank and sometimes whether they are tenured or not, but also as a reflection of national usage. Consequently the term 'professor' may be used in a generic sense in North America but has a much more restricted application in countries in the British Commonwealth other than Canada. Other words used to describe university teachers in some parts of the English-speaking world are 'academic' and 'faculty'. The former includes those members of universities who are engaged in full-time research while the latter is used in some countries to describe a division within the university such as the faculty of arts. We have therefore chosen to use the term 'faculty member', 'university teacher', 'teacher' or 'instructor' when referring to those who have teaching responsibilities in a university or college.

The terms 'course', 'teaching program', 'unit of study' and 'module' are ill defined and therefore tend to be used rather interchangeably, both in this book and the literature generally. They should be distinguished from 'curriculum', which describes all the courses or units of study which an institution requires of its students before a particular degree can be awarded. For example, the University of Glasgow, in its 1993–94 Calendar makes the following statement: 'A minimum graduating curriculum shall consist of seven qualifying courses which the candidate shall have satisfactorily completed.'

Sometimes a full-year course, which may be a compulsory or optional component of the curriculum for a degree, is subdivided into a number of 'modules', each of which must be completed at a satisfactory level before moving on to the next unit. Strictly speaking, a 'teaching program' is the way a teacher organizes resources, learning experiences and assessment tasks so that a maximum number of students will complete the course at levels which reflect their individual abilities and attainments.

The book is divided into three major sections, each of which corresponds to an important aspect of assessment. The first considers the place of various forms of assessment in the total curriculum, the second describes a range of methods which teachers in higher education have found to be successful in achieving the purposes of assessment, and the final section discusses ways of looking critically at the types of assessment being used in particular courses.

Some readers, especially those who are enrolled in a course on the subject and who are using this book as a text, may need to read the book from cover to cover; others will wish to be more selective, concentrating on those sections which meet their most immediate needs. We would, however, encourage the latter group of readers at least to browse through other parts of the book as, hopefully, those sections will stimulate thought about alternative approaches to assessment. In preparing this book the authors have endeavoured to be brief but comprehensive so that readers can assimilate the interdependencies and complexities of assessment while having references for further reading.

There are two other ways in which readers can profit from using this book. The first is for them to try out some of the suggestions with their classes, preferably after discussing changes to their assessment procedures with colleagues. The second is to investigate those references which appear to be relevant to their interests. There is a wealth of literature on the subject, which is unfortunately ignored by a majority of university teachers unless they have a special interest in assessment. An important function of this book is to draw the attention of university teachers to this literature, so much of which has direct relevance to their day-to-day work. Teachers of surgery or philosophy in a university would regard it as a neglect of duty if they failed to keep abreast with developments in their respective fields. Because most academics are both teachers and researchers, they need to keep up to date with developments in teaching and in their special discipline. True scholarship includes both.

Part 1

The place of assessment in higher education

1

Purposes of higher education

Education is what survives when what has been learned has been forgotten.

(BF Skinner)

The advantage of a classical education is that it enables you to despise the wealth that it prevents you from achieving.

(Russell Green)

Introduction

Students undertake education at the tertiary level for many reasons, not all of which would be regarded as important by faculty. For example, if students enrol in higher education to find a mate or to play in a college football team, the appropriate measure of success is obviously not a set of formal examinations! This chapter looks at changing expectations of higher education over the last two or three decades, acknowledging that a university or college degree may serve widely differing purposes.

We do not question the view that for many students, in different countries and different types of institutions, the key purposes of higher education are achieved. On the other hand, there is no doubt that recent changes in demographic patterns, occupational requirements, student motivation and institutional structure have created difficulties for university students, teachers and administrators.

In the United Kingdom, the National Committee of Inquiry into Higher Education chaired by Sir Ron Dearing (1997) stated in Section 5.11 of its report that the four main purposes of higher education are:

1. to inspire and enable individuals to develop their capabilities to the highest potential levels throughout life, so that they grow intellectually, are well equipped for work, can contribute effectively to society and achieve personal fulfilment
2. to increase knowledge and understanding for their own sake and to foster their application to the benefit of the economy and society
3. to serve the needs of an adaptable, sustainable, knowledge-based economy at local, regional and national levels
4. to play a major role in shaping a democratic, civilised, inclusive society.

The situation in the United States, with its great variety of universities and colleges catering for students of widely different educational and cultural levels, is much more complex than in those countries where there is a smaller choice for higher education. Erwin (1995), writing from the James Madison University in Virginia, lists three major problems which need to be addressed when an institution is formulating its admission requirements. These are not limited to the United States but could apply to systems of higher education in many countries:

●   students do not have the basic skills of reading, writing and mathematics to function effectively in the workforce and in a competitive society.
●   there is little consensus about the general education or the knowledge, skills and personal experiences every student should have, regardless of his or her major subject of study.
●   credible measures of student learning are generally available, particularly at an institutional level.

Erwin refers to attempts in the United States, in the United Kingdom and the European Union to identify institutions where the above problems exist. Difficulties arise, he claims, when examinations fail to measure 'higher order models of cognitive and affective development'. We shall discuss these issues in more detail in Chapters 3 to 5 of the present book.

In the same article, Erwin refers to a survey of 37 major corporations and 36 small firms in the United Kingdom conducted by Otter (1992) who identified the following more general learning goals as important for graduation. Graduates should be able to:

access and select information, synthesize and interpret information, demonstrate commitment, demonstrate self discipline, manage personal stress, communicate clearly and accurately, communicate effectively orally, work cooperatively, work alone, accept criticism, understand own strengths and weaknesses, act ethically and possess basic computer skills. (p. 115)

We may well ask ourselves whether the systems of assessment used in our institutions and with our own students are able to verify that students have achieved the above goals by the time they graduate!

Higher education in its social context

Contemporary higher education (HE) does not exist because students want it. HE, as an entity, exists because countries (governments) need it. As noted by Kogan *et al.* (1994), 'Governments have come to see higher education more than ever as an aid to the achievement of social and economic goals and increasingly expect it to be responsive to their agendas.' So the purposes of HE are to meet the needs of government and will be somewhat different according to the country or government. For example, contrast the HE systems of Italy and Germany, or China and India. The models of the twelfth century *do not* apply to the needs of the twenty-first – history will *not* repeat itself. Where HE systems are well established, old models still influence contemporary systems but even these are now changing due to pressures from government and from society – as represented by the currently adopted vocabulary of customers, clients and stakeholders; not to mention employers, parents and students.

Consider some reasonably recent suggestions of purposes of HE. Bligh *et al.* (1981) list three purposes:

1. *cultural:* to pass on the future, the heritage, or a body of knowledge from one generation to the next
2. *functional:* to produce the qualified manpower to benefit a future society or as an instrument of national development
3. *social:* to advance individuals either socially or in terms of their personal development.

The purposes of HE must match the needs of government and of students; the former so that there will be funding, the latter so that there will be sufficient enrolments. In terms of qualified manpower planning (see below), the objectives of HE must also now meet the requirements of professional bodies and, in some countries, legal requirements. Accordingly, for the future development of HE in a context of more and different students; more students studying part-time; more older students (no longer patronized as 'kids' by so-called higher education teachers); and more accountability (cost and quality), the above purposes can be modified to:

- *cultural*: to pass on a body of knowledge from one generation to the next
- *functional*: to produce the qualified manpower to benefit society as an instrument of national development and to 'keep up with competitors'
- *social*: to advance individuals either socially or economically
- *perpetuating*: to perpetuate the national system of beliefs, values and procedures with some evolution – usually in reaction to government policy.

Some three years later, one of Bligh's co-authors, Warren Piper (1984) offered the following variations of HE purposes:

- *functional*: the production of the desired combination of trained person-power; professional and social competence
- *cultural*: fashioning and passing on the culture from one generation to the next; induction of individual into the ranks of the educated
- *social service*: the facilitation of students' progress to their various chosen ends.

Note the change of purpose description and of vocabulary, eg person-power, professional competence, social service.

For sustainable economic (and social) development, it is vitally important that vocational, diploma-level, education is recognized and appreciated as an important part of higher education. The preference for degree-level education can distort the overall mission of higher education which should include opportunities for matching ability with educational programs, and the provision of education for capability which will match development needs.

In a keynote address to a UK conference on 'What do employers really want from higher education?' Harvey (1997) notes: 'Employers are not a homogenous bunch. But certain themes run through, and there is an overwhelming view that graduates add real value to their business.' He further comments that the value comes from the higher level academic skills but the problem is that graduates have 'little idea of the nature and culture of the workplace and find it difficult to adjust'.

In various ways employers are increasingly influencing the HE agenda: expressing dissatisfaction with the graduate as 'product'; specifying expectations of skills *and* attitudes; and becoming HE providers themselves because of perceived deficiencies in the normal higher education system.

What then are the purposes of HE? When Roizen and Jepsen (1985) considered employer expectations of higher education, they introduced their discussion with a justification for manpower planning, which had been argued by Fulton *et al.* (1980):

> The first is that higher education makes extremely heavy demands on society's resources and it is inefficient and inequitable to treat it simply as a luxury consumption good for a relatively small number of people. The second is that even in countries where higher education provision is based on social demand, a very high proportion of the students do themselves consider that it has vocational implications for them. Unless appropriate jobs are likely to be available for students their social demand for higher education is itself based on a misapprehension.

Employers, of course, are affected by the assumptions of manpower planning but often, dependent on country, do not have a truly representative voice; this too is changing and employer federations are increasingly publishing reports and making submissions to governments. As noted by Roizen and Jepsen (1985), some employers feel that HE expansion has gone 'too fast' but they also see that a country needs 'to spend money on higher education to keep up with competitors' – not the same thing.

In a section headed 'The relationship between work and other experience and higher education provision' the Dearing (1997) Report on *Higher Education in the Learning Society* discussed the value of work experience for students in UK universities. The Committee made two recommendations which, if implemented, could lead to the incorporation of work experiences in more undergraduate programs together with recognition that work experience complements the theoretical learning and laboratory experimentation which have traditionally formed the backbone of university courses. These were:

Recommendation 18
We recommend that all institutions should, over the medium term, identify opportunities to increase the extent to which programmes help students to become familiar with work, and help them to reflect on such experience.

Recommendation 19
We recommend that the Government, with immediate effect, works with representative employer and professional organizations to encourage employers to offer more work experience opportunities for students.

Knapper and Cropley (1985) consider that a purpose of HE should be to provide a basis for lifelong education or learning. They contrast the 'old' with the 'new' as polarizations: knowledge for its own sake vs transmission of knowledge; elite professions vs mass higher education; critic of society vs agent for social change; specialist vs general. This purpose of HE was emphasized by the wide range of papers addressing the theme of 'lifelong learning' at the Twenty-first International Conference on Improving University Teaching in July 1996, a point which is also emphasized in the Dearing Report.

Knapper and Cropley (1985) conclude that 'the task is to develop forms of (higher) education that are adapted to current economic, social and political needs of contemporary society' and consider that higher education institutions (HEIs) have a role as one element (only) in their envisaged system of lifelong education. Of course, it needs to be stated that in many countries HEIs will have different characteristics and reputations – recognized in different ways and for different purposes by such stakeholders as government, employers and, indeed, peers.

They list seven 'skills or competencies for lifelong learning' (which have much in common with those sought by employers). These are:

1. capacity to set personal objectives in a realistic way
2. effectiveness in applying knowledge already possessed
3. efficiency in evaluating one's own learning
4. skill at locating information
5. effectiveness in using different learning strategies and in learning in different settings
6. skill in using learning aids such as libraries or the media (ie information technology learning skills)
7. ability to use and interpret materials from different subject areas.

Accordingly, for this book, the purposes of contemporary higher education are considered to be:

A. *Academic*
1. *cultural*: to extend and pass on a body of knowledge and scholar-

ship from one generation to the next in the context of an intellectual culture
2. *perpetuating*: to perpetuate the national higher education system
of beliefs, values and procedures, with some evolution – but
usually in reaction to government policy
B. *Professional*
3. *functional*: to produce qualified employees for national economic
development to benefit society and 'to keep up with competitors'; to certify a student's fitness to enter a particular profession
C. *Social*
4. *social*: to advance individuals either socially or economically
5. *learning*: to broaden students' general education; to prepare
students with attitudes and capabilities for lifelong learning.

Academic functions of higher education

In the present context the word academic is used to describe the
educational and research functions of a university or college, especially when these are devoted to the transmission and extension of
knowledge for its own sake. It is appropriate to list the academic
function first, mainly because so many teachers in higher education
show by the examinations they set that the academic purpose is foremost, even in courses that are clearly designated as vocational, ie
preparation for employment. Reasons for this emphasis on the academic
functions of higher education are not hard to find.

First, incentives and rewards, such as tenure, promotion and
international recognition for faculty, are closely tied to their success
as 'academics'. Consequently, professional practice outside the
university or college and involvement in community activities are
often not given sufficient weighting when applications for tenure or
promotion are being considered.

Second, many academic staff or faculty, particularly in universities, measure their own success as teachers by the number of their
students who qualify to enter doctoral programs or, at a higher level,
receive appointments to prestigious universities. Faculty often do
not wish to be regarded or described as 'teachers'; this explains their
disdain for standards and concepts of teaching professionalism
commensurate with those of discipline and research. And yet, do
not the mission statements of many universities claim that teaching
and research are equally important? Both should be considered as
aspects of scholarship. As noted by Boyer (1990) when reconsidering

the priorities of the professoriate, academic work 'might be thought of in terms of four separate yet overlapping functions of scholarship: discovery, integration, application and teaching' (of knowledge).

Third, most faculty members develop a certain expertise in teaching rather difficult concepts and skills and in testing their students' ability to display the newly acquired knowledge and skills. Consequently they do not have many opportunities for observing at first hand how students from their courses apply their knowledge or skills after graduation. Thus the derogatory meaning of 'academic' refers to theories or studies that have no practical application.

Morgan *et al.* (1980), in describing students' orientations towards higher education, give examples of intrinsic and extrinsic subsets of the academic approach. The orientation may be described as intrinsic when students are seeking intellectual stimulation from their studies, and extrinsic when they are more concerned with the grades they achieve or the availability of work for graduates in their particular field. Of course many students merge these different orientations, but 'passing' is likely to be a dominant motivation.

Professional/vocational functions

Universities have long been concerned with preparing people for entry into the vocations or professions of law, medicine and theology; other professions such as accountancy, agriculture, dentistry, engineering and veterinary science were added during the twentieth century. With the establishment of professionally oriented institutions such as the central institutions in Scotland, polytechnics in England, Wales, Singapore and Hong Kong, and institutes of technology in the United States and Australia, universities in these countries no longer had the sole responsibility for professional education. Some employers claim that college graduates are more fitted for direct entry into the workforce than university graduates. Some of these employers believe that university graduates frequently need orientation to the needs of the industry or profession but that they are eventually expected to be more successful than their counterparts from colleges.

Now that these polytechnics, colleges and institutes are being designated as universities there is a danger that the practical emphasis of their mission will diminish. The newly created universities may strive to attain 'academic respectability' by including more theoretical components in their courses and smaller amounts of field experience. Fortunately there has been a healthy reaction against this trend in some innovative universities in Canada and Australia, particularly when they have had opportunities of developing new degree programs in professions as diverse as architecture, education, engineering, medicine and theology.

An Australian example of this change is the transformation of the Hawkesbury Agricultural College into a campus of the University of Western Sydney. In its early days the former Hawkesbury College focussed solely on agriculture, preparing young men for the various tasks associated with farming in Australia. It was mainly residential and was virtually self-supporting through its own model farm. While still an agricultural college the institution expanded its diploma programs to include home science for young women. Ultimately the gender barriers between the two main streams broke down and further related courses and programs were added.

Under the leadership of Richard Bawden, new approaches to course design, teaching, learning and assessment were adopted with the emphasis being on experiential and problem-based learning. Macadam (1985) describes the changes in the following terms:

> In 1978 their programmes were based on a conventional curriculum of science, applied science, technology and management subjects. Lectures and practical sessions were the means by which students were taught and the programmes were full-time on campus. The School was organized as a number of discipline based departments who controlled resources and offered the subjects that made up the curricula.
>
> By 1985 a complete overhaul of the curricula had occurred. Now the emphasis is on the development of a matrix of competencies focussed on problem-solving, communicating and learning ... Students are expected to undertake projects with an off-campus focus and a semester spent on a co-operator's farm is a feature of the programmes ... The departmental organizational structure has been replaced by a matrix management structure with management teams based on functions. Currently there are teams for program management, outreach, technical and clerical services, College farms, learning package development, curriculum evaluation and staff development. (p. 201)

Concurrent with the curriculum changes at Hawkesbury were similar developments at the CB Alexander Agricultural College, 'Tocal', in the Hunter Valley Region of New South Wales (Drinan et al., 1985). These methods and their relation to assessment will be described in more detail in later chapters. At this stage, however, it is important to note that, where problem-based learning has been adopted, assessment and course development are inextricably linked. Boud (1988) states:

> The notion of assessment as essentially the task of ascertaining what has been learned at the end of a course is challenged by problem based learning. Assessment is required to direct student learning and to give staff feedback on the curriculum as much as it is to measure outcomes ... Assessment is an activity which permeates learning and which needs to be undertaken for learning's sake, not just for the sake of accreditation of achievements. (p. 89)

Bawden (1988, p. 155) describes the close relationship between assessment and course development in the following way: 'The Hawkesbury programmes are in continual evolution with assessment sessions themselves assuming the role of learning opportunities for both students and academics.'

Most faculty recognize at least two purposes for assessment in higher education: one for the direction and enhancement of student learning; the other for confirmation of learning outcomes and the maintenance of standards (accreditation as used above).

One other important feature of professional and vocational education in universities is the increasing emphasis being given to in-service training and professional development programs. This has occurred in three ways. The first is an extension of what has been possible for a long time through evening courses and distance education, namely that corporations and government departments encourage their employees to undertake advanced studies in subjects which are thought to be relevant to the employee's work. Sometimes these courses are actually sponsored by business or government in order to ensure that they will be available when needed. In other cases, even though the cost of the course is borne by the university (or the students themselves), all or most of the students come from one section of government, business or industry.

A second development has occurred mainly in the United States, namely the establishment of private universities specifically for the employees of large (multi-national) organizations. A well-known example of this is McDonald's University; also some of the universities established and operated by religious groups serve a similar function, particularly when their curricula are restricted by the tenets of that religion or sect.

The third development is outside the framework of designated universities; it occurs when a large, usually multi-national firm or a group of related government departments runs a formal learning program for its executives and senior employees. While it is not doubted that some of these courses are intellectually demanding, we would be inclined to regard them as being equivalent to university courses only when some form of assessment is used to ascertain whether a participant has successfully completed the program. Preferably there should also be a set of clearly stated criteria for judging the level of success. This has implications for recognition of prior learning for credit purposes.

Cultural functions

The concept of an 'educated gentleman' as one of the most desired results of higher education has rightly been replaced with the concept of an 'educated adult', even though what is meant by 'educated' is not always clearly defined. For adult or lifelong education, one of the great successes of higher education in the United Kingdom has been the Open University. Another successful development is the Athabasca University in Canada and, in Australia, numerous universities offer distance education courses. By enrolling in institutions such as these, adult students of all ages have been able to broaden their outlook on life through the study of such subjects as history, language, literature, philosophy and the natural sciences. The original purpose of liberal arts colleges in the United States of America was similarly aimed at giving a broader education to future citizens, although these colleges mainly catered for students who had just completed their secondary schooling. In many countries, universities have long made access available for students to complete first degrees or diplomas part-time, usually with classes arranged outside normal working hours. At first the majority of such students studied for professional reasons but, since universities and colleges made entry easier for 'mature age' students, the proportion of those enrolling for 'cultural' reasons has steadily increased.

Because many students now enrol in higher education courses simply to expand their knowledge in a particular field and are not necessarily interested in obtaining a qualification as a result of their studies (in fact, many of these students already possess a degree), the approach to assessment of the performance of such students may have to be different to the assessment of students aiming for a degree. We shall consider this issue at various stages in this book.

Certainly the relatively high proportion of such students in some university or college classes should make one cautious about interpreting dissatisfaction with a course in terms of the number who fail to complete. Perhaps some of those who enrol in and complete only one or two units of study are doing so as part of their desire for lifelong learning.

The contribution of universities to lifelong learning in society is acknowledged in the Dearing (1997) Report on higher education in the UK, as the following quotation from Section 1.10 of that report shows.

> The expansion of higher education in the last ten years has contributed greatly to the creation of a learning society, that is, a society in which people in all walks of life recognize the need to continue in education and training throughout their working lives and who see learning as enhancing the quality of life throughout all its stages. But, looking twenty years ahead, the UK must progress further and faster in the creation of such a society to sustain a competitive economy.

It will be clear from the foregoing description of the three main purposes of higher education that the design *and* the methods of assessment chosen for a particular course need to take into account the main purposes of higher education. Course providers must also keep in mind the most likely reasons for their students' enrolments. Unfortunately there is often considerable confusion in the minds of students and faculty regarding the main purpose of a course, particularly when it comes to setting or preparing for examinations. For example, Snyder (1971) described a 'hidden curriculum' whereby students were told that a course was designed to develop creativity, whereas the examinations in the same course rewarded those who were best able to reproduce lecture notes or selections from the texts. In a similar study Becker *et al.* (1968) reported that a major aim of university students, particularly in professional faculties, was to discover ways of 'beating the system' in order to pass all the required examinations with as little effort as possible. Biggs (1993) describes this form of learning as an 'achieving approach' and writes:

> The achieving approach is pathological because it too is outcome-oriented, not task-oriented. To a student adopting the achieving approach, high grades are the goal, the task being only the necessary medium for achieving them. While this can and should mean proper task-engagement, it does not necessarily do so; students adopting this approach are most concerned about the cost-effective use of their time and effort. Cheating also serves that end. (p. 76)

Various forms of cheating will be discussed in more detail in Chapter 15. It is, however, important to note here that a greater use of new technology in developing learning skills makes it more difficult to ensure that it is the student's *own* work that is being assessed. Doughty (1996) suggests 'a few tricks to try':

1. Assume all text or ideas are from elsewhere and demand references for everything. Demand at least five different sources.
2. At random, and with assessment points, ask students to locate a web page or CD on any topic in another student's essay that is not referenced.
3. Ask for an essay plan rather than the essay.
4. Ask for an essay project diary of events, leads followed, blind alleys entered, etc which demonstrates that learning took place.
5. Do random oral exams on the essay topics, rotating through all students during the course.
6. Mark for quality of arguing a point of view rather than worry about where the material came from.
7. Ask one group of students to locate material and argue a case, and another group to argue the opposite using the same source material.
8. Make 10 per cent of the course assessment mark proportional to the correlation between exam essays and researched essays.
9. Above all try to assess course objectives eclectically, and worry if there are many essays to mark.

Course developers thus have a responsibility to ensure that the types of assessment used in any one course should reflect the broader aims of the total curriculum in addition to the more specific objectives of each particular unit of study. In later sections of this book we will explore how these aims might be met.

The changed curriculum at 'Tocal', one of the two agricultural colleges described earlier, appears to have the effect of providing a broad professional education which goes well beyond the acquisition of the knowledge and practical skills needed on a farm. Drinan *et al.* (1985) claim that, 'through the use of case studies and the concomitant use of small learning groups' the college is seeking to achieve the following educational outcomes 'in addition to the students' acquisition of knowledge':

● motivation to learn
● heightened inquisitiveness
● knowledge of where to find information
● ability to synthesize information

- ability to resolve problems and make decisions
- heightened awareness of the broad world of agriculture
- an holistic view of agriculture
- self-confidence
- better communication and understanding of people
- ability to work with others
- concern for the well-being of others.

With only minor changes, eg the reference to agriculture, the above set of outcomes would be accepted as desirable for almost all professional programs offered in institutions of higher education.

In conclusion, the *purposes* of higher education are often determined by government and reflect HE traditions in a particular country. The *expectations* of HE are shared by government and by other stakeholders – principally employers and professional bodies as end users, and by parents and secondary school staff as sources of guidance for direct entry students; also part-time students. The *providers* of HE, in its different forms, have the responsibility of demonstrating that their provisions are fit for the stated purposes and are not merely self-serving.

While the history of higher education, in its ancient European or Asian forms, will not repeat itself, it may still be worth noting one of the sayings of Confucius (551–479 BC) on true knowledge, when speaking as a teacher to a student: 'Zhong You, shall I teach you what knowledge is? When you know a thing, say that you know it; when you do not know a thing, admit that you do not know it. That is true knowledge.'

––––––––––– 2 –––––––––––

Functions of assessment

I believe that the testing of the student's achievements in order to see
if he meets some criterion held by the teacher, is directly contrary to
the implications of therapy for significant learning.

(Carl Rogers)

Measures of potential or achievement?

When the prime purpose of an undergraduate assessment scheme is
to measure academic quality or potential, the focus may be on
designing a set of tests and assignments which will demonstrate the
quality of mind required for entrance to a postgraduate or doctoral
program. In such an assessment scheme where academic *potential* is
being judged, successful students would be those who have the
ability to undertake complex intellectual activities such as selecting
relevant knowledge of facts and skills from a large amount of material which they have learned and applying this knowledge to the
solution of a particular problem. They should also be able to analyse
and integrate the information which they have recalled with any
other data which is supplied by the examiner to formulate a solution
to that problem.

If, on the other hand, the prime purpose is to measure *achievement*,
the assessment scheme will be designed to measure the performance
of students at a particular point, whether it be at some stage during
their studies or at the end of a program leading to the award of a
degree. It is important to recognize, however, that a high level of
achievement in a particular examination does not necessarily indicate that a student has learned a lot from the course which is being
examined – that particular student may have already possessed the
knowledge or skills prior to enrolling in the course.

In the section which follows we are greatly indebted to John Clift
and Brad Imrie for permission to use excerpts from their book

Assessing Students: Appraising Teaching. The section also contains some hitherto unpublished material entitled *Assessment: Learning and Performance.* This material, modified in places to fit the framework of the present book, forms the bulk of the section which follows.

Measuring levels of achievement – criterion vs norm referencing

Generally the level of student achievement is assessed by requiring students to complete a test or assignment, which is then given a mark. Such a mark often has an *absolute* value ascribed to it, based on what the teacher 'knows' to be the 'standard'. However, as Dressel (1976) has stated rather pointedly, scores from such tests are virtually useless unless they can be fitted into some framework which permits them to be interpreted by the instructor and by the student: 'a grade [is] an inadequate judgement by a biased and variable judge of the extent to which a student has attained an ill-defined level of mastery of an unknown proportion of an indefinite material.'

To counter Dressel's criticisms we would need to ensure that the following five expectations are met:

1. the assessment is based on clearly defined material
2. the relative contribution of each assessment is weighted according to its relative importance
3. the same assessment consistently results in the same grade being assigned
4. the grading procedure conforms to the institutional grading policy
5. it is compatible with the standards applied by colleagues.

This search for a meaningful or valid framework for student achievement resulted in three principal approaches, which may be described as content, 'absolute' or normative frameworks.

A content framework

In this instance, the students 'score' is seen as representing the percentage of a defined sample of knowledge and skills that has been learned. That is, the student's score is established on content-related tasks contained within the test. For example, a qualifying examination may require the student to obtain 110 correct answers out of a possible 120 objective-type questions; all students meeting this criterion are deemed to have qualified.

An 'absolute' framework

This is a special case of a content framework in which the student's 'score' denotes particular levels of achievement specified in the course objectives. The student's score then has reference to an 'absolute' in the shape of desired outcomes or performance objectives. A continuing education course on criminal law has, as one of its objectives, 'that the students be able to explain who is subject to the law'. To meet the pass criteria, the students are required to list without error those who are subject to the law, special circumstances governing any particular groups, and the appropriate references from the Criminal Act.

A normative framework

In this approach a student's performance is measured against the attainment of others. That is, the student's 'score' denotes a position in relation to others who have attempted the same task or tasks. The location of this 'position' relative to others is generally achieved by using a relative standard such as a normal distribution. For example, in the United States of America, the Education Commission for Foreign Medical Graduates used a clinical exercise with 360 questions. In that instance, the pass mark did not depend on how many questions the candidate answered correctly. The examinee's performance was adjusted to fit the current performance of students at United States Medical Schools. That is, an examinee's final score denoted his or her position in relation to other medical students sitting for the same examination (Clift and Imrie, 1981).

The first two scores using a 'score' framework and the third, a normative framework, are often combined by the teacher in final grade assessment. That is, we each may claim to have in mind some required level of content which we believe the student needs to achieve to qualify for a pass. This 'absolute' measure is then modified by fitting all class scores to a selected distribution, usually normal or percentile. There are instances where this is taken a stage further and an acceptable percentage of pass students is predetermined. In the minds of many teachers such a system, based on 'instinct' aided by some spurious mark or grade adjustments, is the means by which standards are maintained. There is no doubt that the teaching profession needs a more sophisticated understanding of the statistics of marking (Nisbet, 1971) to avoid confusing the meanings of the above frameworks. Instinct may then legitimately be transformed into the qualitative professional judgement necessary for the crucial responsibilities we have when we assess student performance and grade students.

The issue of quality is a further complicating factor. Many teachers would subscribe to the notion of maintaining academic or 'absolute standards'. That is, we claim to 'know' (for different subjects and for different institutions and for different qualifications) what level of student performance merits a high distinction, distinction, credit, pass or failure (or an A, B, C, D or F). In theory, then, all students in a course could get distinctions or could fail, depending on how well or how poorly they attained the 'absolute' standards existing in the teacher's mind. This never happens, of course, for cut-off points are usually selected in such a way as to produce an institutionally acceptable number or proportion of students in each grade.

The pass level as a prerequisite for student progress to more advanced courses also has significance for course enrolment quotas and may be a 'policy' decision. As long as the proportion of failures and distinctions conforms reasonably well to other courses and other departments within the institution, and to similar courses in other institutions, the standard of the course may be seen as appropriate. It is, however, well known that some universities and colleges give more 'firsts' than others and that more students get 'firsts' in science than in some other subjects, possibly because of assessment and marking procedures but in some part determined by criteria for research student funding. Thus, the establishment of standards is often a rather uneasy compromise between some 'absolute' existing in the mind of the teacher, the expediencies of producing an appropriate distribution of student grades, and the practicalities of approving the progress of students to courses at a higher level.

Lewis (1972), in talking about assessment procedures, suggests that by

> setting statistical limits in failure rates and distinction rates, we sacrifice educational considerations in the interests of expediency. At the same time we help to perpetuate the lie that all courses are very much the same when in reality some might be very good and others might be atrocious.

Hohne (1975) also makes the point that university examiners prefer to pass and fail almost identical proportions of students year after year rather than ascertain the true calibre of the students and adjust their fail rates accordingly. Assessment practices were also condemned by Birney (1964), who claimed that grade achievement is scarcely related to teaching at all, but that teaching should be related to the development of scholarship (cited by Boyer, 1990). Studies of contrasting teaching methods repeatedly show little effect upon grades but considerable effect upon student satisfaction and some effect on other attitudes such as an increased interest in the subject matter.

In 1963, Glaser pointed out to teachers that, in assessing achievement, they could be looking for two distinct kinds of information. These were: first, whether the students had achieved a particular level of knowledge or a specified degree of competency in the performance of a skill or, second, the relative ordering of the students in regard to their peers.

Ebel (1965) expressed similar views in different words:

> The quantity of a student's achievement can be expressed in *either or both* of two ways:
> 1. as the proportion s/he learned of what s/he could (or should) have learned, or
> 2. as the proportion of the class (peers) who learned less than s/he did.

To the first kind of measurement, using a content or 'absolute' framework, Glaser gave the name 'criterion referenced measurement' (CRM). The second kind of measurement, using a 'normative' framework, Glaser called 'norm referenced measurement' (NRM). The two approaches to assessment are outlined in Tables 2.1 and 2.2.

Criterion referenced measurement is an essential component of teaching strategies such as the Keller Plan or Personalised System of Instruction (PSI), (Keller and Sherman, 1974), which come under the general description of 'mastery models of learning'. The main theoretical basis for mastery learning has been well described by Bloom (1976). Most students, when provided with a systematic program involving frequent 'feedback' of information about their progress, and given sufficient 'learning' time, can achieve mastery of the objectives specified for a course. The particular characteristic of the mastery learning model is the way the testing or assessment activity is built into the teaching program. Therefore, mastery learning does not just use CRM, but incorporates it in an entirely different approach to teaching. Such a course is divided into several areas of study, each with a set of specified objectives which the

Table 2.1 *Summary of criterion referenced measurement from Clift and Imrie (1981)*

CRITERION REFERENCED MEASUREMENT (CRM)

Description A criterion referenced test measures whether a student has or has not reached the criterion or specified level of achievement. Such test scores depend upon the specifying of an absolute standard of quality. This standard is independent of the scores achieved by other students attempting the same test and completing the same course.

Use Criterion referenced measurement is useful:

(a) for evaluating individualized learning programs;
(b) for diagnosing student difficulties;
(c) for estimating student ability in a particular area;
(d) for measuring what a student has learnt;
(e) for certification of competency;
(f) for controlling entry to successive units of instruction;
(g) whenever mastery of a subject or skill is of prime concern;
(h) whenever quota-free selection is being used.

Criticisms Educationalists tend to disagree as to the value or otherwise of CRM. The following criticisms are those that commonly appear in the literature on this topic:

(a) Criterion referenced measurements tell us what a student knows or can do, but do not tell us the degree of excellence or deficiency of the student's performance in relation to peers. These are relative concepts; hence, CRM can provide only part of the information required about a student's performance.
(b) It is unrealistic to expect a teacher to provide the degree of detail necessary in writing instructional objectives for good and reliable criterion referenced measures to be obtained.
(c) Knowledge and understanding do not lend themselves to clear definition and hence, it is extremely difficult to establish adequate criteria of achievement.
(d) Criterion referenced measurements discourage the use of problem-solving questions and encourage right and wrong solutions, with a tendency towards the teacher determining various answers, with the student constrained to choose from another person's selection.

---

student is required to reach by the end of the course. Each area is then broken down into learning units.

For each learning unit there is a set of behavioural objectives for which mastery is essential if the student is to achieve the course objectives. Students undertake readiness tests for each learning unit of the course, and can continue to re-sit these readiness tests until they attain mastery. For this type of learning, students are not penalized for the number of times they have to re-sit a test to meet the

Table 2.2   *Summary of norm referenced measurement from Clift and Imrie (1981)*

NORM REFERENCED MEASUREMENT (NRM)

Description   A norm referenced score measures the student's performance against the scores achieved by others who have completed the same test (not necessarily at the same time).

Use   Norm referenced measurements are particularly useful for:

(a)   classifying students;
(b)   selecting students for fixed quota requirements;
(c)   making decisions as to how much (more or less) a student has learnt in comparison to others.

Criticisms   The following criticisms of NRM have been drawn from those commonly appearing in the literature:

(a)   The final grade received by a student in any one subject conceals the student's misunderstandings, inadequate study skills and potential limitation in that subject. To have meaning for such interpretation, any individual's score needs to be related to the content of the test.
(b)   Any given mark does not signify a definite amount of knowledge and, hence, has little relevance for content of the test.
(c)   Over time, some students who are continually exposed to NRM will suffer a diminishing level of motivation.
(d)   Tests constructed to provide NRM will only sample the course objectives.
(e)   The use of norm referenced measurement hides the fact that some courses are very good while other courses can be very bad, or that teachers set different standards.
(f)   The setting of frequency limits in failure rates and levels of pass is an administrative necessity which overrides individual, educational and often statistical considerations.

---

criterion or level of performance. After each testing session the student receives feedback, and thus each test becomes part of the learning.

Norm referenced measurement is the approach commonly used by developers of standardized tests such as intelligence and many aptitude tests. The procedure followed is construction of a test; a selection of people for whom the test is designed take the test; then, by use of scaling procedures, the scores obtained are used to develop a scale which provides the framework against which individual scores can be interpreted. The standard practice in all educational institutions which have some form of external accountability is to report student attainment by norm reference – percentiles, grades, honours classification. A normal distribution of ability, performance and scores is often assumed for such purposes, despite the implications of progress by selection. A further assumption could be made that the teacher (and the teaching method) has only a random effect on a distribution which (presumably) was normal at the beginning of the course.

The basic principles of a two-stage structure of assessment are most clearly described by Terwilliger (1977). Adoption of these principles would take advantage of the strengths of both the norm and the criterion referenced models, at the same time avoiding most of their weaknesses.

> For any multi-category grading system, a two-stage grading procedure which employs both criterion and norm referenced methods is superior to either method alone. At the first stage, acceptable performances are distinguished from unacceptable performances using minimal objectives with a specified criterion. At the second stage, students who have achieved the 'minimal objectives' are differentiated using more advanced objectives and norms based upon previous students in the same course.

Others find it convenient to classify assessment tasks into three main categories: *diagnostic, formative* and *summative*. This is in general agreement with the approach originally used by Bloom *et al*. (1971) in their *Handbook on Formative and Summative Evaluation of Student Learning*. The following three sections give brief descriptions of each of these three categories and these will be followed by a discussion of other functions of assessment.

Diagnostic assessment tests

Diagnostic tests have as their main function the placement of students in the most suitable teaching programs and, for this reason, they are usually employed at a very early stage in an undergraduate program, preferably before formal study begins. In this way the strengths or weaknesses of each student can be identified and, given sufficient resources, students would be directed to programs which best suit their special abilities. Thus an institution with very large enrolments in certain first-year units is likely to arrange for these units to be taught both at elementary and advanced levels or, less frequently, to include additional remedial work for students whose previous education has provided insufficient preparation for the unit in question.

The State of New Jersey (Lynch, 1990) has required entering students to take placement tests in mathematics and English since 1978. A Basic Skills Council oversees the testing and reports results to the Board of Higher Education annually. In addition, the Council assesses the developmental and remedial programs established by the various colleges and universities to attend to the educational needs of a large and diverse group of students. These reports, published by the New Jersey Department of Higher Education, provide excellent data on student academic preparedness and collegial efforts to place students in the courses best designed to match their levels of ability.

Another discipline where diagnostic tests have proved to be essential is physics. Difficulties may arise when students are being considered for admission to first-year university classes in physics. As is the case with a number of other disciplines there are many branches of the subject, not all of which can be studied at any depth in a broad-based secondary school curriculum, yet some university teachers of physics believe that, without a thorough knowledge of mechanics, it is difficult to understand other aspects of the discipline. Similar cases may be made for the study of mathematics and for languages where specific prior knowledge is essential.

At other times diagnostic tests will be used to guide the teacher in planning or modifying the content or mode of presentation to better suit the needs of students. Evidence based on students' performance in prerequisites, such as final high school examinations, can be quite misleading. This is generally too global and does not provide sufficiently detailed information about specific abilities, knowledge, and weaknesses of individual students. Thus diagnostic measures may take the form of short tests (often multiple-choice) or essays, usually set at the beginning of a course or a section of a course. When classes are small enough it may be sufficient for a tutor or teaching assistant to interview individual students in order to estimate each student's ability in the subject. Diagnostic tests of this type are essential in the creative arts: music, painting, drama, etc and may be administered as part of the general admission procedures to formal studies in the arts.

Ideally, it should be possible to use a diagnostic test to decide whether a student really needs to enrol in a unit which might otherwise be compulsory for persons undertaking a particular degree. Under such circumstances the institution may wish to prescribe some alternative unit which would broaden the student's knowledge or even grant a complete exemption from one or more units, thus reducing the time required to complete the degree.

Formative assessment tests

Exercises, assignments and progress tests given to students throughout an academic semester or year may serve as formative assessment. The main purpose of this type of assessment should be to provide regular feedback to students in order to stimulate learning and to provide students with information which will help them judge the effectiveness of their learning strategies to date. It also alerts teachers to any sections of the course or approaches to teaching where students are having difficulties and which may need further attention. Formative assessment gives students practice in essential skills such as essay writing, computation, problem solving, drawing, use of scientific apparatus or the operation of equipment – without fear of failure.

It is therefore preferable that any marks given for formative tasks should have only marginal, if any, influence on a student's final result. On the other hand, some course coordinators take into account the results of formative assignments when determining the final grade, frequently in response to students' requests. There are three important principles which should be observed when assessing formative tasks:

1. The work should be marked and students informed of the results (grades or marks) as quickly as possible. The purpose of this feedback is to provide students with information on the level of their performance in relation to the teacher's expectations for the class at this particular stage in the course.
2. Teachers should provide detailed and constructive criticism so that students know what is expected of them and how they might improve their performance. These developmental comments need not necessarily be given at the individual level; the teacher's time may be used more efficiently by producing duplicated comments on the assignment and the types of errors detected. This is one example of feedback for development.
3. Models of good performance (behaviour, essays, reports) should also be provided so that good practice can be disseminated.

The following incident illustrates the importance of the first of the above principles. Some years ago one of the authors completed an assignment in a first-year unit he had been asked to monitor. The quality of his answer was then independently judged by the five or six tutors who had the responsibility for grading the work of first-year students in that unit. Marks awarded varied from 8/20 to

17/20, ie from a failure to a distinction or A-. Such variance in marks for the same piece of work points to an obvious lack of consultation on standards among tutors. If it could be shown that some tutors in this subject habitually awarded higher grades than others, as proved to be the case when the matter was further investigated, misleading information was being given to students about their potential in this subject. Unreasonably low marks may either persuade students to work much harder or, alternatively, to withdraw from the program. In a similar way high marks may give students a false sense of confidence in their own ability and knowledge. Students who are given unrealistically high marks in one subject may devote less time to that subject in order to concentrate on another subject where they think they are having difficulties.

It is therefore clear that regular use of formative assessment, used wisely, is an important component of any unit of study. The dilemma for teachers is to judge what is the optimal combination of teaching, private study and formative assessment, a matter to which we shall refer later in the present chapter.

Summative assessment tests

The main purpose of summative assessment is to make a judgement (usually irreversible) regarding each student's performance. The results of the assessment are then expressed as marks (17/20), percentages (85 per cent), grades (distinction or A-) or classifications (qualified to enter a higher level program of study or enrol for a higher degree). Summative assessment may also be defined as a measure of a student's performance or level of achievement at the end of a sequence of study and serves three main purposes.

At the end of each year of undergraduate study it signifies fitness to proceed to higher level courses, most of which have the prerequisite that appropriate introductory or lower level courses should have been successfully passed before a student is allowed to enrol at the more advanced level. Even where no formal statements are made, it is assumed that advanced level students will have had experience of the methods of teaching commonly used in higher education and have developed appropriate skills for advanced study: essay writing in the humanities; statistical analysis in the social and natural sciences; manipulative skills in workshops and laboratories; and appropriate background knowledge in the subject of specialization. End-of-unit examinations, if they are to be useful for certifying fitness to proceed to a higher level, should test whatever skills or knowledge are deemed to be needed before further study can begin.

A second function of summative assessment is particularly important for those students or institutions where the 'academic' purpose of education is foremost. It is particularly applicable in academic programs leading to the award of a degree with honours. In such cases results in earlier years of a study are used to determine:

- whether a student is to be allowed to enter an honours year where students can only be awarded an honours degree on the basis of a further year's study, or
- the level of honours to be awarded when the level of honours is based on performance in one or more years of studies, as is the case in most professional courses.

A third function of summative assessment is important in all professional courses. Success in the final examinations signifies that the graduate is qualified to enter the profession or, as is the case in medicine and related faculties, to gain further clinical experience under supervision before being allowed to practise independently.

Continuous assessment

The use of regular tests and assignments throughout a unit of study, where results for each piece of work contribute to the final result, is frequently referred to as 'continuous assessment'. The advantages and disadvantages of this approach to testing will be discussed in more detail in Chapter 6, but it is worth noting here that this practice can create difficulties for both teacher and student.

One of the chief difficulties with continuous assessment arises when it is allowed to dominate all other teaching and learning activities, to the extent that students do not have time to pursue reading in depth, or even to maintain a healthy balance between academic, social and recreational activities. Furthermore the teaching staff are kept so busy setting and marking tests and essays that they have little or no time for engaging in research. There is also a danger of confusing formative with summative assessment although the latter problem can be partially overcome through the relative weighting given to assessment tasks early in a semester compared with tasks undertaken at the end.

For these reasons some universities, for example the University of Glasgow, make little use of continuous assessment as such but stipulate that satisfactory performance in progress tests must be achieved before a student is allowed to take the final examination. The following quotation from the *1993–94 Calendar* illustrates this point:

> A candidate may be excluded from examination … in a subject by the Head of Department if the candidate has not satisfied the conditions regarding coursework and attendance laid down and communicated to candidates by the professor or lecturer in charge of the course at the start of the session. (p. 109)

Assessment as an aid to learning

Earlier in this chapter we referred to the use of formative assessment in providing regular feedback to both faculty and students on students' progress in a course. The personal example given there illustrates how formative assessment, used badly, can actually be a disincentive to further learning. Four main points were made in that section: first, it is essential that students' work should be graded and returned to them quickly; second, students are helped if they are told where their performance is below expectations or where they have misunderstood assessment tasks; third, it is helpful if students can be shown examples of excellent work (preferably illustrating how different approaches can be equally satisfactory); and fourth, it is essential that tutors or teaching assistants have a recognized standard for marking.

Regular testing of achievement can act as an incentive for more organized study, particularly for students who have not yet learned how to plan their own approaches to private study. There is a danger, however, as we saw in the section entitled 'Continuous assessment', that students in courses where the tests are too frequent will never find the time to read more widely or pursue new and exciting interests. We shall refer to this problem again when we discuss the timing of assessment tasks in Chapter 6.

A much more fundamental interaction between assessment and learning occurs when there is a mismatch between the tasks which students are given to test their progress or achievement and the objectives for the teaching program. An illustration from outside the academic world demonstrates this point. The purpose of a driving school is to teach students to drive a modern car safely under normal traffic conditions. An extreme example of a mismatch would be for the student to be tested by means of a written examination which tests the student's knowledge of the steps needed to start the engine, put the car in motion, increase and decrease speed, negotiate corners and bring the car to a halt. Driving schools would never adopt such a procedure for testing their students, but when we look critically at what happens in some university classes we find examples of an over-dependence on theoretical knowledge at the expense of practical abilities. We could take the analogy of the driving school one step further. Suppose the only test for a driver's licence is given in quiet suburban streets where there is no heavy traffic, where speeds are limited and where the road surface is excellent. Obviously such a test fails to measure the student's ability or readiness to drive in heavy traffic, in poor weather, or on motorways.

In Chapter 3 we shall describe in more detail the links that have been demonstrated between the tasks which students are expected to perform as part of their assessment and the strategies they adopt when organizing their learning. Briefly, if most examination questions require students to *recall* and *repeat* what they have previously memorized, it is only to be expected that in their preparation for the examination students will concentrate on learning by rote and *memorization*. Unless they have a strong interest in the subject matter it is unlikely that they will spend much time in *interpreting* what they read or observe, nor will they seek to find *applications* of the theories they have learned to the wider world.

The example given earlier of the incongruity of using a written examination paper to test driving ability could be applied to many subjects studied at university. Because success in one's study is an important component in admitting a graduate to a profession, it is essential that at least some of the assessment tasks will replicate the types of tasks which form part of the repertoire of the professional person. It is preferable that such tests are used at regular intervals throughout the university course rather than administering them right at the end. Regular exposure to the tasks and thinking expected of a person in the profession will help establish a pattern of thought and an approach to knowledge which is a feature of successful practitioners.

Recording students' achievements

The relative advantages of marks, grades or other methods of recording the quality and level of students' achievements in individual study modules will be discussed in more detail in Chapter 13. At this stage we shall confine ourselves to the final measure of a student's success in a degree program, especially where degrees with honours are awarded.

Whether a student's final performance should be recorded in terms of one of three or four levels of honours, as is the case in most English and Commonwealth universities, or as 'having satisfied requirements for the award of a Bachelor's Degree with Honours', similar to the rules applying for most PhD degrees, is a matter worth debating. The problem with systems that allow for various levels of honours is that in some institutions or faculties the level is determined by the student's overall performance during the total three to five years of undergraduate studies, whereas in other places the level of honours is based solely on the student's performance in the final year of study. (See, for example, the reports issued by the Australian Vice-Chancellors' Committee (AVCC), 1990, 1991, 1992a, b.) Admittedly it is generally necessary for students to have satisfied certain prerequisites in terms of levels of achievement in their earlier units of study before they can be admitted to honours programs, not unlike the requirements for admission to a doctoral program.

Winter (1993) presents a strong case for replacing the system of granting four levels of honours (first, upper and lower seconds, thirds) currently used widely in England with one in which candidates would be deemed to have 'satisfied requirements' for the award of an ungraded honours degree. His argument was partly based on the difficulty of applying any normative measures to work experience programs which play an important part in many professional awards, namely that it is virtually impossible to compare the performance of one student with another whose work experience is in an entirely different environment.

The Grade Point Average, which is used extensively in the United States and some other countries, is a useful device for giving some indication of the level of a student's performance at various key stages in a degree program, and again may be used to determine which students may be admitted to more advanced units of study. Like any other grading system, however, it suffers from inconsistencies between institutions, departments and individual markers.

It should be noted that summative measures are not confined to the end of a degree program, consequently it is quite legitimate to use some summative measures at appropriate stages within the constituent units. As mentioned earlier, the teacher's dilemma is to decide what should be regarded as summative and what as formative, and the extent to which each earlier or interim measure is allowed to influence the final grade. In most degree programs leading to a professional qualification, the profession itself will determine, or at least strongly suggest, much of the subject matter to be included and the levels of attainment expected. Thus the task of allocating suitable weights to each item of assessment must be faced, an issue which will also be discussed in Chapter 13.

(Indirect) measures of teaching quality

Why do some people regard it as unusual or unethical for an educational institution to use the performance of students in examinations as a measure of the quality of the teaching? This issue has received considerable publicity in New South Wales, Australia. During 1996 the state department of education used a battery of diagnostic tests in government secondary schools to measure pupils' gains in levels of literacy and numeracy since they commenced their secondary schooling. On the basis of these measures the department produced a list of schools showing their ranking in terms of the 'value added' component of their pupils' education. Many teachers and parents were annoyed because the list did not contain schools which had excellent results in university entrance exams, namely selective high schools where entry standards were high. As might be expected, the schools which did best in the value added ranking came from those which accepted pupils from all elementary schools in the area, often having had the best students 'creamed off' to the nearest selective high schools or private schools. If both teachers and pupils were highly motivated there was a greater possibility for spectacular gains in literacy and numeracy during the high school years. The point to be gained from this controversy is that it is necessary to use value added measures intelligently.

In the above case, a government department was using increases in test scores to compare one school with another and the teachers' union lodged a protest. There are other circumstances, within a large university class, where the grades awarded by tutors or teaching assistants might be used to compare the quality of their teaching, but even under circumstances such as this, one would need to be sure that the results are not confused by differences in entry level (knowledge), ability or commitment of students in different classes. With well-matched classes following the same curriculum but under different teachers, it could be assumed that the lecturer whose students performed well was a better teacher than one whose students performed poorly. On the other hand, it is sometimes claimed that a person whose teaching technique is poor forces students to undertake more independent study and engage in more active learning than would be the case for students whose lecturer engaged in 'spoon-feeding'.

Arguments such as the above invariably lead to the question: 'What *is* good teaching?' to which one must answer: 'Good teaching stimulates students to learn and instils in them a love of the subject.' Rarely would a final examination provide an accurate measure of these qualities. Some readers will have heard of teachers (at all levels of education) whose students regularly perform very highly in state-wide examinations, yet these students who have scored highly, say in chemistry at high school, lose all interest in the subject and soon forget what they have learned.

Despite the arguments presented in previous paragraphs, most university teachers are aware of wide discrepancies in grading within institutions, within disciplines and even when the same work is graded by the same assessor at different times. There are examples of such discrepancies in the literature on assessment. Warren Piper *et al.* (1995), for example, refer to numerous surveys which indicate that there is a wide variation in standards among examiners, at least in the United Kingdom (Bourner and Bourner, 1985; Chapman, 1994) and Australia (Anderson, 1984; AVCC, 1990, 1991, etc; Nulty and Warren Piper, 1993).

With reference to variations in standards between institutions in the United Kingdom, Warren Piper *et al.* (1995) draw on earlier research by Ramsden:

> Ramsden (1986) argues that the proportions of good (honours) degrees (first and upper second class) are not very accurate indicators of which institutions are of a higher standard than those who produce smaller proportions of good degrees. Ramsden refers to two studies … which found that the proportion of good degrees was more a function of the distribution of results in previous years than teaching quality, student ability or resources. It is difficult to argue that similar distributions between institutions signify a common standard, or that variations in distributions signifies different standards. (p. 71)

Ramsden himself (1986) refers to research sponsored by the Council for National Academic Awards in the United Kingdom which supports the view that 'public sector institutions' (ie polytechnics and colleges) were at that time more efficient in their teaching than the traditional universities, given that the standard of entry was significantly lower for the polytechnics and colleges than the universities. In other words, there is a greater value added component for students' learning in the colleges than in the universities. Now that the public sector institutions (and their equivalents in other countries) have been transformed into universities and are being encouraged to give greater emphasis to research and scholarship – sometimes to the detriment of teaching and public service – it would be interesting to replicate the earlier study in order to discover whether measurable differences in teaching efficiency can be identified. Ramsden (1986) identifies the difficulties associated with the interpretation of such research:

> The error involved in the use of degrees as indicators of effectiveness is simply to forget that they are proxies for output, not the output itself. The evidence is that they do not measure the same things in different departments and institutions. But what are we trying to measure anyway? The real difficulties in comparing standards by looking at degree results and student or institutional inputs are not technical questions of measurement. They are to do with the fact that quantitative indicators are asked to do an educational task which they are not capable of performing. (pp. 109–10)

Finally, with reference to links between teaching quality and student performance in examinations, it is useful to repeat an observation made by Clift and Imrie (1981):

> Earlier in this book, we stressed that assessment is a major teaching responsibility. Assessment for learning, as well as for grading, implies that students understand what is required, that the tasks are relevant to course objectives and content, and that student learning and performance can improve as a direct result of the assessment. For grading, assessment should provide valid measures and descriptions of student knowledge, ability and skills.
>
> If any part of teaching is to be assessed, then it should be the 'business' of quality control of assessment. A minimum requirement would be the moderation of the formal procedures of assessment for grading. Again, colleague participation is entirely appropriate for mutual appraisal to improve this requirement of institutional education.
>
> Ideally, departments or groups of teachers should form moderating groups with the responsibility of monitoring all assessment information. Such information would include assessment information supplied to the students at the beginning of a course, draft examinations, tests and assignments, together with solutions, marking schemes and control procedures. (pp. 128–9)

Seventeen years later one is tempted to ask to what extent these ideals have been incorporated into the regular practice of university and college teachers.

3

Cognitive educational objectives, learning outcomes and levels of testing

> If someone offers to furnish a sure test, ask what the test was which made the sure test sure.
>
> (Author unknown)

Approaches to learning

Research on student learning – as reported by such people as Pask (1976), Marton and Säljö (1976a, b), Svensson (1977), Laurillard (1979), Ramsden and Entwistle (1981), Entwistle and Ramsden (1983), Newble and Jaeger (1983), Schmeck (1983), Bowden (1984), Bowden and Ramsden (1986), Bowden *et al.* (1987), and Scouller and Prosser (1994) – has demonstrated links between the students' approaches to learning and their performance in assessment tasks. As we reported in the previous chapter, the converse also applies: the format of assessment can determine the way students set about their learning. A simple example will demonstrate this point. A university teacher may tell students that it is essential that they must be able to *evaluate* apparently opposing theories or explanations for a set of data, yet if the examinations consistently ask students to *describe* the different theories, students will respond to the latter and not develop skills of evaluation.

One of the earlier investigators of student learning, using strictly controlled laboratory conditions rather than classroom observations, was Pask (1976) who identified two basic learning strategies which he called 'serialist' and 'holist'. In Pask's earlier papers he described a *serialist* approach as one in which students learn, remember and reca-pitulate a body of information in a relatively fixed sequence. Consequently they find it almost impossible to tolerate irrelevant information unless they are equipped with unusually large memory capacities. He defined a *holist* approach as one in which students learn, remember and recapitulate as a whole. Students who use the holist strategy, he claimed, are more likely to grasp general principles than are serialists, but their memory for details is not as accurate (Pask and Scott, 1972).

According to Daniel (1975), who has interpreted some of Pask's work for a wider audience, the existence of the serialist/holist dichotomy is further attested by the evidence that if holists are presented with a teaching program designed for serialists (or vice versa), there is a highly significant decrease in the amount of learning compared with that which occurs when the program is matched to the characteristics of the learner. When students are presented with a learning task designed to allow a choice of either a serialist or holist approach, the two groups perform equally well. Moreover, when each group is asked to teach the newly learned material, they do so following the procedures, serialist or holist, which they themselves have followed.

While it is unrealistic to expect tertiary institutions to allocate students to classes which are appropriate to their learning strategies (assuming that students really do fall into the categories described by Pask), it is not unreasonable to examine carefully all systems of teaching which expect students to follow a rigidly predetermined sequence of learning tasks such as is found in some laboratory courses.

More or less concurrent with Pask's original research, a different approach to the investigation of how students learn was being devel-oped by Marton and his team in Gothenburg, Sweden. Marton and Säljö (1976a, b), in describing their earlier work, identify two levels of approach to learning tasks or levels of processing information, namely 'deep' and 'surface'. A *deep approach*, they claimed, is charac-terized by an intention on the part of the student to seek the author's meaning when reading a passage from a reference, to consider the evidence presented and conclusions drawn by the author in order to reach a personal conclusion, and to attempt to relate the new knowledge to the student's previous knowledge or experience in the new world. A *surface approach*, on the other hand, is used when a student concentrates on memorizing discrete facts or ideas, or concentrates on completing a set task. Students who undertake their learning tasks in a superficial manner may fail to recognize the hierarchical structure of the text and they are likely to confuse examples with principles.

More recent research by Laurillard (1979), Ramsden (1979), Hounsell (1979) and Säljö (1982) has cast considerable doubt on the stability of the serialist/holist and deep/surface dichotomy, in that some students have been observed to demonstrate what a number of them call a 'versatile' approach to learning tasks, using whichever strategy they think is the most appropriate. Despite the fact that some students are able to demonstrate versatility, there is still the problem that other students habitually use learning strategies which are inappropriate for achieving higher level objectives such as the ability to analyse a complex set of data or to integrate new learning with their previous knowledge.

Following the line of research developed by Marton and his team, Bowden *et al.* (1987) describe students' approaches to learning in a number of faculties along a continuum ranging from 'superficial learning' to 'learning for understanding':

> Rarely do groups of academics, when talking about the qualities they expect their students to develop, fail to mention such capacities as understanding, critical thinking, integration of concepts and ideas, intellectual independence [and] knowing how to find out rather than merely knowing. Yet when the objectives of tertiary study are discussed and the practices of university and college departments investigated, the question is raised as to whether the relation between assessment methods and students' approaches to learning is always considered when academics set examinations and other assessments … Unfortunately there is a good deal of recent evidence to suggest that the quality of student learning in tertiary institutions is adversely influenced by inappropriate assessment methods. (p. 397)

An even stronger indictment of the frequent mismatch between the objectives of the curriculum and the assessment methods used comes from Scouller and Prosser (1994):

> Although staff report that they want their students to be analytical, critical and creative thinkers, problem-solvers able to understand and apply principles and key concepts to new problems; and to be independent and autonomous learners, students are receiving a different set of signals if examinations demand primarily recall of factual information and lower levels of cognitive processes. In fact, assessment has been identified as possibly the single most potent influence on student learning, narrowing students' focus to concentrate only on topics to be examined (that is, *what* is to be studied) and shaping their learning approaches (that is, *how* it is to be studied). (p. 268)

The distinction between superficial (or surface) learning and learning for understanding (or deep learning) is best illustrated in the summary of the research project described below.

Superficial learning

In the article by Bowden *et al.* (1987), from which an earlier quotation was taken, the authors describe an investigation of first-year students' approaches to learning. The students were asked to think about the assessment of their first-year courses and the extent to which the assessment encouraged them to learn in particular ways. They were then invited to select from an inventory of 20 items the ones which best described their most typical study habits for particular courses. Nine of the 20 items in the inventory were designed to illustrate a superficial approach to study, such as an emphasis on memorizing. The other 11 items focussed on learning for understanding.

In this particular survey the researchers found that the five 'superficial learning' items chosen repeatedly were, in order of their frequency:

1. to memorize the main points in the study material
2. to try to absorb a large amount of factual information
3. to concentrate on trying to remember as much information as possible
4. to learn by heart the material you were studying
5. to concentrate on facts and details rather than issues and arguments. (pp. 398–9)

Learning for understanding

Of the 11 items in the inventory which were associated with learning for understanding, the five which were most frequently chosen by students were:

1. to really understand what you are studying
2. to try and integrate all the facts and details you covered
3. to reflect on key points in the study material
4. to link different themes and concepts together
5. to try to understand the implications of what you are learning. (Bowden, Masters and Ramsden, 1987 pp. 402, 404)

University teachers and all who are interested in higher education may well compare the above two lists with their own expectations for students, asking themselves whether the ways their courses are structured, taught and assessed are more likely to induce students to adopt superficial learning strategies or strategies which will enhance deep understanding of their chosen field of study.

Before we leave this section on students' approaches to learning it is important to point out the distinction between 'learning styles' and 'learning strategies'. One of the earlier descriptions of this difference is in an article by Entwistle *et al.* (1979) where they say:

> Clearly there is still a strong element of intention in any description of the learning process or processes adopted by a student, but it seems important to distinguish between *strategy* and *style*, where *strategy* is a description of the way a student *chooses* to tackle a specific learning task in the light of its perceived demands, and *style* is a broader characterization of a student's *preferred* way of tackling learning tasks generally. This definition of strategy of course rules out the possibility of developing any general scale to measure it. (p. 368)

Schmeck (1983) distinguishes between strategy and style somewhat differently and adds a significant comment about the effect of the learning environment on a student's strategy:

> From my theoretical perspective, a learning style is a predisposition on the part of some students to adopt a particular learning strategy regardless of the specific demands of the task. Thus a style is simply a strategy that is used with some cross-situational consistency. In turn, I define a *learning strategy* as a pattern of information-processing activities used to prepare for an anticipated test of memory ... Some researchers have argued that a learning style (or predisposition) is less important than the immediate situation in determining which specific learning strategy a student will adopt. Within the university, the immediate situation includes characteristics of course content, the instruction, and the test. (pp. 233–4)

We suggest that involving students in discussions of learning style and learning strategy would provide a sound basis for both students' intellectual development and quality assurance of the teaching program.

Educational objectives

It is acknowledged by teachers and students alike that some tasks are more difficult or more demanding than others, either because they test a wider range of knowledge or the level at which a student is expected to perform is higher in some tasks than in others. This phenomenon was recognized over 40 years ago by Benjamin Bloom and his associates (1956) who identified and classified the main types of objectives which students were expected to achieve. Since then there has been much discussion on the concept and value of objectives and a call for replacing the emphasis on *educational objectives* with one on *learning outcomes*. For example, Allan (1996) reviews earlier work on the subject and presents a strong case for putting the emphasis on the outcomes (for the student) of learning experiences, not all of which would have occurred within the context of a formal teaching program. She claims that learning outcomes in higher education are much broader than what is learned in the classroom and which is assessed by traditional methods. These desired outcomes embrace:

> personal transferable outcomes, including acting independently; working with others; using information technology; gathering information; communicating effectively; organizational skills; and generic academic outcomes – making use of information; thinking critically; analysing; synthesizing ideas and information. (p. 107)

In the above statement Allan underscores the generally acknowledged belief that the benefits of university education are much broader than what teachers hope to achieve in their particular courses. In calling for greater attention to be given to learning outcomes she says:

> This is not to undermine or denigrate the role of the lecturer, but rather to emphasize the role of the student in accepting responsibility for his/her own learning and to acknowledge that learning might take place in a variety of settings. There is no explicit expectation that the course/module must necessarily be completed in order to achieve the outcomes, some of which may be claimed through Accreditation of Prior Experiential Learning (APEL) schemes. (p. 104)

While we accept Allan's contention that learning outcomes are much broader than educational objectives we would stress that, when designing assessment tasks, course planners must focus on the objectives of their particular teaching/learning programs. They must be able to specify what students should be able to do as a result of their learning experiences, under what conditions the students will perform these assessment tasks and at what level of competence.

In this chapter we shall attempt to demonstrate how the various categories of objectives described by Bloom and those who succeeded him are applicable in most fields of higher education. We shall also report on more recent research which identifies links between conditions of assessment and the levels of objectives achieved. What Bloom and his colleagues did was to consider the many types of objectives commonly found in education and put them into a manageable number of categories. These categories have been used by course planners and test designers at all levels of education over the ensuing years and, while other schemes have been proposed (some of which will be discussed later), it is certain that Bloom and his associates have had a profound influence on educational practice and this influence is still very evident almost 40 years later.

Over the intervening period there has been considerable research on the relationships between educational objectives, students' approaches to learning and assessment, including quite justifiable questioning of some assessment techniques which encourage learning styles that are quite inconsistent with the original objectives (see, for example, Balla and Boyle, 1994). Nevertheless the original recognition that the quality of learning can be assessed at different levels is worth pursuing and taking into account when designing tests. Hence the reasonably detailed treatment of types and levels of objectives in this chapter.

Among the many types and levels of educational or instructional objectives Bloom identified three major classes or 'domains': cognitive, affective and psychomotor. Bloom claimed that within each major domain there existed a hierarchy or 'taxonomy' of objectives, but the initial publication of *Taxonomy of Educational Objectives* (Bloom, 1956) concentrated exclusively on the acquisition and use of knowledge – the cognitive domain. Construction of taxonomies for the affective and psychomotor domains was not completed until much later, namely 1964 and 1966 respectively.

Bloom's cognitive objectives

Because the taxonomy of the cognitive domain has had, and continues to have, such an influence on test design, particularly in the realms of science and technology, each of the levels in that domain will be briefly described here, with some applications being made to assessment in higher education. Bloom (1956) referred to six levels of objectives in the cognitive domain and the descriptions which follow are based on their abridged definitions in a later publication (Bloom *et al.*, 1971, pp. 271–3), the applications being added by the present authors.

1. Knowledge

> ability to recall specific items of information, to describe known ways of dealing with this information, or to enunciate previously learned general principles or theories

'Knowledge' is usually regarded as the lowest level of the cognitive objectives and therefore thought by some to be the easiest to test. Most questions asking for a definition are at this level. On the other hand, those questions which test the higher levels of the cognitive domain, eg questions asking the student to 'compare and contrast', 'write brief notes on …', solve problems or write essays, also depend initially on a student's ability to recall and describe relevant items of information, principles or theories. One of the difficulties with more advanced courses is that students are expected to learn a very large amount of factual information and the size of this task may interfere with their ability to engage in critical thinking or the integration of concepts and ideas (Bowden *et al.*, 1987; Bowden and Ramsden, 1986).

Even though 'knowledge' is at the lowest level of Bloom's cognitive objectives, it would be quite misleading to assume that questions at this level are necessarily simple. The following revision questions from Nelson *et al.* (1967) ask students to recall quite difficult items of factual information.

- Trace the steps involved in the translation of a DNA code in the nucleus into an enzyme out in the cytoplasm.
- Make a list of the biomes described in this chapter, then name one or more indicator plants and animals for each. (pp. 98, 297)

2. Comprehension

> ability to demonstrate one's understanding by translating or paraphrasing, interpreting information or extrapolating from given data in order to determine likely implications or effects

Many examples from higher education can be given at the 'comprehension' level of the cognitive domain. Translating is, of course, an important part of many tests and examinations in the foreign languages and paraphrasing is a requirement in English as well as in foreign languages. It should be recognized, however, that a typical translation of a prose passage from one language to another involves the student in activities which would be classified at a higher level than is implied by Bloom's use of the word translation. In fact each of his next four levels would be used as a student analyses the intentions of the author of the passage to be translated, applies the rules of grammar, makes judgements about the most appropriate ways of conveying the original meaning in another language, and creates a new piece of prose. When students are asked to write short notes on various items, a question type which appears in most disciplines at the tertiary level, they are engaging in a type of translation exercise (in Bloom's sense of the use of the word). Interpretation and extrapolation are important in mathematics, history, sociology, physics and other natural and social sciences.

The following revision question on bones and muscles illustrates the level of comprehension (Villee, 1967): 'Which muscles contract and which relax when you hold your arm out at the side? When you throw a ball?' For this question to be answered in a satisfactory manner a student would need to recall the names and functions of the relevant muscles and bones, understand the concept of muscular contraction and relaxation, and extrapolate from this knowledge in order to describe which muscles are contracting and which are relaxing for each of the described positions and movements.

Many multiple-choice questions measure the 'comprehension' level of Bloom's cognitive domain as is shown in the following example (Mathews, 1977):

'Whenever the factors of production are combined to produce any given commodity, the cost to society is to be reckoned in terms of the alternative goods which those factors could have produced.' This statement seeks to explain the concept of:
a) average cost
b) factor cost
c) opportunity cost
d) comparative cost
e) marginal cost. (p. 52)

3. Application

ability to apply abstract principles to particular and concrete situations

A frequently used term of criticism for certain proposed plans of action which a person judges to be impractical is that they are 'too academic', by which the speaker generally means that the idea may be good in theory, but it cannot be put into practice. The word is also used to describe some courses in higher education when it is thought that they have no application in 'the real world'. The ability to apply previously learned principles to the solution of new problems is really an objective for all courses in higher education; well-designed exercises or examination questions test students' abilities to reach this objective. For example, students' ability to apply abstract principles to a particular situation is tested in the following question (Keeton *et al.*, 1968):

> A well-known example of convergent evolution between two different plant families is that involving cacti and euphorbias. The two types of plants look so much alike that the average person normally calls both 'cacti', yet they are really not closely related. Can you think of reasons why these two plants, which live in the same sort of habitat, might have evolved the particular characteristics that both possess in common? (p. 266)

The next set of questions commence at the level of 'knowledge' in that students are asked to recall definitions of four engineering terms which they had probably committed to memory. The examples of machine tools for these operations would also be a recall exercise for the majority of students, but the last part of the question tests their ability to apply their knowledge of terminology to concrete situations.

> a) With respect to machine cutting describe what you understand by:
>   i) Surface forming
>   ii) Surface generation
>   iii) Climb milling
>   iv) Conventional milling.
> Give examples of machine tools on which such techniques may be employed.
> b) What factors dictate the choice of machining and machining method over other manufacturing processes? (Australian National University, *Manufacturing Technology*, 1993)

In the following question on short stories, candidates are asked to apply a particular hypothesis to stories they have studied during the previous semester:

> The plot of a short story usually involves a conflict or struggle between opposing forces. The discerning reader can see it develop in a pattern during the course of the narration, whether its events proceed chronologically or are rearranged, eg with flashbacks.' Discuss the nature and development of any TWO short stories studied this semester in tutorials or lectures. (Australian National University, *Introduction to English Literature*, 1992)

4. Analysis

clarification of a complex situation by breaking it down into its constituent parts, identifying any relationships between the parts, and identifying any organizational structure inherent in the original situation or set of data.

From the above description it will be seen that 'analysis', as defined by Bloom, is again a common objective in higher education. When a student is confronted with an examination question or an essay topic, the first task is clarify what the question is asking. In advanced laboratory and field studies, students are presented with large amounts of data upon which they must impose some organization once any interrelationships between the various sets of data have been recognized. For an effective analysis to be carried out a student must be able to work at Bloom's first two levels of 'knowledge' and 'comprehension', but we would not agree that application is also a prerequisite for 'analysis'. The following question from criminal law requires students to analyse the data, drawing on their knowledge of the relevant laws, interpreting that knowledge and applying it to the specific case.

> Jim and Tina went to a party. Both had too much to drink. After the party, there was a discussion as to who should drive Tina's car home. Jim insisted on doing so and Tina reluctantly agreed. She thought he looked drunk, but he denied this. Jim drove dangerously, but Tina decided it was best to say nothing. Jim then noticed a hitch-hiker ahead. He stopped and picked him up. Jim then resumed the drive and, soon afterwards, lost control of the car and hit a tree beside the road. Both Jim and Tina were uninjured, but the hitch-hiker was knocked unconscious. Jim panicked and urged that they should leave the car (with the hitch-hiker inside). After some argument, Tina agreed to leave the car and they decided to walk home. Police evidence indicated that the car had been left in a 'dangerous position'. A few minutes later another car hit Tina's car, killing the hitch-hiker.
>
> Assume that Jim is guilty of an offence under s.4(1) of the Motor Traffic Act 1909 (NSW). The relevant part of this section states: Any person who drives a motor vehicle upon a public street … in a manner which is dangerous to the public, shall be guilty of an offence under this Act.
>
> Discuss the liability of Tina for this crime and the liability of Jim for manslaughter. (The police have decided not to charge the driver of the second car as they concluded he was not criminally liable for the accident.) (Australian National University, *Criminal Law and Procedure*, 1993)

The next question provides students of engineering economics with some basic data, an hypothetical situation (the effect of having no toll) and a problem to be solved. Students must demonstrate their ability to represent these data by means of a diagram which they judge to be appropriate and then solve the problem.

> A bridge has the capacity to carry 1,000 vehicles per hour without congestion but cannot carry more than this without 'complete congestion'. Travel is free during the off-peak hours (totalling 20 hours in the day) and there are less than 1,000 crossings per hour. Peak crossings are priced at $1.00 per crossing during the peak period which lasts for 4 hours per day. 1,500 vehicles per hour would use the bridge at a zero price in the peak-period if the capacity was available.
> i)   Represent these data on a diagram.
> ii) What would be the value to bridge users of expanding capacity to 1,500 crossings per hour given that the bridge lasts for ever, that there is a peak period for each of the 365 days of each year, and that the discount rate is 10 per cent? (Australian National University, *Engineering Economics*, 1993)

5. Synthesis

> bringing together a number of facts or ideas to create a new pattern or structure such as a unique communication, a proposed set of operations or a set of abstract principles which are derived from the original data

The writing of essays in the humanities or social sciences, laboratory reports in the natural sciences, or proposals of solutions to problems in engineering or mathematics are all examples of the level termed 'synthesis'. Very little opportunity, if any, is provided for students to work at this level if they are only tested by multiple-choice questions. Even so, essays can be mere repetitions of previously learned lecture notes, whether written under examination conditions or given as a term assignment, in which case they are really only testing a student's ability to recall and reproduce factual information, the lowest of Bloom's cognitive levels. Lecturers who believe that all tertiary students should be able to demonstrate the skills described by Bloom under the heading of 'synthesis' will therefore take steps to ensure that their students are challenged to create 'unique communications' at many stages during their academic studies. It could be argued that analysis and synthesis are the objectives which are the most demanding and should therefore be placed at the top of the hierarchy of cognitive objectives.

The following two examination questions illustrate ways in which students' ability to achieve the cognitive objective of synthesis may be tested. In the first example, the candidates are asked to demonstrate their knowledge of historical events and interpret these in order to produce what may be a unique exposition for each student. Likewise, the question on political science requires students to demonstrate an extensive knowledge of both political theory and political events, not necessarily confined to the one country, to point out where the events are consistent with the theories being espoused by the government of the time and which are inconsistent with the government's policies. Furthermore, as this is an honours paper, it is reasonable to assume that the examiner expects students to suggest reasons why there is this lack of consistency and perhaps to advance a new hypothesis which accounts for the apparent lack of consistency.

> To what extent was slavery, and then segregation, influenced by blacks' behaviour and attitudes? (Australian National University, *US History*, 1992)
> What is your understanding of the relation between political theory and the practice of politics? (Australian National University, *Political Science Honours*, 1992)

6. Evaluation

> judgments about the value of materials or methods for a given purpose

Evaluation, in the sense described here, is a necessary prerequisite for both effective analysis and synthesis. For this reason one might question the ranking of Bloom's taxonomy of the cognitive domain which has been accepted by some of his followers. On the other hand, as the following examples show, students must use all levels of cognitive skills to answer the following evaluation type questions.

> Explain and evaluate the separation of ownership and control which characterizes the company form of business enterprise. (Jackson and McConnell, 1980, p. 134)
> Gaffikin suggests: 'Management may find variable costing statements very useful for analytical purposes. A principal benefit is that variable costing usually causes net income figures to move in the same direction.' Demonstrate how this statement is true. Discuss the advantages and disadvantages of adopting a system of variable costing. Which do you prefer and why? (Australian National University, *Engineering Management*, 1993)

Other cognitive taxonomies

Much research has been conducted on taxonomies, particularly the cognitive taxonomy. Applications have been diverse. One recent example (Benson *et al.*, 1992) describes a model for guiding students in writing reviews of family literature, based on Bloom's cognitive taxonomy. Another example (Reeves, 1990) examines the implications of the cognitive and affective taxonomies for teaching business ethics. Following Imrie (1995), three examples of modification and application of Bloom's taxonomy are now described briefly.

The first example (Table 3.1) is the RECAP model (Imrie, 1995, p. 179) which is an adaptation of Bloom's taxonomy and provides a two-tier structure (after Terwilliger, 1977) for both in-course (coursework) and end-of-course assessment (eg examination, project), linked to four levels of learning referred to by the acronym RECAP: REcall, Comprehension, Application, Problem solving. RECAP covers all the abilities of Bloom's taxonomy with direct correspondence for the first three levels (knowledge, comprehension, application) but groups Bloom's top three categories (analysis, synthesis, evaluation) together as problem-solving skills.

Tier 1

The course objectives state the minimum essentials which students should achieve. Objective, short answer and structured questions are

Table 3.1   *The RECAP Model (Imrie, 1995)*

RECAP	Skill level	Bloom's category	Assessment level and task
TIER 1	Recall Comprehension Application	Knowledge Comprehension Application	Assessment of minimum essential skills using, eg objective, short answer and structured questions.
TIER 2	Problem-solving skills	Analysis Synthesis Evaluation	Assessment of more advanced skills using, eg supply questions.

usually suitable for assessing these skills; mastery testing (to see if students have achieved basic competence, at mastery level, in the skills being assessed) may be appropriate. (Mastery testing will be discussed again in Chapter 7.)

Tier 2

The course objectives focus on skills which are important for problem solving. Essay, structured, and case study questions are examples of procedures suitable for assessing these skills. Both criterion-referenced and norm-referenced assessments are appropriate at this level.

In its design, Bloom's taxonomy goes from the simplest to the highest skills. Another way of visualizing this is shown in Figure 3.1 which is reproduced here with the permission of Cedric Hall of the Victoria University of Wellington, New Zealand. *Knowledge* (the ability to recall what has been learned) is seen as the simplest or most basic skill and is needed for the next level, comprehension. *Comprehension* (the ability to show that what has been learned is understood) is needed for the next level, *application*. Note that the top three categories, *analysis, synthesis and evaluation*, are different kinds of higher skills which follow on from *application*.

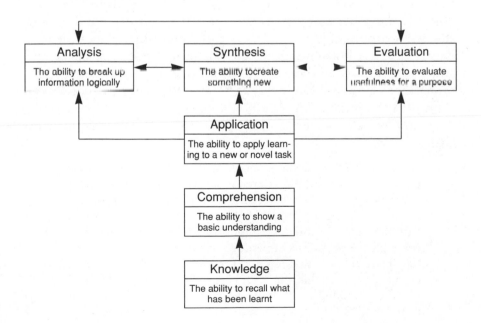

Figure 3.1   Interrelationships between Bloom's cognitive levels

As students progress towards meeting course objectives, their skill levels change. What is at first an application task for a student may only be a knowledge (recall) task later. Even the most complicated skills eventually become automatic with on-the-job practice as the practitioner moves from 'novice' to 'expert'.

Petter (1982) provides an example of a pedagogical analysis with reference to law school curriculum in Canada in the context of the Bloom (1956) and Krathwohl *et al.* (1964) taxonomies. He maintains that:

> It is highly desirable, if not essential, that law schools provide for all six levels of cognitive learning objectives within their curricula. Law schools, after all, are training grounds for lawyers and, in order to prepare lawyers to act effectively on behalf of their clients, it is necessary that they teach their students to:
> 1. know the law
> 2. comprehend it
> 3. apply it to particular fact situations
> 4. break it down into its component parts
> 5. reorganize it and employ it creatively so as to serve clients' interests
> 6. evaluate the strength of its authority and its probable impact on clients.

Petter's conclusions were that there should be provision for both domains but that 'only one out of eleven levels of cognitive and affective learning objectives appears to be consistently addressed ... knowledge, the bottom step on the cognitive ladder'. In effect, the conclusion seems to be that faculty have not discharged their professional responsibilities to assess student performance at the appropriate or intended levels.

A simpler scheme using only three categories was derived by Crooks (1988) from Bloom's taxonomy, namely:

> a) Recall or Recognition – students to demonstrate that they know particular information ... to recognize or recall ... not required to demonstrate that they understand or can apply the information.
> b) Comprehension or Simple Application – students to demonstrate that they can comprehend and/or apply information, formulae, principles or skills. Essay questions which focus largely on recall of information but which require students to be able to write coherently ... are placed in this category.
> c) Critical Thinking or Problem Solving – students to make use of principles, skills, or their creativity to solve problems or work with ideas in ways which are clearly more than routine exercises. The key point about questions at this level is that they must

involve (from the student's point of view) original situations or perspectives.

In the grid (Table 3.2) Crooks shows how an examiner might determine the proportion of marks allocated for each of his three levels and each aspect of the subject matter. Using the three-level taxonomy advocated by Crooks makes it much easier to construct an assessment planning grid which is a relatively simple means of ensuring that each important area of content is tested at each level of objectives. For example, in the sample grid shown by Crooks, the examiner is able to predetermine the proportion of marks which will be allocated for each area of content and each level of objectives. There is no need for the marks to be divided evenly; the allocation depends on the relative importance attached by the examiner or course coordinator to each cell in the table. Another examiner may well decide to allocate a greater proportion of marks to ecology and less to vertebrates, for example, and have more marks for critical thinking about ecological issues. With grids such as these it is easier to ensure that the total pattern of assessment achieves what has been predetermined by the course coordinator.

Table 3.2 *Content vs objectives grid (Crooks, 1988)*

Content Area	Recall, Recognition	Skills, Comprehension, Application	Critical Thinking Problem Solving	Row Totals
Biochemistry	3	12	0	15
Cells/Tissues	4	13	3	20
Genetics & Reproduction	2	10	3	15
Invertebrates	4	6	0	10
Vertebrates	5	11	4	20
Plant Life	2	6	2	10
Ecological Issues	0	7	3	10
Column Totals	20	65	15	100

For professional and vocational education, where attitudes and values are particularly important, there are two taxonomies which provide an inclusive framework. The first (EPC, 1989) is a teaching/learning analysis for quality in engineering education that could be generalized to other fields. The paper describes three types of cognitive learning: knowledge, skills and understanding. In the affective domain are attitudes and values, which are personal qualities. The EPC taxonomy identifies the above categories as types of learning and links each with resources needed, processes of learning, and assessment of outcomes. The EPC paper also makes reference to deep learning and surface learning with the former being the 'key issue in achieving quality in education'. As noted previously, the key pedagogical issue is that of 'understanding'. Two domains (cognitive and affective) are presented with an emphasis on understanding which 'involves grasping concepts and being able to use them creatively' (corresponding to 'originality'). In discussing assessment, the author(s) of EPC (1989) make the following statement:

> To test for understanding it is necessary to set students new challenges. Unfortunately this is not easy ... The result is that although most academics intend to teach understanding, and encourage students to be 'deep' learners, the examinations they set can often be dealt with successfully mainly by the exercise of memory and well-practised skills – that is, by adopting a 'surface' approach to learning.

EPC (1992) presents a taxonomy of examination styles which indicates potential to 'test levels of different kinds' and takes into consideration staff concerns such as 'staff time per student'. Subsequently, Sparkes (1994) reported a further development of know-how as a distinct type of learning.

Another inclusive taxonomy is the 'experiential taxonomy' which was developed by Steinaker and Bell (1979) to provide an integrated framework related to actual learning experience with due consideration for the varying and time-dependent interactions of cognitive, affective and psychomotor learning. This taxonomy sets out educational objectives related to the stages of learning experience and development outlined in Table 3.3. At the dissemination stage in the scheme described by Steinaker and Bell, assessment requires the student (in some specified way) to demonstrate learning and there should be clear correspondence between the actual and the intended outcomes in terms of the 'qualities/skills' that the course seeks to develop in students. The level of the award can

Table 3.3 *The experiential taxonomy (Steinaker and Bell, 1979)*

1.0 EXPOSURE (initial level)
    1.1 Sensory
    1.2 Response
    1.3 Readiness
	3.0 IDENTIFICATION
	    3.1 Reinforcement
	    3.2 Emotional
	    3.3 Personal
	    3.4 Sharing

2.0 PARTICIPATION
    2.1 Representation
        2.1.1 Covertly
        2.1.2 Overtly
	4.0 INTERNALIZATION
	    4.1 Expansion
	    4.2 Intrinsic

	5.0 DISSEMINATION (final level)
	    5.1 Informational
	    5.2 Homiletic

then be justifiably related to the aims, objectives and content of the course. They described their taxonomy as one 'that could speak to the totality of an experience'. As such, the experiential taxonomy provides a powerful structure for the management of learning experiences to improve teaching performance and methods, and for the organization of educational development. The reader will note some similarities to the taxonomy of affective objectives (Krathwohl *et al.*, 1964) to which we will refer again in the final section of this chapter and which will be described in more detail in Chapter 4.

A final example in the cognitive domain is the SOLO taxonomy – Structures of the Observed Learning Outcomes – which was developed by Biggs and Collis (1982). According to Gibbs (1992) it has been used as a framework for judging the quality of essays, answers to technical questions, medical diagnoses or students' accounts of their reading.

A possible relationship between the SOLO taxonomy and deep or surface learning is seen in Table 3.4 where Ramsden (1992) applied the structural levels of the SOLO taxonomy to the assessment of an essay or 'open-ended' problem.

Table 3.4 *Levels in the SOLO taxonomy (Ramsden, 1992; based on Biggs and Collis, 1982)*

Prestructural	Use of irrelevant information or no meaningful response.
Unistructural	Answer focuses on one relevant aspect only.
Multistructural	Answer focuses on several relevant features, but they are not coordinated together.
Relational	The several parts are integrated into a coherent whole; details are linked to conclusions; meaning is understood.
Extended abstract	Answer generalizes the structure beyond the information given; higher order principles are used to bring in a new and broader set of issues.

In Table 3.5, Entwistle and Brennan (1971) focuses more on the type of learning, but one can see parallels to the SOLO taxonomy in their descriptions of each level. In this case qualities of learning are linked with levels of learning for assessment of student performance.

Table 3.5 *Levels of learning (Entwistle and Brennan, 1971)*

Level	Description
Deep active	Student demonstrates an understanding of the argument and shows how it is supported by the evidence.
Deep passive	Student mentions the main argument, but does not relate evidence to conclusion.
Surface active	Student describes the main points made without integrating them into an argument.
Surface passive	Student mentions a few isolated points or examples.

Concluding comments on cognitive objectives

From a pedagogical point of view, there should be clear and justifiable links between objectives, assessment and outcomes. It is the responsibility of the teacher (or course planner) to select teaching and assessment methods which are appropriate to the needs of the students within the context of the educational institution and the particular study program being followed. Assessment of student performance (both formative and summative) provides the principal domain of interaction between students and teachers in that context.

One occasionally hears criticisms from university teachers that their students are unable to demonstrate the type of problem-solving skills which Imrie (1984) described as Tier 2 in the RECAP Model which was summarized as Table 3.1. In their assignments and answers to examination questions the students are said to be very good at remembering and repeating material from lecture notes and textbooks, but unable to solve problems which they have not previously seen or discussed, even when they have the knowledge and skills needed to solve these problems. Under such circumstances it is the *teacher's* responsibility to organize the course in such a way that students will be encouraged to think for themselves, to 'internalize' what they have learned so that their understanding of the subject matter is no longer at the 'superficial' level similar to that described by Bowden *et al.* (1987) and mentioned in the first section of this chapter.

An example from the first-year university experience of one of the present authors will illustrate how problem solving as such may not measure deeper levels of understanding. At the time of this experience, students in Chemistry 1 were required to demonstrate their abilities in three major branches of the discipline, namely inorganic, organic and physical chemistry. As a student, this author felt that he had a reasonable grasp of the inorganic section, enjoyed and understood the organic, but had no grasp of the theoretical basis of physical chemistry. A perusal of previous examination papers showed that each question on this final section had two parts: the first testing one's knowledge of the theory and the second being a problem, supposedly based on the first part. The student found that by following relatively simple rules, it was possible to solve all the problems (thus scoring 100 per cent for the second part of each question) without any real understanding of the principles which were supposedly being tested! One must ask whether a change in

61

teaching methods or exam format was required if the objectives for that particular course were to be achieved.

Royer *et al.* (1993) has made a comprehensive study of procedures for enhancing cognitive skills and techniques for measuring these skills. As well as considering whether cognitive theory can support cognitive instruction and valid assessment, he considers whether cognitive assessments are 'authentic', ie 'involve performances that have educational value in their own right' (Wiggins, 1989).

Royer also considers measures of metacognitive skills. It is worth noting that Nisbet and Shucksmith (1984) describe metacognition as a 'seventh sense' but conclude: 'All that can be claimed for metacognition is that it is likely to prove useful in the task of "learning to learn", an educational objective of increasing importance in a period of rapid technological change.'

Bearing in mind that this was in 1984, the much more recent concept of 'graduateness' uses a metacognitive vocabulary. However, as previously noted, both the assessment methods and the practitioners need development. Royer *et al.* (1993) acknowledge that not all cognitive skills (as defined) are 'transferable' so it is worth noting that by the end of the 1980s, Hind (1989a, b) had produced a tutor's manual *and* a student guide on transferable personal skills which he described as a new term!

The distinction between Bloom's highest level of cognitive objectives, *evaluation*, and the affective objectives, as described by Krathwohl *et al.* (1964), is sometimes blurred. In Bloom's terminology, as we have seen, 'evaluation' refers to judgements made, on academic grounds, about the worth of a particular proposal – whether it takes into account all relevant data and whether a logical sequence of arguments is used. By way of contrast, Krathwohl's affective objectives relate to students' attitudes, which may or may not be influenced by their levels of cognitive achievement. Some university teachers believe that affective objectives are inappropriate to the formal processes of higher education, taking the view that it is not the function of university teachers to prescribe appropriate attitudes for their students, but there are probably more who would acknowledge a need for developing in their students a willingness to consider new ideas, to report their findings honestly and to be considerate in their dealings with others, particularly students, clients or patients. An example of the overlap between cognitive and affective objectives is described by Reeves (1990) who examines the implications of the cognitive and affective taxonomies in teaching business ethics. There is also the 'totality' of a student's experience as addressed by Steinaker and Bell (1979) and noted earlier. It is therefore quite appropriate that a book on assessment in higher education should pay some attention to measuring the attainment of affective objectives. We shall do this in the next chapter.

4

Measuring the outcomes of non-cognitive educational objectives

The worth of a book is to be measured by what you can carry away from it.

(James Bryce)

In the previous chapter we referred to Bloom's (1956) *Taxonomy of Educational Objectives* in which three domains were identified: cognitive, affective and psychomotor. Much of the emphasis in higher education is on the attainment of cognitive objectives and, because these objectives influence and are influenced by the types of assessment used, there is more discussion of cognitive objectives than non-cognitive. Nevertheless, with changes in traditional curricula and the incorporation of schools of art, music and drama into a greater number of universities, we must not overlook the importance of non-cognitive objectives, even in traditional university disciplines.

Affective objectives

Affective objectives are defined by Krathwohl *et al.* (1964) as those 'which emphasize a feeling tone, an emotion, or a degree of acceptance or rejection'. 'Affective objectives', they add, 'vary from simple attention to selected phenomena to complex but internally consistent qualities of character and conscience.' The authors identify five major levels at which students respond to educational objectives in the affective domain. The names of the levels and the subdivisions within each level are those used by Krathwohl *et al.* (1964); the descriptions which follow them are the present authors' interpretation of a summary by Bloom *et al.* (1971). It may be used as a guide for tertiary teachers who wish to compare the levels reached by students at different stages in a course, or indeed within a single lecture or tutorial. The difficulty for a college or university teacher is not so much in recognizing the importance of affective objectives as in deciding whether to include them as part of the formal scheme of assessment and, if they are to be assessed, in what way and with what degree of weighting.

1. Receiving

a sign is present that the student is prepared to learn

This may be indicated by the student's presence at classes. Krathwohl's group note that this basic level of 'receiving' may itself become manifest at three sub-levels, namely:

a) *Awareness* of visual or oral stimuli from the lecturer, without necessarily being able to recall the nature of the stimuli.

Most of us can recognize that this is the *highest* level managed by at least some of our students in the less exciting parts of our lectures and therefore we seek ways of varying the stimuli in order to raise the level of our students' responses.

b) *Willingness* to receive stimuli from the teacher with no attempt being made by the student to avoid the stimuli.

Attempts to avoid the stimuli from the lecturer would include occasions when a student masks out the sound of a lecture by engaging in conversation with another student or listening to music through headphones.

c) *Controlled or selected attention* occurs when a student shows signs of attending to some stimuli in an environment where there are many.

Students may, for example, only pay attention in a lecture when the lecturer displays new material by means of an overhead projector (or unexpectedly leaves the room!).

2. Responding

the student displays a minimum level of commitment to the material being taught yet may appear to be gaining some satisfaction from the subject.

66

As with 'awareness', 'responding' may be demonstrated at three sub-levels:

a) *Acquiescence in responding* – a passive obedience by the student to any instructions from the teacher.

Examples of acquiescence would be writing down definitions or examining a specimen in a laboratory.

b) *Willingness to respond* – the student voluntarily obeys instructions, not because the student fears any kind of penalty or reproof.

c) *Satisfaction in response* – a student appears to derive some satisfaction from his or her voluntary response to the teacher or the instructional materials.

It is sometimes difficult for a teacher to distinguish between Stages 2 b) and 2 c), at least over a short period. Over a longer period evidence of students' satisfaction or enjoyment is shown by their willingness to undertake further work on a particular topic.

3. Valuing

an appreciation by the student of the worth of pursuing particular educational objectives

As with other major levels, this level may be further subdivided into:

a) *Acceptance of a value* – indicated when a student is prepared to be identified with certain beliefs or points of view

b) *Preference for a value* – intermediate stage between acceptance and commitment, and

c) *Commitment* – belief is expressed in action on the part of the student.

4. Organization

an attempt by the student to arrange a set of values into a hierarchical system so that relationships between different beliefs held by the student become clear

Where there are apparent conflicts, the student identifies which belief is the more important. Two subdivisions of this level have been identified:

a) *Conceptualization of a value* – the student can see how one set of values relates to another or how a new attitude or belief fits into the student's previously held set of beliefs

b) *Organization of a value system* – the student is beginning to develop a philosophy of life which incorporates a 'complex of possibly disparate values' which the student attempts to bring into an ordered relationship with one another.

5. Characterization by a value or value complex

the highest level of the affective objectives which is reached when the student consistently behaves in accordance with the set of values which he or she has adopted

There are two sub-levels, namely:

a) *Generalized set* – an unconscious cluster of attitudes which guides a student's actions without conscious forethought on the part of the student
b) *Characterization* – the value system has become the student's philosophy of life.

It should be clear from the above descriptions that each level of Krathwohl's affective domain is likely to be evident in almost any course in higher education. Their importance in fields such as theology, counselling, medicine, social work and law is obvious. An essential part of the day-to-day work of a graduate in each of the above professions is with individual clients, where ethics, beliefs and value systems of consultant and client may be in conflict, or at least need to be recognized. One would therefore expect that at some stage during their professional training undergraduates will be required to demonstrate their acceptance of certain values in other people, and their preference for and commitment to a value system which is not inconsistent with the values of the relevant branch of their chosen profession. For example, it was recognized by Krathwohl *et al.* (1964) that commitment to a particular attitude or belief is shown in a student's attitudes.

There should be actions on behalf of the value, belief, or sentiment – actions which by their very nature imply a commitment. For example, as a consequence of the social studies objective 'Identification with a current social problem', one student volunteers to assist a juvenile-delinquent group worker in a neighbourhood community center and devotes every Saturday during the school year to his work, while another student becomes interested in capital punishment and reads widely on the subject, attends lectures and public meetings, and talks with public officials and criminologists. (p. 150)

The researchers state that there may be occasions when a student has no opportunities for demonstrating directly the type of commitment being sought, in which case the teacher must devise ways of testing students' beliefs and attitudes through such activities as rôle plays or socio-drama. Testing the higher levels of affective objectives by means of formal examination questions, or even by reports on projects similar to those described in the above quotation, would be a less valid method of assessing these objectives than would direct observation of a student's actions over time. The difficulty for the teacher is in awarding a mark or grade as it is virtually impossible to compare students who are engaged in very different types of activities. The most logical solution would appear to be for the lecturer to draw up a set of guidelines which state the minimum acceptable standards for community involvement (or whatever the activity is) and use these guidelines to determine whether each student has satisfied course requirements or not with regard to 'commitment'.

Psychomotor objectives

Although originally recognized and defined by Bloom's team in 1956, a limited taxonomy for this domain was not produced until ten years later (Simpson, 1966) and the more detailed version six years after that (Harrow, 1972). Krathwohl *et al.* (1964) define psychomotor objectives as those 'which emphasize some muscular or motor skill, some manipulation of material and objects, or some act which requires neuromuscular coordination'. As is to be expected, more attention has been given to the psychomotor domain by teachers of very young children, by those responsible for training apprentices and armed service personnel and by sports coaches than by other university teachers. In some traditional university courses it has long been recognized that certain manipulative skills were essential, particularly in subjects such as dentistry and surgery, but the existence of a hierarchy of skills may not always have been acknowledged.

A comparison of the taxonomies developed by Simpson (1966) and Harrow (1972) with other classifications which are less well known reveals quite different approaches (Harrow, 1972). The taxonomy described by Harrow is more detailed and, while designed to cover the maturation and development of neuromuscular coordination in children, it is readily applicable to higher education.

69

The terms she uses to describe the six main levels and their sub-categories are virtually self-explanatory. Consequently we will reproduce them here with only the briefest of explanations when there is any likelihood of confusion. The examples are selected from those given by Harrow (1972). The levels and their sub-categories are as follows.

Reflex movements

As Harrow rightly points out, reflex movements are not normally the concern of course designers, although in those rare cases when a student is lacking a particular reflex due to a birth defect, faulty maturation, disease or an accident, their absence could seriously inhibit the development of higher-order manipulative skills.

Basic-fundamental movements

These include changes in locomotory patterns, bending and twisting the body, and manual dexterity, all of which are normally developed within the first few years of life, and are therefore of much greater interest to parents of young children and to pre-school teachers than they are to teachers in higher education. Nevertheless teachers at the secondary and tertiary levels are becoming more aware of the importance of these skills as more students are encountered with physical handicaps. A certain level of manual dexterity is required for typing, when using the keyboard for entering data on a computer or for manipulating apparatus in science laboratories, and very high levels of manual dexterity are required when playing a musical instrument or dissecting specimens in a biological laboratory.

Perceptual abilities

Harrow describes four types of discrimination – kinaesthetic, visual, auditory and tactile – and adds a fifth sub-category which she describes as coordinated activities (eg eye-hand or eye-foot coordination). It is not difficult to imagine how these abilities need to be developed to high levels of sensitivity in sports psychology, the training of air pilots, musical performance, and craft work, to give a few examples from some of the newer disciplines in higher education.

Physical abilities

The types of physical abilities described by Harrow – namely, endurance, strength, flexibility and agility – are all important for athletes, ballet dancers and players of musical instruments, and normally the level of performance improves during secondary and tertiary education as students in more traditional fields of study engage in extra-curricular sporting or musical activities. Some, if not all, of these physical skills are also essential in medicine, dentistry, physiotherapy, veterinary science, forestry and mechanical engineering.

Skilled movements

At this level reasonably complex movements or 'adaptive skills' have to be learned. Harrow differentiates between 'simple' skills (eg typing, skating, sawing, piano playing), 'compound' (eg tennis, violin playing) and 'complex' (eg aerial gymnastics, high diving).

Non-discursive communication

There are two sub-categories at this level, namely 'expressive movement' (including posture and carriage, gestures and facial expressions) and 'interpretive movement' (including aesthetic and creative activities). These range from non-verbal communication skills which are so important in the training of teachers, counsellors, lawyers and medical practitioners to the more difficult expressive and interpretive movements required of actors and dancers.

Relationships between the domains of objectives

In describing the various domains and levels of objectives we have chosen to give a greater emphasis to the cognitive domain as this is an essential ingredient of all university study. The examples of test questions and learning experiences illustrate a continuing need for university teachers, course designers and constructors of test questions to ensure that the level of understanding expected of students is being achieved and that students are not forced into superficial learning strategies by the nature of the assessment tasks. The authors believe that the cognitive domain considerations in this book are much wider than those addressed by many practitioners.

Consequently we include recommendations and examples of a full range of taxonomies which specify, for example, 'understanding', 'know-how' and 'problem solving'. The experiential taxonomy, which was described in the previous chapter, combines both cognitive and affective student experiences as does the taxonomy for professional education, which is described below.

As was hinted earlier, objections have been raised to the apparently rigid separation into three domains as proposed by Bloom and those who followed. The areas of higher education where alternative approaches have been advocated include medicine (eg Engel and Clarke, 1979), engineering (Carter, 1985) and training for the armed services (Hartley, 1984). In each case these authors demonstrate the futility of trying to separate objectives into the three domains, claiming that successful graduates in their respective fields are required to demonstrate, often in the one operation, their possession of appropriate and adequate knowledge and skills coupled with desirable attitudes. Their position is well summarized by Hartley (1984) who writes:

> Breaking learning into domains is an artificial classification ... (which) does not always truly describe real situations. The performance of physical skills involves knowledge, attitudes, motivation and motor skills. (p.41)

A good example of the above dictum may be seen in the modern approach to the training of athletes in higher education institutions. In preparing potential record-breakers attention is given to increasing an athlete's knowledge of how the body responds to stress. Each athlete's previous performance is analysed and attitudes which will enhance success are encouraged while attitudes likely to interfere with physical performance are discouraged. At appropriate stages in the training program, and particularly just before peak performance is required, a series of closely supervised training sessions is used to develop the highest levels of coordination and endurance in appropriate sets of muscles and nerves.

A taxonomy of objectives for professional education

Carter (1985, p. 137) criticizes the Bloom *Taxonomy* for failing to distinguish between knowledge and skills. Although Carter himself uses the term 'taxonomy', his pattern of the various types of objectives commonly found in professional education (in his case, engineering) could better be described as a matrix (see Table 4.1).

72

Table 4.1 *Summary of a taxonomy of objectives for professional education (Carter, 1985)*

	Mental Characteristics	Attitudes and Values	Personality Characteristics	Spiritual Qualities	
Personal Qualities	Openness Agility Imagination Creativity	Things Self People Groups Ideas	Integrity Initiative Industry Emotional resilience	Appreciation Response	**Being**
	Mental Skills	**Information Skills**	**Action Skills**	**Social Skills**	
Skill	Organization Analysis Evaluation Synthesis	Acquisition Recording Remembering Communication	Manual Organizing Decision making Problem solving	Co-operation Leadership Negotiation & persuasion Interviewing	**Doing**
	Factual Knowledge		**Experimental Knowledge**		
Knowledge	Facts Structures Procedures Concepts Principles		Experience Internalization Generalization Abstraction		**Knowing**
	Cognitive		**Affective**		

As may be seen from Carter's matrix, most of the higher levels in Bloom's cognitive domain are classified by Carter as 'mental skills'. The type of psychomotor objectives originally identified by Bloom and later described by Harrow are termed 'manual skills' and are included with certain cognitive skills under the heading 'action skills'. Carter's 'manual skills' probably do not encompass the higher psychomotor skills described by Harrow nor does he give reasons for including manual skills with organizing, decision making and problem solving when he describes action skills. The only one of his examples of a manual skill where the close links between Bloom's three domains can be readily demonstrated is surgery which, to be effective, demands high levels of cognitive skills and an attitude of care for the patient, as well as delicate neuro–muscular control.

Despite the fact that Carter makes no reference to Harrow's higher psychomotor objectives (or to Harrow's work at all), Carter's matrix is a most valuable contribution to educational thought and, in our opinion, of more direct use to teachers in higher education than

STUDENT ASSESSMENT IN HIGHER EDUCATION

any of the earlier books on educational objectives. Its great strength is in the importance this matrix gives to what Carter calls 'personal qualities' or 'being', which includes the personality characteristics of integrity, initiative, industry and emotional resilience, and the fact that he links this section of his matrix so closely with the group of objectives he calls 'social skills' (cooperation, leadership, negotiation and persuasion, interviewing). In fact the highest point in his matrix of objectives would be seen in this group of skills because successful development of these is dependent on acquiring a suitable body of knowledge and the necessary attitudes.

In an explanation of his category, 'spiritual qualities', Carter states:

> the category includes qualities other than those of a religious character. It is concerned with the capacity for awe and wonder, with the ability to appreciate, value and respond to both the world of nature and the highest levels of human achievement. Some would wish to add that most important of all is the ability to respond to the One who is the Author of all these things. The importance of spiritual qualities may not lie so much in their utility as in their importance in the development of a mature and balanced person. (p. 145)

It would be generally accepted that it is unfortunate when skilled or semi-skilled workers have an aversion to their jobs. Interest in the job will mean that a person is more likely to take pride in each task, will seek opportunities for further learning and, if the job involves contact with other people, will be cooperative with other members of the team and sympathetic in dealing with members of the public.

Relating objectives to assessment procedures

These two chapters will not be complete until the reader spends some time looking through the descriptions of the various taxonomies, checking against a course outline and asking which of the objectives are important in the course being planned or taught.

Beard and Hartley (1984) give a number of examples of relationships between objectives, learning activities and assessment in higher education quoting from courses in history, medical science, French language, design and art. They also list a set of more general objectives specifying aspects of knowledge, skills and attitudes which students should develop during their years at university. A selection from these objectives will illustrate how Beard and Hartley relate objectives to methods of teaching, students' learning activities and the type of assessment to be used or feedback given to the student.

For the more comprehensive list the reader should consult both the original work and an earlier publication by Beard *et al.* (1974).

As examples of higher order mental skills (not to be confused with the psychomotor domain described earlier) Beard and Hartley state that 'university teaching in general should enable the student to be verbally articulate and to make his [*sic*] own independent judgements'. These skills, they claim, may be developed through 'giving papers, effective argument in discussion groups and tutorials, meeting contradictions, and contrasting points of view'. Students' acquisition of skills may be assessed through 'criticism by other students and tutors, by "compare and contrast" questions in examinations and by the evaluation of arguments'. Under the heading of attitudes the authors state that 'an aim in university teaching is to foster in the student enthusiasm for learning'. Student activities which are likely to develop this attitude are non-assigned reading, extra-curricular meetings (eg science clubs) and their acquisition of this attitude will be judged by the 'extent of extra-curricular activity' or 'posing new problems for (the student's) own investigation'.

The types of assessment which Beard and Hartley list as the most appropriate for testing the above objectives are informal and rarely contribute to a student's final grade. In fact some objectives are really only achieved, and therefore measurable, after a person has completed a course and entered the workforce. For this reason many professions such as teaching, law, theology, engineering and medicine insist on a transition year of postgraduate training, satisfactory field experience, a period of probation when first entering the profession, or some combination of these before a person is deemed to be qualified to practise.

— 5 —

Stages of intellectual and ethical development

Ethics is not definable, is not implementable, because it is not conscious; it involves not only our thinking, but also our feeling.
(Valdemar W Setzer)

Never let your sense of morals get in the way of doing what's right.
(Isaac Asimov)

Research conducted by Perry at Harvard College during the mid-1960s suggested to him that students typically pass through about nine stages (or 'positions') of intellectual and ethical development during their college years (Perry, 1970). Perry and his team noted a transition from a position of reliance on the teacher or some other person as an authority on factual and moral matters to one where the student exhibited self-reliance within the student's own personal value system. In a later publication (Perry, 1981) he reduced the original nine positions to four, namely *dualism, multiplicity, relativism* and *commitment*.

Because these stages or, perhaps more accurately, contrasting attitudes by students to authority have implications for the approach to teaching and the types of assessment used, they will be described in more detail below. Whenever it is relevant, each of Perry's stages will be linked to typical behaviours of university and college students as observed by the authors or as described in the literature on higher education. For example, Whiteley and Yokota (1987) related Perry's stages to the development of character among first-year university students in an American college.

Dualism

This position is marked by a dependence on the authority of teachers and textbooks in academic matters, the student typically

77

taking the view that teachers, particularly at the university level, know the subject matter to be learned and that it is the student's task to commit to memory the material presented in lectures or read in the textbooks. It is not difficult to see the link with the superficial approach to learning which was described in Chapter 3 or Bloom's lowest level of cognitive objectives which he called 'knowledge' and which is described in the same chapter. Students are said to have the belief that 'hard work and obedience bring success'. In the ethical field, students at this first stage hold dualistic views in relation to the universe: right vs wrong, good vs bad, truth vs falsehood. This dualistic approach to ethical matters has some parallels with the two lowest levels in Krathwohl *et al.*'s (1964) affective domain, namely 'receiving' and 'responding', which were described in Chapter 4.

While most lecturers in higher education would recognize some elements of dualism in their first-year students they would also know from experiences in the home and the community that young men and women in their late teens are often rebellious against traditional authorities, frequently substituting for the authority of the church and the home the authority of the peer group. Moreover, those teachers with experience of mature-age students in their university or college classes will recognize that people who are quite mature in relation to their business or family activities will revert to a dualistic position when faced with unaccustomed methods of learning at college or university.

It would therefore appear that it is possible for a person to be at Perry's first position in some areas of life but at the same time be at higher levels in other areas. This is not very different from a child who for some modes of thinking works at Piaget's pre-operational level yet in other contexts works at a concrete operational level.

Designers of first-year college or university courses need to recognize that novices in a discipline commonly hold a dualistic approach to their learning. This approach is contrary to the generally accepted view that scholarship is much more than the transmission of accumulated or revealed knowledge from previous generations. Teachers of first-year students must therefore seek opportunities for helping students to progress beyond this dualistic approach to knowledge which is linked to rote learning. For example, part of almost any introductory unit of study should be devoted to a consideration of conflicting evidence or theories in order to develop critical attitudes in students. Assessment exercises should reinforce these attitudes. Consequently any form of assessment which merely asks students to reproduce rote learning is to be avoided or at least kept to a minimum.

As students discover, somewhat to their amazement, that their professors do not know all the answers to students' questions or that there is disagreement between what they are told in lectures and what they read in their texts they pass through a transitional phase of *uncertainty*. Typical explanations for their teachers' inability (or is it unwillingness?) to answer students' questions and for these discrepancies between authorities are either that their teachers are setting the students exercises in discovery or even that the teachers are not as knowledgeable as the students had previously imagined!

Students may find other tentative solutions to the problems created in their minds when so-called authorities differ. The students realize that new truths are continually being discovered and that either their lecturer is unaware of these new discoveries or that further research is needed before their questions can be answered. Students working in areas of pure and applied science are particularly likely to adopt this position during their earlier years at university or college as they are very much aware of the rapid rate of scientific discovery. According to Perry, they still do not really doubt that an answer, a set of absolute truths, exists.

Multiplicity

As students encounter more areas of knowledge where uncertainty exists, some explain the diversity of viewpoints among authorities by adopting the view that everyone is entitled to his or her own opinions and that therefore no particular opinion can really be wrong. Multiplicity can be a dangerous stage if students remain at this level as they have not properly grasped the need for arguments to be supported by data. Some students, according to Perry (1981), believe that the authorities want them to use certain modes of thought; the facts don't matter but the method of acquiring them does. Perhaps this attitude of thought is encouraged by teaching methods, particularly in some courses in school science and mathematics, which emphasize process over content. For these reasons it is important that assessment tasks include questions which require students to demonstrate their knowledge of opposing theories, where these exist in the discipline, and the need to examine the extent to which any one theory accounts for the available data or evidence. Many essays in the humanities and in some professional disciplines are particularly helpful in teaching students the value of a critical approach.

Relativism

Students at this stage in their mental development perceive that new knowledge must be viewed in relation to all other knowledge. At Perry's lowest subdivision of this category, students still think of an absolute truth or authority in fields such as physics or morals, but acknowledge relativism in other areas, such as art or literature. At the highest level, everything is relativistic but the student sees no need for commitment to any particular set of values. In a sense there is a certain legitimacy for the relativist position. It is a significant advance on the two earlier phases of dualism and multiplicity in that students are now being encouraged to consider new evidence or theories in the light of their existing knowledge.

Problem-based learning and its assessment will be treated later in this book (Chapter 11). It is, however, relevant to mention it here as it would seem to the present authors that there are strong links with Perry's phase of relativism. Boud and Feletti (1991) describe problem-based learning in the following way:

> Problem-based learning is a way of constructing and teaching courses using problems as the stimulus and focus for student activity. It is not simply the addition of problem-solving activities to otherwise discipline-centred curricula, but a way of conceiving of the curriculum which is based around key problems in professional practice. Problem-based courses start with problems rather than with exposition of disciplinary knowledge. They move students towards the acquisition of knowledge and skills through a staged sequence of problems presented in context, together with associated learning materials and support from teachers. (p. 14)

For learning to be successful in courses of this nature students must be able to seek out relevant information from all available sources, weighing up the relative importance and significance of each. In fields such as accounting, architecture, engineering and medicine, where problem-based curricula have been used successfully, there may well be more than one correct answer to a given problem, but there are also solutions which are obviously incorrect and some which are better than others. Both dualism and multiplicity fail to explain the type of learning that occurs in problem-based courses where students have to recognize the key elements in a problem, relate it to their existing knowledge, seek data which might be relevant to its solution, design or select appropriate tests and suggest a viable solution.

In a world of relativistic values, the concept that one person's opinion is as good as another's becomes increasingly unsatisfactory and a thinking student sees that some form of decision about one's beliefs is inevitable. Thus there is really a transition stage between relativism and commitment.

Commitment

Perry (1981) describes the level of commitment as 'an affirmation, choice or decision ... made in the awareness of relativism'. This decision might be about one's 'career, value system, politics or personal relationships'. By implication the description must also apply to one's academic studies. There is a danger that students will superficially accept a value system that is presented by their academic teachers and advisers rather than make commitments of their own, in which case they are really working at one of Perry's lower levels, probably that of multiplicity. One of the tasks of a university or college teacher is to present course material in such a way as to help students make their own commitments to value systems which are consistent with the discipline. Assessment tasks should facilitate rather than inhibit this. For example, many years ago when one author was responsible for a class of future high school science teachers, one of his students opted to write an essay on the difficulty some people have in reconciling their religious beliefs about creation and their desire to accept an evolutionary explanation for the origin of species. This particular student presented a poorly argued essay which simply reiterated the teacher's own views on creation and evolution without any attempt to justify those views or compare them with alternate explanations. The essay had to be rewritten! In this case one might describe the student's attitude as one of compliance rather than commitment.

Initially commitment may be limited to beliefs about certain fields of knowledge or areas of one's life. Thus a value system applicable to the study of English literature is not seen as applicable to the study of psychology, and even less to mathematics or engineering. This inconsistency where students hold differing attitudes to 'truth' in different areas of knowledge may stimulate them to seek links between their different fields of study. Some university departments provide formal opportunities for students to discover these links through courses such as the philosophy of science, the history of mathematics or the science of history. There is a danger, however, that students will view such courses as a set of facts to be learned, thus reverting to the lowest level of Bloom's cognitive domain or the first position in the Perry hierarchy. Again it is essential that students in these linking courses be challenged by means of their assessment tasks to think through the implications of the theories they are studying, to question them if necessary and, where possible, to compare them with alternative theories.

The views of a student at the highest level of commitment have been described by Perry (1981) in the following way: 'This is how life will be. I must be whole-hearted while tentative, fight for my values yet respect others, believe my deepest values yet be ready to learn. I see that I shall be retracing this whole journey over and over – but I hope more wisely.'

It is unlikely that many of our students will actually reach this ulti-mate position in all aspects of their life by the time they reach their final years of higher education. If it is seen as a desirable objective, those responsible for planning the total curriculum and those who are in a position to influence extra-curricular activities will seek to ensure that their students will think for themselves and develop their own philosophies of life in the light of the knowledge, skills and atti-tudes they have gained during their college years. At this stage the various taxonomies are seen as stages towards the goal of an inte-grated personality, the facets of which are better described by Carter's matrix which was reproduced in the previous chapter.

In some respects, parallels may be found between Perry's stages of development and those described earlier by Piaget and Inhelder (1969) or even the less well-known 'developmental tasks' identified by Havighurst (Havighurst 1953, Chickering and Havighurst 1981) for various critical stages in one's life from infancy and childhood through adolescence to adulthood and old age.

For some students the challenge of moving through these posi-tions to higher levels is too great. They exhibit instead various levels of avoidance behaviour which Perry calls temporizing, escape and retreat. He describes these in the following way (1981):

- *temporizing* – postponement of movement for a year or more
- *escape* – alienation, abandonment of responsibility; exploitation of multiplicity and relativism for avoidance of commitment

- *retreat* – avoidance of complexity and ambivalence by regression to dualism coloured by hatred of otherness.

Most of us who have had any experience with students in higher education, or for that matter, adolescent children, will recognize the above avoidance mechanisms. Among the responsibilities of teachers and counsellors in higher education is to be aware of these stages in the normal development of students and to watch out for those who are having problems with their beliefs. While Perry's positions do not purport to be a taxonomy of objectives, it is not difficult to identify a certain amount of overlap between his levels and the levels of affective objectives described by Krathwohl *et al.* (1964).

Before leaving the Perry schema, additional mention should be made of his *transitions* from one position to the next above it. He gives much greater emphasis to these in his 1981 outline of the stages of cognitive and ethical development than in his original (1968–70) description, saying that the transition stages emphasize the active parts of developmental progression (Perry, 1981). It is during these periods of transition that students are most likely to question the adequacy of their current intellectual and ethical beliefs. These beliefs are challenged by the newly acquired knowledge and the fresh insights on life which result from meetings with students and faculty from different backgrounds and with different beliefs.

Part 2

Some assessment methods

——— 6 ———
Timing of assessment tasks

There's nothing remarkable about it. All one has to do is hit the right keys at the right time and the instrument plays itself.

(JS Bach)

Before moving on to a description of the types of assessment commonly used at university level we should briefly consider the question of the most appropriate time in a unit of study for assignments and examinations. As would be expected, there has been, and continues to exist, a considerable variation in practice.

At one end of the spectrum is the custom of using a relatively formal examination to test each student's learning, usually at the end of a semester or year, or even after three or four years of university study. In the most extreme versions of this approach to summative assessment, there was no other formal assessment of students' knowledge or skills during their time at university. A much more common approach, however, is for students to submit regular essays or other assignments, at least as part of the ongoing formative assessment. (See Chapter 2 for a brief description of both formative and summative assessment.)

In some of the older universities in England, for example, the formative assessment consists of a weekly 'tutorial' during which each student meets individually with his or her tutor and presents a paper for constructive criticism by the tutor. In other places where the emphasis is also on formal final examinations but where the ratio of students to academic staff is too high for individual tutorials, other methods have to be adopted. Thus the formative assessment may consist of group discussions in larger tutorial classes, essays marked by tutors or teaching assistants, objective tests administered in lecture periods, or some combination of these.

At the other end of the spectrum we have 'continuous assessment' (see also Chapter 2) where there may be no final examinations as such, the mark or grade being determined on the basis of scores in individual tests or assignments scattered throughout a course of study. The use of continuous assessment, both as a regular indication of students' progress and as a measure of their achievement in a teaching program leads to a confusion between the distinctive purposes of formative and summative assessment.

In addition, the teacher must choose between the various options that exist for determining the final grade, ranging from a simple addition of scores in each component test to some process of weighting or statistical manipulation of individual scores. Procedures for combining marks to produce a final grade will be discussed in more detail in Chapter 13.

Reasons why both continuous and end-of-unit assessment continue to exist, even within the one institution or department, are that each method has its advantages and disadvantages. Before adopting a particular approach or combination of techniques, a university teacher should weigh up the contributions made by each type to students' learning and to the achievement of specific objectives in a unit of study. These are outlined below; for a fuller treatment readers should consult one or more of the references cited.

Difficulties with continuous assessment

Major difficulties encountered when a system of continuous assessment operates include:

1. students have little time for any in-depth reading as they are constantly preparing for the next test without receiving adequate feedback on their performance to date
2. teachers have an intolerable marking load and therefore have insufficient opportunities for research or for considering ways of enhancing teaching
3. *some* tests used in continuous assessment encourage students to engage in 'superficial (or surface) learning' (see Chapter 3) which concentrates on committing a series of facts to memory so that these facts may be reproduced in answers to such questions as 'List the causes of …'
4. there is little opportunity for measuring each student's grasp

of broader principles in the chosen discipline or their knowledge of the relationships between different areas of subject matter

5. although the absence of a final examination may reduce stress among students at examination time, the general level of stress is likely to be increased throughout the academic year

6. where relatively few students have the same combination of subjects, it is virtually impossible to organize assessment tasks so that workloads for each student will be spread evenly over a semester or term

7. assessment tasks which are not undertaken under supervision provide greater opportunities for plagiarism as there are no effective procedures, particularly with large classes, for preventing students from copying the work of others, unless the tasks are individually different. The problems of plagiarism will be discussed in Chapter 15.

Advantages of continuous assessment

Most of the difficulties outlined above are recognized by university teachers and students. Despite this fact, there are evidently sufficient numbers of students and teachers who believe that the advantages of continuous assessment outweigh the disadvantages for a number of academic departments and individual teachers to abolish final examinations and replace them with some combination of assessment tasks which are spaced fairly evenly throughout the year. The advantages claimed for continuous assessment, some of which are direct contradictions of items in the above list of disadvantages, are said to be:

1. results of tests can be returned to students soon after each test is completed (but essay marking takes longer and may cause difficulties if the next essay is due before comments on an earlier one are returned to students)

2. students and teachers are kept informed of all students' progress, both in relation to the objectives of the unit and to other students throughout the unit (this is the essence of formative assessment which was mentioned earlier in this chapter and discussed in more detail in Chapter 2)

3. each section of a unit can be tested in more detail than would be possible with one final examination, so that if remedial work

needs to be done that can be prescribed at the most relevant time

4. if a student is sick or unavoidably absent on the day of a progress test it is easier to arrange for an alternative test to be administered than would be the case with a larger final examination

5. when essays or practical projects are a component of the continuous assessment, students can be guided by their tutors in the initial stages of reading or gathering data.

Just as it is possible to list advantages and disadvantages of continuous assessment, so one can compare the advantages and disadvantages of final assessment. In this way, it is easier for a teacher to select the form of assessment which is most applicable to the needs of the students and the objectives of the course. In those institutions where it is the practice to consult with students concerning the type of assessment to be adopted, it is highly desirable for the teacher to discuss with the class the advantages and disadvantages of each type of assessment. One would expect that such a commonsense approach would be adopted by all university teachers, but from our experience, this is not always the case.

Difficulties with final assessment

1. Where the final grade for a unit of study is determined substantially or wholly by a student's performance in a final examination there is a possibility that some students will be at a disadvantage due to medical or emotional problems that day, especially if these problems are not sufficiently serious to warrant students being given permission to take special examinations.

2. For some students, the level of anxiety provoked by a major examination which is the major determinant of one's grade is too great altogether so that their performance in the examination is not a true measure of their ability or knowledge.

3. A final examination with a limited number of choices may not adequately reward those students who had concentrated their study on other aspects of the subject; consequently teachers should carefully consider whether the examination questions are a reasonable sample of both content and objectives (see Table 3.2; see also the section on validity in Chapter 14).

4. On the other hand, a final examination (or list of major essay topics) which gives too much choice will make comparison of one student with another less reliable. (This problem is discussed in more detail in the section on reliability in Chapter 14.).

Advantages of final assessment

1. Students are encouraged to read more widely than would be possible if they were constantly preparing for the next test.
2. A final examination provides better opportunities for students to demonstrate their knowledge of the whole field of study and the interrelationships between different sections.
3. Students are encouraged to practise learning strategies which result in 'learning for understanding', sometimes called 'deep learning' (see Chapter 3).
4. A final examination is a better measure of the levels students have achieved by the end of a study unit, compared with progress tests which can only measure levels of performance at particular stages in the unit.
5. The higher levels of anxiety referred to above (the second disadvantage) may be substantially reduced by providing students with information at an early stage in the course about the format of the final examination and samples of the types of questions which will be asked.

It will be seen from the above comparisons of continuous and final assessment that, because each has its advantages and disadvantages, there are no compelling arguments why one should be chosen in preference to another. In practice, many institutions have adopted a form of continuous assessment which records the completion of a series of required tasks and this is complemented by a final examination which is an indication of a student's level of attainment at the end of a unit of learning.

If marks are awarded for progress tests or completed tasks, there should be a positive correlation with the final grade. By the time students reach the end of a unit, they should know whether they are passing the unit or are in danger of failing. The grading scheme may even be arranged so that better students will have already demonstrated that they should be awarded a Pass or a C grade on course work alone. The final examination or essay is then used to determine whether a student is worthy of a merit grade such as a Credit, Distinction or High Distinction, an A or a B.

Timing of assignments and progress tests

Once a decision has been made concerning the most desirable combination of continuous and final assessment it will be necessary to choose the optimal stages in a unit for administering the different tests and assignments. In some universities it is a requirement that teachers will discuss with their students the types of assessment to be adopted at the beginning of each unit of study. Whenever large numbers of students are enrolled it is obviously impossible to take into account all their wishes and even a majority decision, if such is allowed, may have a sizeable minority of students who would not favour the scheme adopted. There are therefore good reasons why the basic form of assessment should be determined, or at least strongly recommended by the course coordinator or the teacher and then discussed with each new group of students, at which time an assessment timetable will be given for the unit of study.

In determining the most appropriate pattern for assessment within any given course we recommend that the following factors be taken into account.

1. The length of the course.
2. The need to provide for a realistic workload for students and staff.
3. The need to provide opportunity for practice of skills and use of knowledge, also for practice (without grading commitment) with different forms of assessment, such as objective questions, essay questions, structured questions, etc.
4. The provision of a degree of flexibility in the program to enable staff and students to cope with unexpected peaks in workload.
5. The need to allow sufficient time between tasks, such as assignments, tests, essays, etc, so that the student can benefit from the assessment of the task before being required to complete the next task.
6. Opportunities for staff and students to recuperate and review their work during vacation periods.

Decisions to be made concerning 'in-course' assessment

Finally, in relation to timing of assessment tasks, we suggest that university teachers or course planners who are contemplating the use of continuous or 'in-course' assessment should consider the following questions, which were adapted from an earlier list devised by Mortlock and Storer (1973). These questions admirably summarize the main issues raised in the present chapter.

1. How much should 'in-course' assessment count towards the final result for the year?
2. What variety of work can be set for assessment? What percentage of the set work should contribute towards final assessment?
3. If tests are used, when and where should they be held? What supervision is necessary?
4. Who should set the assessable work? Who should mark it? How will standards of marking be checked?
5. What information about 'in-course' assessment should be supplied to students to assist them in planning an equitable distribution of work throughout the semester or year?
6. How much interruption to the normal lecture, tutorial, practice class system will 'in-course' assessment cause?
7. Should all assessable work count equally, or should various pieces of work be given varying weights?
8. How should the pass be decided for each piece of work or test?
9. How is 'in-course' assessment to be evaluated?

Most of these issues will be discussed in more detail in later chapters.

7

Essays

I am returning this otherwise good typing paper to you because someone has printed gibberish all over it and put your name at the top.

(An English Professor, Ohio University)

In the opening section of this book we considered the purposes of higher education, relationships between educational objectives and learning outcomes, and stages in students' intellectual and ethical development. Our aim was to provide the background knowledge that would help faculty to select (and justify) the most appropriate forms of assessment for achieving the chosen objectives. Chapter 3 introduced readers to those educational objectives which emphasize the acquisition of knowledge and the ability to use that knowledge in the solution of complex problems, principally in the cognitive domain. The chapter contained examples of examination questions which tested the achievement of progressive levels of cognitive objectives. The fact that many of these examples were essay questions demonstrates that this form of assessment may be used at any level in the cognitive domain and, in many cases, the affective domain (which was described in Chapter 4).

The current chapter, when read in conjunction with the earlier chapters on objectives, looks more closely at the value of essays in different types of assessment, as a result of which the reader should be able to identify when it is appropriate to set essays and when it is better to use some other form of assessment. We shall also pay attention to the difficulties of establishing a fair system of marking essays.

Essays are popular methods of assessment, at least among teachers in some universities, if not among their students. Their chief weaknesses, which have been well documented, are that they cannot be marked quickly and that it is difficult to achieve reliability in marking. For these reasons some institutions make little use of essays as measures of students' performance in final examinations even though they may make regular use of essays during the year, paradoxically counting the marks gained in these essays towards the final grade. Essays are frequently used to test whether students are able to recall and select appropriate data, principles or theories, to demonstrate relationships, and to explain the significance. They test students' ability to develop a cogent argument which is supported by evidence gained from their reading or from data provided by the examiner. Essays also indicate whether students can express complex ideas logically, using the type of language and arguments which are appropriate for the particular discipline.

Thus when deciding whether essay questions are the most appropriate means of assessing a student's achievements and capabilities, university teachers must carefully consider which of the many learning objectives for a teaching program can best be measured by an essay and which should be measured by other means. For example, it is much easier to write an essay on discipline in the classroom than it is to control a class of unruly children, or to describe the care of mentally ill patients than it is to treat these people in appropriate ways. Hence the practical requirements in so many professional and vocational courses.

Types of essays

Perusal of assignment topics and examination papers in many disciplines and universities reveals an almost infinite variety of essay types, some examples of which will be given later in the present chapter. A useful summary of the major types of essays used in undergraduate education is given by Cockburn and Ross (1977b). Their categorizations are reproduced here with the permission of Professor Ross.

1. *Short answer* essays examine mastery of facts, principles, single concepts. They may be used as exercises in diagnosis or analysis.
2. *Essay outlines* examine the ability to organize material, to construct coherent arguments, to select relevant information from a wide field of study.
3. *Standard* essays examine the ability to describe and to analyse the relationship between ideas and events; to give a coherent account of a topic; to select and to weigh evidence in support of an argument; to diagnose and to suggest solutions to problems;

to solve familiar types of problems; to express critical judgements; to make comparisons.

4. *Extended* essays allow the examiner to present a more complex problematic situation or one that requires more extensive preparation or research.

5. *Extended time* essays allow students to think deeply about the problematic situation and therefore can be used to examine the ability to solve less familiar problems, to analyse or critically to appraise less familiar material.

6. *Dissertations* examine the ability to make an integrated study in depth over a wide field.

7. Essays that allow complete *freedom of response* examine the ability to reach independent conclusions, to create a new synthesis of ideas and events, or to set out and justify new ideas or interpretations.

A few brief comments on the above may be helpful to readers who have little experience in setting essay questions or whose own background as students has been limited. Where appropriate, examples are given to illustrate each category.

Short answer essays

Ideally, these should test a student's grasp of a single concept. They are necessarily longer and more detailed than a definition, which merely tests a student's ability to memorize a series of words and does not indicate the level of the student's understanding of the topic. The key word in Cockburn and Ross's description of short answer questions is 'mastery'. There are many ways in which mastery may be defined but in this context we suggest that short answer questions can only give an *indication* that a student has attained mastery of a concept or principle rather than *proof* of that mastery or an accurate *measure* of the level of ability. For example, mastery might be indicated if students could show that they were able to apply a concept appropriately in a different context to that in which the concept was learned (Nicol, 1994).

The following examples of short answer essays give an indication of the possible wording and depth of treatment expected:

Write brief answers to any four (4) of the following seven (7) questions. *Each question is worth 5 marks*.

a) What impact has capital market research (CMR) had on the setting of accounting standards?

b) Briefly comment on the distinction between measurement and disclosure issues in accounting theory.
c) Outline one empirical study in support of current cost or exit value accounting. Explain whether this study uses a semantic or pragmatic methodology. (Australian National University, *Accounting*, Year 3 Semester 1, 1991) (Approximate time allowed: 12 minutes)

Rank the four major causes of death in Australia and comment briefly on the significance of each. (Australian National University, *Issues in Contemporary Social Structure*, 1991) (Approximate time allowed: 6 minutes)

Currently, general practitioners in private practice are under pressure from several quarters. List some of these pressures and briefly describe their effects. (Australian National University, *Issues in Contemporary Social Structure*, 1991) (Approximate time allowed: 6 minutes)

If it were possible to eliminate the entire bacterial population of the large intestine of a human, what effects on the health of that individual would be likely to occur? (Australian National University, *General Microbiology*, 1990) (Approximate time allowed: 7 minutes)

Essay outlines

Outlines are, by definition, not essays as such. They are therefore unable to achieve many of the objectives of essays which were described in the introductory paragraphs of this chapter. Despite these limitations, they are useful devices for introducing students to essay planning; they demonstrate a student's ability to outline the most suitable approach for writing the essay, and they give an indication of the student's general understanding of the topic. It would be unusual to use essay outlines for summative assessment; they are much more suited to formative (see Chapter 2 for the distinction between formative and summative assessment). Using essay outlines for formative purposes allows teachers to provide almost instant feedback to students on their ability to plan an essay – in fact, where students and teachers are able to communicate via e-mail, the time involved for both is much reduced.

The first two of the following questions are adaptations of full essay questions from two final examination papers, changing them from standard essays to essay outlines; the third question is quoted *verbatim*:

You are to give a talk on the radio to an audience of non-specialists. Outline a script showing how you would discuss some philosophical interests of autobiography. (Australian National University, *Philosophy and Literature*, 1993)

List what you consider to be the most important developments in the history of twentieth-century social psychology and make brief notes to justify your selection of each. (Australian National University, *Psychology*, 1993)

Give a brief summary of the advantages and disadvantages of the various processes used to store radioactive waste from nuclear power stations safely. (Australian National University, *Inorganic and Material Chemistry*, 2nd Year Final Examination, 1990) (Approximate time allowed: 12 minutes)

Standard essays

These are described adequately in the quotation from Cockburn and Ross at the beginning of this chapter. They may be used at almost any time in a course, except immediately before a final examination when the completion of an essay would interfere with students' preparation for the exam. Another reason why essays should not be set near the end of a course is that there is no time for teachers to mark the essays and provide feedback to students on their performance before the final examination. The following question illustrates the type of essay topic which tests students' knowledge of the topic gained from two or three major sources. Implied in the question is a requirement that students will be able to compare and contrast conflicting theories and, if possible, either propose a resolution of this conflict or provide sound arguments to justify the theory which the student supports. Other examples of standard essay topics from different disciplines are given at the end of the present chapter.

> What are some of the Bible's own explanations for the emergence of the Israelite people? How can these explanations be criticized from a modern historical and/or archaeological point of view? (Australian National University, *Biblical Literature*, 1st Year Final Examination, 1993) (Approximate time allowed: 45 minutes)

Extended essays

When extended essays are to be answered under examination conditions, it is preferable to allow students the full examination time (generally three hours) to write the single essay. It is also desirable to give them a relatively generous 'reading time' during which students select the topic on which they will write and prepare an outline of the essay. One would expect that if one examination session were to be devoted to answering a single extended essay, there would be at least one other session which examines a student's performance in the remainder of the course. If the latter had already been tested in a series of progress tests it might be acceptable for the final examination to consist of the single extended essay.

It is possible to envisage two contrasting types of extended essays which are to be written under examination conditions. The first is designed to test a student's ability to write a substantial exposition of some aspect of the discipline which that student has chosen to study extensively. One would expect the student to demonstrate an ability to marshal appropriate facts, theories and arguments and present these in a logical and organized way. Students may be permitted to bring into the examination room a limited set of notes to assist them in providing appropriate references to support their arguments. Some examiners have a rule that students may bring into the examination room no more than a single A4 sheet (30 x 21 cm) or sometimes a card which is half that size. The paper or card may have writing (or typing) on both sides. Research by Trigwell (1987) demonstrated a positive correlation between the amount of work a student had put into constructing the 'crib card' and their subsequent grade in the examination. For example, those who had copied out another student's crib card did not benefit from the exercise, nor did those who had used their crib card to record very basic information relating to the subject being studied.

If an extended essay is going to be included in a formal examination the teacher should tell the students early in the course that one of the assessment requirements is such an essay and it will be based on a student's in-depth reading. At the same time the teacher should supply a suggested list of topics, including some key references.

A second type of extended essay may not have the same amount of choice for students as the one which is based on specialized reading. In this case it is usual for the teacher to provide students with substantial amounts of data which, combined with students' skills and knowledge gained from the course, are used to solve a particular problem. There may be more than one way of solving the problem, in which case the better students should be able to indicate their awareness of alternative approaches and present arguments for the one which they espouse.

In the question which follows (from Hall and Imrie, 1994), the problem is stated in a few words, namely a hypothetical appointment to a post in educational administration, yet a satisfactory answer requires an extended essay. In order to answer the question a student would need to be aware of the current situation in New Zealand, the resources available and the likelihood of adverse reactions to proposals which had implications for increased government spending or changes in technical teachers' duties.

> You have just been appointed adviser on technical education in New Zealand.
>
> Identify and justify three top priority measures for the assessment of students in technical education.
>
> For each priority, describe the policies and structures you would put in place to bring about what you see as the important goals. (20 marks)

Extended time essays

These are normally set as either an optional or compulsory part of the course work. Whether they are optional or not depends on how flexible the assessment arrangements are for that course and the nature of the objectives. For example, if the objectives include a requirement that students should be able to gather, select and analyse data, these objectives will be reflected in the type of assignment set. Arguments may be presented for giving students a wider choice of topics when essays are required as term papers than would be the case in a formal examination or perhaps even as an assignment. In this case, 'term paper' refers to a major essay or report on a project which has occupied a substantial part of each student's time during a course and which makes a considerable contribution to the final grade. The Department of Commerce at the Australian National University gave the following advice to its students in 1992 regarding what the Department calls 'research reports':

> A research report is an argument. It must first state a question (and, if necessary, break it down into its component parts), advance arguments, present evidence, critically examine arguments and evidence, and reach a conclusion. A research report does not merely narrate events or describe institutions. Nor is a research report simply a collection of facts or a list of points.

During the first semester of the first year of studying accounting, the Department requires students to submit two research reports, each with a maximum length of 1,200 words, the first being due towards the end of the fifth week of the semester and the second towards the beginning of the ninth week (there is a two-week teaching break between weeks 6 and 7). The second research report for that particular semester is one where the above advice is most appropriate. The requirement is stated as follows:

> Evaluate the major problem areas involved in the application of the matching principle to both the accrual basis of accounting and the cash basis of accounting.

An example of a major essay which requires students to interpret the literature on the subject comes from the first-year course in political theory at the Australian National University. The following is one of the topics set in 1992, each of which had a short list of suggested readings:

> Is the collapse of the Soviet regime in Russia of any real significance for the political ideals of socialism?

The third example of an essay which is to be written during the year comes from the Geography Department at the Australian National University. In this case, there is no reading list, but students are given three background statements from someone who has undertaken research on developing countries. These statements are meant to set the scene for writing the essay, but it would be necessary for students in this course to substantiate their assertions with references to other relevant literature and their own knowledge of the chosen country. The following 2,000-word essay was set in the second semester of 1992, was due at the end of the eighth week, and provided up to 40 per cent of the marks for the course (the other 60 per cent were allocated from the final examination):

> Explain the reasons for uneven development in one of the following countries: Nigeria; Kenya; Thailand; Fiji.

Background
The British geographer, David Smith, in *Where the Grass is Greener* (1979: 99) pointed out that development theorists usually ignore 'two fundamental geographical aspects of the development process that have an important bearing on the level of development achieved by individual nations'.

According to Smith, one is the *'tendency to view nations as homogeneous entities in which all the people will gain from development.* (Emphasis added.) The reality is that the impact of Western-style capitalist development can be uneven spatially so that some people in some places may lose rather than gain ...'

The second of the frequently overlooked geographical aspects of the development process is that *'the nations themselves are too often viewed in isolation whereas their level of development can only be understood in the context of external relations with other countries.'* (Emphasis added.)

When students must submit a number of essays at intervals throughout a course there is an advantage in requiring all students to write on the same topic. By doing this the teacher is better able to compare one student's performance with that of other members of the class and also to gain some indication of whether the class as a whole has grasped an essential component of the subject. There is, of course, a greater danger of students copying each other's work, a serious offence which is harder to detect in large classes and which is ultimately to the detriment of all students enrolled in any program where there is widespread cheating.

One way in which copying may be reduced, or even eliminated, in a large class that is divided into a number of tutorial groups is for each tutorial group to be given a different topic from other groups. Such a practice would enable the tutor for each group to discuss with the group what is required in the essay and possible approaches to the essay topic. During these discussions the tutor would need to emphasize the importance of students presenting their own work. Penalties for infringements would be clearly delineated and enforced. The problems of plagiarism will be discussed in more detail in Chapter 15.

Dissertations

Dissertations, or theses, will be discussed in some detail in the next chapter as they normally occupy a major portion of a student's time at senior undergraduate (eg honours) level or in postgraduate studies, particularly for higher degrees.

Essays that allow complete freedom of response

Broad-ranging essays such as these are more suitable for use in advanced courses or in those courses which include in their objectives the development of independent thought among students. The following topics allow students considerable freedom in their approach.

Is there a place for Western-style democracy in the Pacific Islands? (Australian National University, *Pacific Politics*, Semester Examination, 1991) (Approximate time allowed: 60 minutes)

Examine the concern with nature in writings connected with the Revolution in France. (Australian National University, *European History*, 1991) (Approximate time allowed: 90 minutes)

Give an account of the Resistance Movement in France during the Occupation. Why did the political forces represented in it not remain in coalition together after 1947? (Australian National University, *Political Science*, 1991) (Approximate time allowed: 30 minutes)

Setting essay questions

In setting essay questions, whether it be for assignments or for examinations, it is important to give students an indication of the amount of time they are expected to spend on the essay and, where relevant, the approximate length. In this way students will be given *some* indication of the depth of treatment expected by the examiner. Another way that students can be given an indication of the depth of treatment expected is for the teacher to distribute to the class copies of what the teacher judges to be successful essays, together with notes on why other essays failed to answer the question successfully. This is an approach which one of the present authors (Miller) used regularly with students enrolled for correspondence courses in science education at the University of New England (Australia) in the 1960s. This type of feedback is much more useful for essays completed during the teaching period rather than essays set in final examinations.

An alternative to the above approach was suggested by an anonymous reviewer of an early draft of this chapter. It is particularly valuable as a tutorial exercise for senior students who regularly attend classes. In this case the tutor circulates a number of (apparently) unmarked essays from previous classes in that unit and students are asked to mark the essays and give reasons for their decisions. An exercise such as this can help students to develop their judgement about the quality of work which is expected in the present unit.

There are times, however, when the examiner expects students to follow a predefined structure in their answers to a more general question, in which case the main question will be followed by a series of sub-questions or instructions. Lockwood (1992) refers to this technique as *structured essays*. The following two examples, the first for use in plant physiology and the second in ecology, illustrate the technique. They were generated in a workshop on assessment conducted by Lockwood at a conference on higher education in Gippsland, Australia, in 1992.

What is an essential element, and what experimental problems are encountered in deciding whether a particular element is essential or not? List the elements essential to crop plants. There has been some disagreement about whether chlorine, silicon and sodium are essential elements to plants: discuss their role, if any, in plants and describe their behaviour in the soil. (Approximate time allowed: 20 minutes)

Describe the effects of the coming of Europeans to Australia on the Australian environment over the period from 1788 to the present day. In your answer you should refer to:

a) the introduction of exotic fauna and flora
b) the effects of these on the original ecosystem
c) the effects of insecticides, growth hormones, fertilizers and other agricultural chemicals
d) the effects of urbanization and transport networks. (3,000 word assignment)

As may be seen from the examples given so far in this chapter, some essays are more suitable for use in final examinations, some as assignments or term papers, while others may be used in either context. It is important that teachers recognize the difference and refrain from setting inappropriate questions. This raises the question of what features make a particular question more suitable for a term paper than an examination, and *vice versa*.

We suggest that essay questions designed for use in final examinations should have the following characteristics:

- Questions should aim at testing the higher levels of learning, such as evaluation, application, appreciation and problem solving.
- The majority of questions set should relate to the essential aspects of the course and not the 'could know' or 'nice to know' material.
- Rather than limit the examination to one or two complex questions, which restrict the range of course material that can be covered, the examiner should consider the use of shorter, less complex questions.
- The design of the paper should allow for reading time (some questions take longer to read/interpret than others) and for the physical processes of writing and calculating.

Numerous writers on assessment have developed lists of 'key words' which, if used wisely, tell students what is required of them and, at the same time, provide markers with clear guidelines for checking whether a student has answered the question satisfactorily. The list of key words in Table 7.1 is adapted from many sources including Rowntree (1987) and Jones and Grant (1991). We have attempted to define some of the terms in ways which are particularly applicable to essay questions. Naturally many of the words have quite different meanings when used in other contexts. In some cases, eg 'define' and 'list', the operation forms only a small part of the essay, probably in the introduction, after which the student is expected to expand on the definition or explain why certain items are included and others excluded from their listing.

Table 7.1 *Some key words to use in setting essay questions*

analyse	appraise	assess	compare
consider	contrast	criticize	debate
define	demonstrate	describe	diagnose
discuss	distinguish	elucidate	enumerate
evaluate	examine	explain	explore
identify	indicate	illustrate	interpret
hypothesize	justify	list	outline
present	prove	reconcile	relate
review	specify	state	suggest
summarize	support	survey	trace

In brackets after each of our definitions is a word or list of words which could be regarded as synonymous with the original term. In some cases the word being defined has a similar but slightly different meaning to another word. We have then used the abbreviation 'cf.' (= compare) before the alternative word. For further elaboration, readers may wish to consult Jones and Grant (1991, pp. 12-23) in which they discuss the importance of key words, giving synonyms for each and examples of how they might be used in setting and answering examination questions.

● *analyse*: critically examine an argument, hypothesis, piece of literature, work of art or musical composition in order to identify its key elements (diagnose, examine)
● *appraise*: discuss the value of a particular hypothesis, procedure or work of art (assess, evaluate)
● *compare*: list any key similarities between two or more objects, ideas, techniques, or artefacts, and to note any features which can be used to distinguish one from the other

- *contrast*: describe the distinguishing features between two or more objects, ideas, techniques, or artefacts (distinguish)
- *criticize*: list, discuss and judge the relative merits and faults of a piece of work (appraise, examine, evaluate)
- *define*: give a precise description of an object or activity such that the entity being defined is distinguishable from similar entities (cf. describe, identify)
- *discuss*: present reasoned arguments for and against a proposition (consider, explore, cf. evaluate)
- *enumerate*: identify and write out the key components of a trans-action, process or theory either in historical order or in order of their importance (itemize, list, specify)
- *explain*: outline reasons for a particular action; clarify a complex or apparently contradictory set of data (define, elucidate, justify, resolve)
- *hypothesize*: advance a tentative proposition which could explain the occurrence of a number of phenomena and which can be tested by further observations or experimentation (cf. suggest)
- *justify*: set out the evidence or reasons for adopting a particular course of action or making a specific assumption (prove, vali-date)
- *outline*: write brief notes describing the successive stages in a process, main points in an argument or key incidents in a narra-tive (summarize, trace)
- *reconcile*: show how two apparently conflicting theories or sets of data are compatible (cf. relate).

Major essays and essay questions set in final examinations should also attempt to measure the level of each student's learning as a result of the whole course rather than their ability to reproduce from memory. Thus an emphasis on integration of knowledge gained from different sections of the course would be most appropriate. Successful students should be able to demonstrate their ability to select information or arguments which are relevant to the topic and to present the information and arguments in a logical manner which is clear to the reader. The following essay question is an example of one which measures these skills:

> North and South Vietnam, America and China were all partly to blame for the outbreak of the Vietnam War. Explain each of their roles in the events which led immediately to the entry of American forces into the war.

To answer the above question in a satisfactory manner a student must be able to demonstrate a knowledge of political, economic and social circumstances in each of the countries listed in the years immediately preceding the involvement of US and other forces in the conflict.

Some essays topics will also test students' ability to evaluate a major theory which has been studied or a set of procedures advocated for solving a problem, as in the following question:

> Outline the main arguments Harris (1966, 1971) advances about India's sacred cattle and the criticisms of his thesis by Simoons. (Australian National University, *Anthropology B8: Social Change*, 1st Semester, 1991) (Approximate time allowed: 90 minutes)

One final point needs to be made concerning the setting of essays in examination papers. This concerns the amount of time allowed for the paper as a whole and the individual questions which make up that paper. If the heading to the paper gives the direction *Answer 'x' out of the following 'y' questions*, it is essential that all questions on the paper be of approximately the same length and of comparable levels of difficulty. Sufficient reading time should be allowed for the students to make an informed choice and to complete the physical processes of writing and any necessary calculating or drawing, in addition to planning and other mental processes required for preparing a satisfactory answer to the question.

Essay marking

Improving reliability

We have already referred to the difficulty of using essays as a reliable measure of students' performance. In earlier research on this subject, Dunstan (1959) demonstrated a lack of agreement within a team of markers when each was marking the same essay. A complementary research project by Hartog and Rhodes (1935) showed that markers rarely gave the same mark when assessing the same essay a year later. It is unfortunate that reports such as these have received wide publicity, as they have tended to bring essays into disrepute in some quarters. Contrasting research by Gosschalk *et al.* (1966) and by Britton *et al.* (1970) suggests that the most reliable grading of essays occurs when, prior to marking, lecturers spend time discussing with their colleagues criteria which are likely to influence their judgements, but they do not attempt to attach a weighting to each criterion. They then read each student's essay and award a mark based on their total impression.

Clift and Imrie (1981) refer to the work of McDonald and Sansom (1979) who experimented with a technique for improving both the calibre of students' essays and the consistency of marking by tutors in Murdoch University, Western Australia. McDonald and Sansom persuaded a group of university teachers to attach to each assignment topic a list of criteria which would be used in the assessment of students' performance in that assignment. They summarize their findings in the following way (SRHE, 1980):

> All tutors and 80 per cent of the students found them useful. Tutors mentioned that they were encouraged to consider aspects of the essay that they might otherwise have ignored, the attachments made them aware of the common agreed assessment criteria, and they could mark work knowing that students had been encouraged to assess their work themselves according to the same criteria. Over three quarters of the students surveyed felt that the attachments helped to explain their grade and indicated which aspects of the essay were good and (which were) deficient, and two thirds felt that they provided useful information for the preparation of other assignments.

A contrasting view on marking has been advanced by Partington (1994) who discusses the practice of double-marking students' work and says that:

> the rules of marking are, or should be, determined not by the individual examiner, nor by any random pair of examiners, but by the teaching syllabus. The syllabus will specify learning targets for the students, probably expressed as both *content* (topics, themes, areas, knowledge and so on) and *skills*. Each piece of assessed work is designed to assess part or parts of that syllabus. (p. 59)

Following on from the above, Partington asserts that:

> Assessment criteria and weightings to be attached to each aspect of the student's work should really form part of the published syllabus which directs students' learning. A marking scheme for each piece of work which fits together with the syllabus should be devised at *the same time as the questions*. (Italics in the original article.)

An anonymous reviewer, when commenting on an earlier draft of this chapter, drew attention to another procedure which some faculty have found helpful when determining the most appropriate grades for essays in a relatively small class. In this case the marker reads each essay and provisionally puts it with essays of a similar broad calibre. Once all the essays have been checked the marker is now able to compare more thoroughly essays of similar quality before deciding on an order of merit (if that is what is being sought) and final allocation of a grade or mark. While this method of marking has been used on occasion by the present author, it no longer has the appeal of apparent simplicity. Determination of criteria for success seems to occur *after* each essay has been read and (provisionally) assessed, rather than before marking begins, or even before the essay is set.

Perhaps the differing views on marking which have been described in the preceding paragraphs may be attributed to the contrast between *norm-referenced assessment*, which compares each student's performance with the student's peers, and *criterion-referenced assessment*, which measures the performance against an agreed set of criteria. These contrasting approaches will be mentioned again later in the present chapter and in more detail later in the book.

In discussing the marking of essays, Cockburn and Ross (1977b) suggest criteria which may be used when determining the grade to be awarded. They acknowledge that for different subjects and marking schemes new lists of criteria would need to be prepared. Nevertheless their list, which is reproduced in Table 7.2, may be of assistance to those with little experience in marking essays.

Table 7.2 *Criteria for the award of grades*

GRADE	DESCRIPTION
A+/A	Excellent critical and conceptual analysis; comprehensive survey of relevant issues; well argued; well presented; relevant reading effectively incorporated.
A–/B+/B	Good critical and conceptual analysis; good survey of relevant issues; satisfactory presentation; relevant reading effectively incorporated.
B–/C+/C	Rather more descriptive than critical and conceptual; analysis lacks clarity in parts; evidence of relevant reading but not always effectively used.
C–/D+	Perfunctory; largely descriptive; disorganized and lacking in detail.
D/D–	Perfunctory; almost entirely descriptive; narrow in conception; poorly argued.
E	No evidence of understanding; little evidence of a serious attempt.
O	Not presented.

Some faculty members (or departments in which they work) use an entirely different system for the allocation of grades from those described above. Instead of using criterion-referenced assessment – judging each student's work against a predetermined set of criteria for each level of performance – they prefer to use norm-referenced assessment, comparing each student's performance with that of the class as a whole. In adopting the latter system of grading, the assumption is frequently made that marks (and grades) will follow a normal distribution, ie relatively small numbers of students score highly or fail, while most of the class earn a passing grade. This may be the case when very large numbers of students are tested, but there is no certainty that normal distributions will apply to examination results in situations where the students have been through rigorous selection procedures, are highly motivated or are well taught. We shall discuss the implications of these different approaches to assessment in a later chapter, but at this stage it would be helpful to demonstrate a marking scheme developed by Hall and Imrie (1994) in which norm-referenced assessment is combined with criterion referenced.

Table 7.3   *Description of grade standards for a test combining criterion-referenced and norm-referenced information*

Grade	Mark	Description
A	75+	Top 10% of students who passed.
B	60–74	Next 20% of students who passed.
C	50–59	The student has met course objectives concerned with:
		matters of safety on-the-job performance minimum essentials in course work.
D	<50	The student has not met the objectives listed under grade C.

With reference to the standards for grading, Hall and Imrie (1994) write: 'When you give students their results from a norm-referenced test, also give them a description of the grade categories, as illustrated. Students should be given a clear idea of how they compared with other students.'

Table 7.3 demonstrates clearly how norm referencing might operate but, in regard to maintaining standards from year to year, it is *not* logical to work with fixed proportions for grades (or honours classifications). Even though the quality of students may change from one year to the next, the standards expected should not.

Jones and Grant (1991, p. 48) refer to six areas in which markers' comments may be useful to students. They are listed here in order of importance:

1. misunderstanding the question
2. faulty structuring of the essay
3. inadequate grasp of concepts
4. lack of knowledge
5. bad communication
6. details of presentation.

Unfortunately some of us, when marking essays, put all our efforts into the correction of spelling errors and grammatical faults (each of which needs correction), ignoring the far more important issues such as those listed by Jones and Grant.

Beard (1976) lists 17 factors which might be taken into account in the marking of essays, and although the list was originally prepared for teachers of English, most could be used in marking essays in other subjects. Edited examples from her list are:

● evidence that the question has been read thoroughly
● clear listing of main points in a logical order
● concise arguments
● references and quotations used in context and either cited correctly or, if paraphrased, this would be acknowledged
● generalizations based only on suitable evidence
● written within the framework of the subject, eg literary criticism rather than history or philosophy.

One of the commonest reasons why students fail to achieve satisfactory marks for essays is that they do not answer the basic question posed by the essay. This is more likely to occur when essays are used as examination questions than when they are used as assignments during term. Under the stress of examination conditions, students may imagine that an essay is asking them to write 'about James Joyce' rather than to 'show how the writings of James Joyce distinguish him from other significant writers of the same period'. Those who misread the question will describe the life and writings of Joyce, often with few references to other writers of the period, and even if these others are mentioned there will be little or no attempt to describe the distinctive features of Joyce's works and how these contrast with his contemporaries. When essays are used as in-course assignments students would be expected to support their own arguments with a balanced review of any literature on the subject including, of course, appropriate quotations from the works of James Joyce and other authors of that period. Students would be penalized for making unsubstantiated claims.

Fortunately, more and more academic departments are attempting to overcome the problem that students, especially those in their first year at university or college, need clear guidance as to what is expected in a term paper and what is expected in their answers to examination questions. The Department of Commerce at the Australian National University, for example, in its Course Outline for Accounting 1 (*Accounting: A Financial Information System*), includes nearly four pages of helpful suggestions under the headings 'Guide to Research Report Writing', 'Guide to Referencing', 'Common Faults' and 'Comments from Markers in Prior Years on Research Reports'. The Department of Political Science in the same university includes a six-page 'Guide to Essay Writing' in its main Course Guide and seven pages on plagiarism and related problems. The Geography Department in the same university provides each batch of students with an *Undergraduate Information Guide* which contains a list of 'Criteria for Assessment of Assignments' and a one-page interpretation of 'The Grading System and its Meaning'. This has some similarities to the two examples given earlier in the present chapter, but incorporates much more detailed descriptions of what is required for the award of each grading level. It is reproduced at the end of this chapter as Table 7.4 with the permission of Professor Diana Howlett, the Head of the Department.

Wherever possible, students should be told how their essays will be marked and, generally speaking, students have a right to know afterwards the basis on which their marks were awarded. There may be occasions when a lecturer will wish to make the essay topic deliberately open in order to test students' ability to interpret what information is needed and how it would best be presented. Even when the lecturer's purpose is to encourage creativity, the students should be informed that the examiner is looking for evidence of this quality.

Helpful comments

Lecturers are often criticized for failing to provide sufficient feedback on the quality of a student's work or the level of attainment reached by the student. Simply giving marks such as seven out of ten, or β++, or comments such as 'Good Work' or 'You could do better than this', do not really tell students much about how their work compares with other members of the class, whether it comes up to the teacher's expectations or, most important of all, what the students need to do to improve their performance.

If the class is small enough and there are not too many essays to be marked at the one time, it is possible for the teacher to write quite specific comments and suggestions on each student's essay and to arrange for each student to receive his or her marked essay at an interview session in the teacher's office. (There are times, however, when such a practice would be ill advised, particularly if there is any possibility of a charge of sexual harassment against the teacher.)

With larger classes an alternative procedure to individual comments and interviews has to be adopted. One practice which the author has found to be quite successful is to give each student a mark or grade for the essay, write a small number of comments which apply only to a particular student's essay, and provide for the class a set of notes which describe the criteria used in determining grades, a listing of common errors and suggestions for acceptable approaches to the essay topic(s) which had been set. If the class agrees, it is also helpful to have one or two of the better essays photocopied and distributed to members of the class, particularly if there is more than one satisfactory approach to the assignment.

As more and more universities make extensive use of computing facilities in teaching and assessing performance there is an advantage in requiring students to submit assignments using the electronic mailing facilities (e-mail) of the Internet. With a system such as this in operation, the teacher can easily generate a file of comments and select the most appropriate comments for individual assignments. It is also a simple task to distribute representative essays by e-mail so that students may see what is required to gain an A or, for that matter, why some essays are given a lower rating. A similar use of e-mail facilities for the submission of essay drafts is described in the section which follows (Holmes *et al.*, 1992).

Possibilities of draft essays

If an objective of a particular unit of study is for students to achieve their greatest potential, then it is reasonable to encourage students to submit essays in draft form so that tutors or teaching assistants may make constructive criticisms before the student revises the essay for its final presentation. In this way students are being encouraged to take their writing seriously as they are following the actions of professional writers who send a draft paper or chapter to colleagues before submitting their work for publication.

There are two obvious difficulties with this practice. First, when a student makes substantial changes to an essay after receiving helpful suggestions from the tutor one must ask just how much of the revised essay is the student's work and how much can be attributed to the tutor? Provided the objectives of the course require students to reach certain specified levels, it should not matter whether the tutor has give considerable help; provided the student has considered the tutor's suggestions the objectives will have been achieved. In any case, there will be other opportunities to test the student's own levels of knowledge and skills.

A second problem with draft essays is that they increase greatly the marking load for tutors or teaching assistants. If the university or college values the use of draft essays it will be prepared to reimburse people for the time spent in the additional marking or in making extensive comments on students drafts. It may not therefore be reasonable to expect tutors to spend extra time dealing with draft submissions unless this practice is regarded as part of their workload for which they are adequately paid.

An interesting adaptation of the draft essay is described by Holmes *et al.* (1992). As part of a course in neuro-science students were required to write an essay using computers. The essays were not necessarily printed out but were submitted to their instructors via the computer network in the University of Texas at Houston. Instructors, if they wished, could send back comments and suggestions to each student, or to the class as a whole, using the same network, and students whose work was unsatisfactory were given the chance to resubmit. The authors of the article claim that this exercise improved students' writing skills and their familiarity with computers and word-processing packages.

Redemptive work

A variation on draft essays is to allow students whose initial essays were inadequate to resubmit after extensive revision. The practice is, of course, quite common in marking theses or other major reports in postgraduate courses, but not as popular among teachers of undergraduate courses. There are four major difficulties with the idea of allowing undergraduate students to resubmit unsatisfactory work. The first is the same as that given in the previous paragraph, namely that workloads could be greatly increased for teachers of large classes; the solution is the same – payment of an additional allowance when there is an increase in the marking load.

The second is the definition of 'unsatisfactory'. Should students be allowed to decide for themselves whether an assignment or grade is unsatisfactory or should this be the prerogative of the marker? Some students who were aiming for a very high grade but were only marked moderately highly may feel that their grade would be improved if they were allowed to revise and resubmit. Why should the only students who are allowed to resubmit be those who had failed or received a lower-grade pass? If a policy of redemptive essays is to be fair to all students anyone should be allowed to resubmit an assignment, within certain time constraints.

Mention of time constraints provides a link with the third difficulty with redemptive work, namely that students who complete their work in minimum (or at least the allocated) time should not be at a disadvantage compared with students who are allowed to resubmit their work after revision. At the beginning of this section, reference was made to revision and resubmission of postgraduate reports and theses, but usually this is only allowed within a strict time limit which is known to all students.

A fourth matter to be resolved in relation to redemptive work is whether 'unsatisfactory' assignments should be revised or completely rewritten. By the time a student is given the opportunity to resubmit most students whose work was satisfactory will have received their marked work, hopefully with helpful comments on it from the teacher. There will thus be a strong temptation for unsuccessful students to obtain a copy of a satisfactory essay or answer to an assignment and use that material in the revised work resubmitted. This is less a problem with postgraduate students as they are more likely to have been given different assignments which are more in line with their particular specialization.

Some examples of essay topics

The following essay questions have been selected from recent examination papers in a selection of disciplines taught at the Australian National University. The questions are reprinted with the permission of the University. The questions are included here in order to provide readers with opportunities for looking critically at the way teachers in disciplines other than their own assess students' knowledge and, as a result, readers may be challenged to experiment with a wider range of question formats. As an interesting exercise, readers may wish to consider which of these essays are more challenging to the students and whether any could be improved by a slight change in the wording.

From the humanities

What do you make of the claim that *Northanger Abbey* is principally a work *about* literature rather than a work *of* literature? In so far as it is the former, what are its main criticisms of contemporary literature and its readers, and its main assertions about the value of the novel? In so far as it is the latter, what seem to you to be its chief qualities and/or shortcomings? (*Nineteenth- and Twentieth-century Literature* (Honours), Annual Examination, 1995) (Time allowed: 60 minutes)

What are the 'wisdom' books of the Hebrew Bible, and what sort of wisdom do they aim to teach? (*Biblical Literature*, 1st Year Final Examination, 1993) (Approximate time allowed: 45 minutes)

Select two of the three poems listed below. Note differences between them in their use of language, paying attention to vocabulary, word–order, devices of verse and other kinds of patterning. Comment on the contribution made by the features you have noted in one of these poems to the overall impression the poem makes on you. (*Introduction to English Literature*, 1993) (Approximate time allowed: 60 minutes)

The women's movement of the 1970s offered a radical critique of the structures of power in society. What were the elements of this critique, and what agendas for reform grew out of it? (*History*, 1st Year Annual Examination, 1993) (Approximate time allowed: 60 minutes)

What would you say to the claim that Wordsworth's poetry is important chiefly for its treatment of momentary experiences which cumulatively give life its value? If you agree with this claim, illustrate its validity by close reference to five or six of what you see as the more important of these moments in the poetry? If you disagree, what do you find of most importance in the poetry? Again, illustrate with reference to five or six passages. (*Nineteenth- and Twentieth-century Literature* (Honours), Annual Examination, 1995)

From foreign languages

What advice would you give to a government in a newly independent country (five indigenous languages, none reduced to writing, colonial language was French) which intends to introduce Esperanto as its official language? Give reasons for your advice! (*Linguistics*, Year 1 Semester 2, 1991) (Approximate time allowed: 90 minutes)

Comment on the grammar of the words underlined in the following passages:

a) *Phaselus ille, quem uidetis, hospites ait fuisse nauium celerrimus.*

b) *nec deprecor iam, si nefaria scripta Sesti recepso, quin grauedinem et tussim non mi, sed ipsi Sestio ferat frigus.* [3 more sections to this question] (*Advanced Latin* C, 1991) (Approximate time allowed for whole question: 36 minutes)

From the social sciences

The post-Vietnam period has seen the emergence of neo-Realism as the new orthodoxy in International Relations. Discuss neo-Realism with particular reference to the issues of structuralism, order, hegemony and the global political economy. (*International Relations Theory*, Semester Examination, 1993) (Approximate time allowed: 60 minutes)

Discuss the respective roles of the state, the community and the family in ensuring that the basic needs of individuals are met. Your discussion must draw on the experience of any one or more Asian societies. (*Individual and Society in Contemporary Asia*, Annual Examination, 1995) (Time allowed: 90 minutes)

Examine the relative importance of economic, social and political crises in the making of the Russian revolution of 1917. (Australian National University, *From Lenin to Stalin: Soviet History 1917–1937*, Semester Examination, 1993) (Approximate time allowed: 60 minutes)

From the physical sciences

Describe the evolution of a massive star from the end of its main hydrogen burning stage to its eventual death. Include different scenarios depending on the star's mass. (*Physics*, 1st Year, 2nd Semester, 1990) (Approximate time allowed: 30 minutes)

a) Derive an expression for the magnetic dipole moment of the classical ground state. The expression is known to give the right answer in good agreement with experiment, but for the wrong reasons. Comment on this. What are the dimensions and units of magnetic dipole moment?

b) Describe the Stern-Gerlach experiment. Why was it done and what essentially did it show? (*Chemistry A11*, 1991) (Approximate time allowed: 30 minutes)

From the natural sciences

There are numerous issues in environmental geology concerned with hazardous earth processes. Discuss three natural hazards of concern to humans and how better knowledge of the geological setting and history can help overcome or predict those hazards. Examples discussed in lectures were: catchment hydrology and associated erosion, human activities associated with the coastal zone, global change, earthquakes, landslides, and volcanic activity. (*Environmental Geology*, 2nd Semester, 1995) (Compulsory question; time allowed: 60 minutes)

Is there a relationship between the species diversity, stability and complexity of communities? (*Community Ecology*, 1993) (Approximate time allowed: 36 minutes)

What does contemporary research tell us about the operation of the primary visual cortex in visual perception? (*Psychology B08, Cognitive Processes*, 1991) (Approximate time allowed: 36 minutes)

The Precambrian involved a period of about four billion years. The remainder of geological time involved only six hundred million years, yet evolution seems to have been far more productive of new types during the latter time interval. Would you agree with that statement? Give reasons for your answer. (*Palaeontology and Stratigraphy*, 2nd Semester, 2nd Year, 1991) (Approximate time allowed: 36 minutes)

From economics and commerce

Describe the interaction between historical events and legislation, affecting auditing, in nineteenth-century Britain. What can Australian legislators learn from that experience? (*Auditing*, 1989) (Approximate time allowed: 27 minutes)

Decentralization offers a number of advantages to firms. However, the assessment of performance in decentralized operating units presents difficulties. Discuss critically these difficulties and some of the suggested performance measures with respect to profit centres. (*Accounting: Managerial Decision Making*, 4th Year, Semester 1, 1993) (Approximate time allowed: 45 minutes)

What form do you think a famine-mitigation program should take which results in the limited funds available for famine relief reaching those who need assistance most? Explain your answer in some detail. (*Development, Poverty and Famine*, Final examination, 1993) [Paper allowed 45 minutes study period and approximately 40 minutes per question; there was a choice of 3 questions out of 12.]

With new manufacturing technologies and management philosophies, many companies are recognizing the limitations of traditional financial performance measures and are creating new performance measurement systems outside of the domain of conventional management accounting.

Why? What are the implications for performance measurement systems design and the effective integration of an organization's Accounting Information System within its Management Information System? (*Management Control and Performance Evaluation*, 2nd Semester Examination, November 1994) (Time allowed: 40 minutes)

From law

What implications does liberal ideology have for the way in which we should assess the quality of the legal system? (*Law in Context*, 1st Year, Final Examination, 1993) (Approximate time allowed: 45 minutes)

Belinda invents a rainmaking machine. She develops a design, and decides to build two prototypes herself, one for her own use, and the other for sale to Fred. Belinda incorporates under the name Belinda Pty Ltd. Each machine requires 5 popdoodles, which are manufactured by Malcolm and Co (Malcolm). The popdoodles cost $30,000 each. Belinda places two orders, each for 5 popdoodles, from Malcolm. She tells Malcolm that the popdoodles must be capable of being fitted to the standard Albacord crop-dusting aircraft. Malcolm insists that the contracts be made on its own order form, which contains a term to the effect that the contract between itself and Belinda excludes all implied terms, statutory or otherwise. The contracts provide that the popdoodles be supplied in four instalments over two months, and that Belinda will pay ⅓ on signing the contract, ⅓ at the end of the first month, and ⅓ at the end of the second month.

Malcolm delivers two popdoodles in the first instalment, and Belinda incorporates one into each of her machines. Then Malcolm delivers two more, and these prove unsatisfactory because Malcolm has used the wrong thread pitch on them — they do not fit the Albacord. She contacts Malcolm, which apologizes, but says that it will not be able to do much about it as its new milling machines don't make threads to match the Albacord. Malcolm suggests that Belinda get someone to make adaptors for her.

Belinda has found a better and cheaper supplier of popdoodles – Ace Suppliers – and is keen to get out of the contracts with Malcolm. Advise Malcolm. Do not discuss merchantable quality. (60 marks) (*Commercial Law*, Final Examination, 1994)

Published criteria for grading

Reference has been made already in the current chapter to the need for making the criteria used for grading assignments as clear as possible for both markers and students. Table 7.4 is more detailed in its description of the quality of work expected when a particular grade is being awarded. It could be applied in grading a major essay or a student's overall performance in a semester unit.

Table 7.4 *The grading system and its meaning*

Grade	Percentage Value	Interpretation
High Distinction (HD)	80%+	Work of exceptional quality showing clear understanding of subject matter and appreciation of issues; well formulated; arguments sustained; sketch maps and diagrams where relevant; relevant literature referenced; marked evidence of creative ability and originality; high level of intellectual work.
Distinction (D)	70–79%	Work of unusual quality showing strong grasp of subject matter and appreciation of dominant issues though not necessarily of the finer points; arguments clearly developed; relevant literature referenced; evidence of creative ability; solid intellectual work.
Credit (Cr)	60–69%	Work of solid quality showing competent understanding of subject matter and appreciation of main issues though possibly with some lapses and inadequacies; arguments clearly developed and supported by references though possibly with minor red herrings and loose ends; some evidence of creative ability; well prepared and presented.
Pass (P)	50–59%	Range from a bare pass to a safe pass. Adequate, but lacking breadth and depth. Work generally has gaps. Frequently work of this grade takes a simple factual approach and does not attempt to interpret the findings. At the lower end, indicates a need for considerable effort to achieve improvement.
Fail (N)	<50%	Unsatisfactory. This grade characterizes work which shows a lack of understanding of the topic. Inadequate in degree of relevance, sometimes completeness, sometimes both.

Some concluding comments

The length of this chapter gives some indication of the importance the authors give to the use of essays as an assessment tool, which in turn reflects the predominance of essay questions, both in assignments and in formal examinations. Essays are valuable instruments in both formative and summative assessment. They provide students with practice in marshalling and interpreting data, developing tentative conclusions and evaluating alternative hypotheses. Thus essay writing is a good preparation for the preparation and evaluation of reports in industry and in research, tasks which are an important component of employment for university graduates or further study.

Practice in writing essays is also important as it helps students to develop their powers of written expression. Too many students enter universities with little or no experience of writing the type of essay which is expected in higher education, and some undergraduate programs, particularly in the sciences, provide few opportunities for students to develop these skills until they reach the honours level. While the development of communication skills may not be one of the stated objectives of a particular university course, it is a skill which will be useful throughout life. There is, however, a problem with this emphasis on communication skills. It arises with students whose language ability is limited, either because their first language is not English or because they come from a social group where language usage varies from the norm. Such students may become highly competent in the technical aspects of the discipline being studied, but unable to express themselves in clear English. Should they be penalized for the poor quality of their spelling and grammar or their imprecise use of words?

One's answer to the above question will depend partly on the purpose of the course and partly on the likely destination of its graduates. In most instances the teacher should draw each student's attention to any errors but determine a grade which largely reflects the extent to which the student has dealt with issues inherent in the essay topic. The grade might also be influenced by the teacher's judgement of how well the student appears to have grasped the basic concepts in the discipline which are relevant to that essay. Occasions when the quality of English would influence the level of the mark will be where objectives of the program include the development of communication skills. If a substantial proportion of students in the class have come from a country where English is not the official language, the course designer must decide whether graduates of this program will need to be able to express themselves in English in order to keep in touch with colleagues in other countries and the literature on their discipline.

Essays are time consuming for students and also for those who mark the essays, but there are very few teaching and learning programs which would not be enhanced by using them at some stage to assess students' understanding and achievement.

——— 8 ———

Theses

It is a good morning exercise for a research scientist to discard a pet
hypothesis every day before breakfast. It keeps him young.

(Konrad Lorenz)

In this chapter we shall consider some of the problems which may
arise when examiners are required to make judgements about the
quality of a thesis, whether it be associated with the award of a bachelor's degree with honours, a postgraduate diploma, a master's
degree or a doctorate. Naturally the expectations regarding the
quality (and usually the size) of the thesis will be greater for the
higher degrees, but most of the principles relating to the assessment
of a thesis are common to all levels.

Arguments for and against a thesis in postgraduate studies

It is generally accepted that a thesis is an essential component of
a higher degree, particularly a PhD, but there is no consensus as
to whether a thesis should be required at the Masters level or lower.
In its report on the teaching of economics in Australian universities
and its examination of standards for the award of a bachelor's degree
with honours, a working party of the Australian Vice-Chancellors'
Committee (AVCC) listed the main arguments for and against the
inclusion of a thesis in honours programs (AVCC, 1992b). While
these particular lists were developed in relation to the teaching
of economics and to a bachelor's degree with honours, they are just
as applicable to other fields and levels of study when 'economics' is
replaced by the name of the other discipline. Similar sets of reasons,
with appropriate modifications, could be advanced in relation
to theses at higher levels. The main arguments for requiring a thesis

for the award of an honours degree in economics are (AVCC, 1992b):

1. Honours graduates are an elite group, most of whom will go on to independent professional work. The opportunity to do a sustained piece of independent research with the benefits of supervision is thus an apprenticeship which is likely to be of benefit in future study and employment.
2. The thesis, because of the magnitude and quality of independent work which is required, and the provision of supervision, distinguishes the honours year from the previous years.
3. The thesis provides an opportunity for the student to bring together many of the aspects of economics which have been learned in earlier years as separate subjects.
4. The thesis is a valuable instrument for assessment because it provides an environment wherein the distinctive qualities of the first-class graduate can be exhibited – namely originality, mastery of economic ideas and a feel for how to use them, and creativity. It is much more difficult to detect such qualities in an examination or in short pieces of written work.
5. The thesis develops and tests the ability to organize and execute a sustained piece of research and to present complex material well.
6. The thesis is the one durable part of the honours year which the students recognize as their own distinctive work. Students do not regard their exam scripts in this light.

The AVCC working party lists only three objections to the inclusion of a thesis in an honours program. These are (AVCC, 1992b):

1. Opportunity cost: the time students put into their thesis may be better spent on instruction in subjects which take them to the frontiers of the discipline.
2. The difficulty in ensuring consistent assessment and supervision across students.
3. The difficulty of separating out the supervisor's contribution for the purposes of assessment.

Choice of a topic for investigation

The amount of freedom given to students in the choice of a topic for investigation varies greatly, both between and within universities. The worst situation is when students who enrol for a higher degree are told by their adviser to come back when they have found a topic they would like to investigate. The only advantages of this approach are that the student will be forced to consider a wide range of options and may spend some time reviewing each of the major topics studied during the undergraduate years. The disadvantages are obvious. First, much time can be wasted because the student lacks direction in the search for a topic. Second, even when the student has provisionally chosen a topic, that topic might be rejected by the department either because there is no suitable person to supervise it or because the topic is not sufficiently challenging and would therefore be unsuitable for training in research procedures.

At the other end of the spectrum there are university departments, particularly those which are science based, where a potential postgraduate student is given a very restricted choice of topics. The reason for this is that the student needs to be attached to an existing research team and therefore must investigate a topic which will contribute to the work of the team. The main advantages are that the student gains valuable experience as a team member, often working with highly respected researchers; a student in a team is more likely to make a valuable contribution to the overall research efforts of the department than a student working more or less alone; and there is no time lost in searching for a topic. Arguments against such a procedure are that the student may lose initiative, and credit for the student's research is more likely to go to the team (or its leader) rather than the student who made the discovery.

Moses (1985) describes in some detail steps which might be taken and questions which might be asked when guiding a postgraduate student in the choice of a research topic. She introduces the section on 'Selecting the Research Topic' with the following recommendation from the British Swinnerton-Dyer Report on Postgraduate Education (1982) which appears to be a satisfactory compromise between the two extreme practices described above:

> The choice of research topics should be heavily influenced by the staff and, where appropriate, also from outside the academic institution; this is to ensure that the topic is a suitable subject for research training, that it is likely to prove a rewarding investigation, that it is of practical benefit where this is possible, that competent supervision is available and that the work can be completed within the time available. (pp. 11–13)

Decisions about research procedures

Choice of appropriate procedures is naturally closely linked to the choice of a topic for investigation. Nevertheless it is important to recognize that there are frequently a number of ways that a particular topic may be investigated and it is the responsibility of the supervisor (or supervisory panel) to inform the student of the advantages and disadvantages of the alternatives available. The ultimate choice of investigatory procedures will preferably be made by the student as part of the final judgement of the quality of the thesis and will take into account whether the research methods used were appropriate for the particular problem being investigated.

It is not our purpose in this book to provide details of different research procedures; that is the function of other types of publications, usually more closely allied with a particular discipline. Later in this chapter, however, we will briefly discuss some differences between quantitative methods, which rely heavily on statistical techniques, and qualitative methods, which rely more on the investigator's observations and perceptions. Nevertheless, it is important that students, acting on the advice of their supervisors, ensure that any populations selected for observation or experimentation are as representative as possible. The size and nature of the population being studied will determine the type of statistical analysis (if any) which is most appropriate.

Although the final interpretation of the results is the student's responsibility, one would expect students to discuss their findings and likely conclusions with colleagues and with academic staff, generally at a compulsory seminar led by the student some time before the thesis is concluded.

Quality control

The assessment of major extended research and writing tasks is an important facet of postgraduate education. With a system of external examiners, the people responsible for making summative judgements about the quality of students' work are normally different from the supervisors or advisory groups who make formative judgements. Even though the formative and summative aspects of assessment are more completely separated in postgraduate studies than at the undergraduate level, there is still a need for all postgraduate examiners, at least within the one discipline, to have shared expectations about common standards. Regular use of external examiners in the United Kingdom for all levels of higher education seeks to maintain a reasonably high level of quality control in postgraduate courses.

In her report on a survey of PhD students and supervisors in the United Kingdom, Phillips (1993) states:

> The different ways that academic staff spoke about the thesis appeared, ultimately, to form a kind of consensus that the design, thought and explanation all had to be well done. There was some reference to three key elements which should incorporate technical proficiency, originality and conceptual development. (p. 16)

She adds that 'most of the students were confused about what was required of them and commented that it would be useful if they were provided with guidelines on method and form in the beginning'. We strongly support this view and recommend that each university should publish a statement of postgraduate students' rights and responsibilities (a charter for students) and a complementary list of the rights and responsibilities of supervisors (a code of ethics?). Within any one university there will, of course, be variations between academic departments in their expectations and these should be included in departmental handbooks.

When the National Committee of Inquiry into Higher Education (Dearing, 1997) considered the need for greater quality control over academic awards in the United Kingdom, it recommended the establishment of a 'national framework of qualifications' (Rec. 22). The Committee noted that there were four main messages in a report on academic awards from the Higher Education Quality Council (HEQC).

1. UK awards are not perceived as national awards in mainland Europe because they are awarded by individual institutions.
2. The establishment of a UK framework of qualifications would be likely to lessen some current problems of international recognition of qualifications, and to enhance confidence in standards.
3. A typical continental degree tends to be defined as a programme of a minimum of four years of study, although the levels of achievement for such programs are not defined.
4. The expansion of UK higher education has weakened the argument, previously accepted in Europe, that highly selective entry for UK students supported the standing of the three-year honours degree. (Dearing 1997, Section 10.40)

To a limited extent some quality control of honours degrees is being encouraged in Australia through a number of 'Academic Standards

Panels' set up by the Australian Vice-Chancellors' Committee. (Reference has already been made to some recommendations of the Economics panel.) Each panel established by the AVCC is responsible for reporting on standards in one discipline. The panels have found that discussions with subject specialists in individual universities have helped stimulate change, especially where a particular institution has a noticeably different proportion of first-class honours graduates in a given discipline from other institutions teaching that discipline. To date reports have been published by these panels on the following disciplines: physics, history, psychology, economics, computer science, biochemistry and English.

Each panel devised a series of questions to be answered by the appropriate academic department prior to a visit from the panel when honours courses would be discussed in more detail. As an example of the types of questions asked, the list of questions used by the history panel is quoted below (AVCC, 1991):

- What are the expectations of students' performance?
- How does the structure of an honours course (eg early specialization, combined honours degrees) relate to quality?
- How does an honours subject get into the curriculum?
- In what ways does an honours subject differ from those offered at pass level?
- What is a satisfactory thesis proposal? What scope is there for original work in the thesis?
- How is examination of the thesis organized? What quality control mechanisms exist? What does a supervisor actually do?
- What distribution of staff time is apportioned to honours teaching?
- Do students have input into the design of the honours program?
- How satisfied is the department with the number and gender of honours graduates?
- Is there any evidence that particular fields of study are over-represented in first-class honours results?
- What skills do honours graduates have to offer employers? (pp. 22–3)

The above questions recognize the fact that honours programs in history, as with a number of other disciplines, are quite labour intensive in that they require supervisors to devote substantial amounts of time to their students (AVCC, 1991). They also attempt to address the emphasis of the Australian Government on a need for 'relevance' in publicly funded university courses. With little or no modification these questions could, and indeed should, be asked about all honours and other postgraduate programs.

As a result of these disciplinary reviews the AVCC (1995) has produced a three-page document entitled *Fourth Year Honours Programs: Guidelines for Good Practice*. While the document was intended for use by Australian universities and deals specifically with honours programs rather than postgraduate study, much of what is said could apply equally well to any academic program where a thesis is required. Among the major guidelines are the following:

1. Purposes and organization
   1.1 The primary goal of honours programs should be on research training. Within this broader context of introducing students to research, departments should formulate and explicitly state the objectives of their Honours Program. The content of the program, and the assessment processes, should clearly reflect the objectives.
2. Responsibilities and expectations
   2.1 Honours programs should contain a mix of advanced theory, professional training (where appropriate), research training, and a research project leading to a thesis (in some fields, for example the performing arts, an alternative form of presentation may be appropriate). No overall guidelines are appropriate, but each discipline should establish appropriate upper and lower boundaries for the proportion of the total assessment allocated to the thesis component. The thesis components of most current programs fall in the range 30 to 70 per cent.
3. Assessment
   3.1 Departments should provide regular and systematic feedback to students on all elements of their performance in the honours year as it proceeds.
   3.2 The supervisor's role as an examiner should be delineated, and the policy on the number of examiners and the use of external examiners clearly specified.
   3.3 Departments should develop explicit criteria for the assessment of theses, including definitions of performance at the various grades of honours. All examiners, particularly external examiners, should be provided with a clear statement of the criteria and standards.
   3.4 The assessment process should include written reports on the thesis incorporating a short statement of the reasons for the grade or mark awarded to the thesis. Students should be apprised of the results for each component of the classification of honours award.

3.5 Departments should maintain written records of the criteria used for grading honours performance to facilitate comparability from year to year. Written records of the considerations entered into in reaching final grades for students should be maintained.

The difficulties experienced by postgraduate students in ascertaining what standards are expected of them and in reaching those standards have been examined by a number of other people, including Zuber-Skerritt and Knight (1986), Moses (1984), Nightingale (1984) and the Science and Engineering Research Council (SERC) (1983).

Zuber-Skerritt and Knight (1986) conducted a series of workshops for postgraduate students at Griffith University in Queensland, during which they discovered that the two main points at which students require help from their supervisors are in defining the research problem and in commencing the first draft. Part of the technique used by Zuber-Skerritt and Knight was to encourage students to discuss with each other what they thought might be problems worth investigating, why their particular problems were important and how they might go about solving their problems. Using these methods the investigators were able to help students to focus on and define their problems more succinctly.

The same authors also quote the report of the Science and Engineering Research Council of Great Britain (1983) in which SERC identified the four chief causes of failure to complete postgraduate studies in minimum time. These are (Zuber-Skerritt and Knight, 1986):

1. a slow start
2. perfectionism in the student
3. distraction due to reading unrelated texts and references
4. inadequate collection of data due to poor planning. (pp. 90–1)

Any assistance which supervisors can give their students so that the students themselves can define their own research tasks at an early stage would help alleviate three of the four problems identified by SERC. The problem of perfectionism is not so readily overcome, particularly in these days when so many postgraduate students compose their theses on computers where it is so easy to make changes. Nevertheless it is the supervisor's responsibility to discuss with each student the dangers of attempting too high a standard of reporting. After all, there will be opportunities for the student to refine and develop the ideas presented in the thesis after the degree has been granted and the new graduate selects parts of the thesis for publication in a series of journal articles.

Moses (1984) lists a number of steps which should be taken in order to improve the quality of postgraduate supervision. The most important of these is for institutions and departments to make available to supervisors, external examiners and students a set of guidelines (as was also recommended by Phillips, 1993) which indicate institutional and/or departmental expectations concerning the postgraduate studies and areas of responsibility for both supervisors and students. She suggests a series of common questions which should be answered in these guidelines, three of which are reproduced here.

- How, and on what grounds, can the student change the supervisor?
- Are there provisions for supervisors' absences (eg on study leave)?
- What help can the student expect from the supervisor with regard to the selection of the research topic, selection of methods, with data analysis, with the actual writing of the thesis? (pp. 162–3)

Moses also refers to the value of coursework in the higher degree program, particularly courses which are designed to ensure that students have adequate research skills before undertaking the main research for a thesis. Although course work has long been accepted as a necessary component of higher degrees in North American and some Asian universities, it is interesting to note that it is now being used more widely in British and Australian institutions.

Other recommendations by Moses, based on her long experience in assisting teachers of postgraduate students, are that departments should establish postgraduate studies or research committees which will be formally responsible for the arrangement of supervision and monitor the progress of students, that joint supervision should be used instead of individual supervisors wherever possible and that regular meetings be scheduled for students with their supervisors or supervisory teams with written contracts being used as an aid to the planning of each student's work.

Nightingale (1984) conducted a detailed study of requirements for postgraduate study at one Australian university (Macquarie), comparing arrangements in that university with those which are practised in comparable institutions. Even though Macquarie University has relatively clear requirements for the award of higher degrees, Nightingale found evidence of overlap between requirements for masters' and doctoral degrees and lack of clear criteria for determining the standard expected in a dissertation, a situation which was not unique to Macquarie.

Evaluating a literature survey

An essential component of all theses is an up-to-date survey of relevant literature on the thesis topic, the purpose of which is to set the present project within the context of recent research or scholarship in the field. Most students need considerable help in conducting this survey. Its length should be proportional to the expected length of the thesis or extended essay and the amount of time spent in preparing the survey should be almost as much as that spent in gathering and analysing data. In addition to any reading done specifically for the thesis, it is our view that students working for postgraduate awards should continue to read as widely as time permits samples of literature describing recent developments in their chosen discipline. Moses (1985) reminds us that arts students will have had more experience in using the literature during their undergraduate years than typical science students and recommends that science students should be encouraged or required to build up a card (or computer) index of articles from current journals.

Breadth and depth of reading

A need for an appropriate blend of breadth and depth in reading is implied by the statements made in the previous paragraph. Unless a student who is writing a thesis is certain that his or her future career will continue to be in the line of research undertaken for the thesis, it is of utmost importance that the student's reading should not be limited to topics related to the thesis. As the AVCC panel which investigated economics honours degrees in Australian universities pointed out (1992b, p. 34), one must take into account the types of careers into which economics graduates will eventually move. (Similar arguments would, of course, apply to most other disciplines and to all levels of postgraduate awards.) The panel listed four types of careers for which an economics major prepares people, namely:

1. as a generalist administrator or manager in the private or public sector
2. as a high school teacher of economics

3. as a private or public sector 'tradesperson' economist called upon to apply the essential ideas of economics in their daily work
4. as an academic or other high level professional economist doing original work in a research or policy environment.

For each of these goal paths there is a need for a mix of general and specific knowledge in the discipline, with the proportion of specialized knowledge increasing the more one's career is headed towards research. The Economics Panel expanded on the reasons for both breadth and depth in a student's studies with a listing of the three main ends that honours programs are seen to be serving (and, as before, we may apply these statements to other disciplines and for higher degrees). The three main ends are (AVCC, 1992b):

1. a general intellectual goal of stimulating the mind's powers to understand and interpret the world (in its broadly 'economic' aspects) and to think creatively and argue coherently about it. At this level, the particular subject-matter and analytical orientation of the economics discipline is simply the context for a more basic intellectual object. We ought to expect that our best students will come to apprehend, and to have affection for, the life of the mind; and our honours programs ought to be designed with that expectation in mind.
2. a more specific goal of equipping students for further training, should they wish it and be capable of it. Part of the object here is to help students to an intelligent view of whether they do wish it and of what their capacities may be. We take it that most students who go on to further training will aspire to an academic career (or a career in economic research and policy).
3. the goal of equipping students for the career of professional economist. This goal involves developing the ability of the student to undertake independent economic analysis, to apply the techniques and skills of modern economics and generally to perform competently as a professional economist in the work place. (p. 35)

Within the above constraints the assessor must take into account the breadth of cover and the amount of detail in the literature survey. For example, has the student demonstrated an awareness of the major contributors to this particular part of the discipline? Is the student aware of any major changes or developments in our understanding of the topic being investigated, particularly when there have been paradigm shifts? Is there an appropriate balance between the quotations and reports of the student's own investigations or interpretations?

Judging research skills – qualitative vs quantitative research

Judging the calibre of a student's research skills tends to be by indirect methods except in those cases when the student is enrolled in a doctoral program lasting at least three years, most of which are devoted to a substantial research project in which the student is the chief (or sole) investigator. Some doctoral programs do not provide this opportunity, either because they have a large course-work component or because the research undertaken by the student is part of a larger team project where the professor or some other senior academic is chief investigator. With honours programs, opportunities for the student to conduct meaningful research are even more limited, partly due to time constraints, but mainly because an important function of the honours year is to teach the student research skills which are relevant to the discipline.

The immediate problem is therefore to identify those skills which are deemed to be essential in the branch of the discipline in which the student is enrolled. Because much of the research in science-based subjects depends on the investigator gathering and analysing data using appropriate statistical procedures, there was once a belief among some educationists (many of whom have a background in psychology and statistics) that a quantitative approach to research is the most appropriate method to use in a majority of disciplinary areas. A typical investigative procedure would be to compare the performance of an experimental group (or set of procedures) with a control group, much as an agronomist might compare the growth of crops with or without the addition of a particular fertilizer. The logic for this type of investigation in the social sciences is described clearly by Lindquist (1953) and is outlined in the opening sentences of his book:

> The major purpose of psychological experiments is to describe the effect of certain experimental treatments upon some characteristic of a particular population, or to test some hypothesis about this effect … In most experiments, the observed 'effect' is described in terms of the changes or differences in the mean value of a certain 'criterion' variable. For example, the effects of different experimental conditions under which a certain task is performed may be measured in terms of the mean time of completing the task.

Fortunately, there is now a greater acceptance of the value of qualitative studies, which are based on the traditional anthropological approach to research. The epitome of this technique may be seen in an anthropologist who lives for an extended period with the society being studied, learning their language and customs and seeking to compare and contrast these customs with those of other societies. In the realm of educational research, this approach was developed more or less concurrently by investigators in the Universities of Lancaster, Edinburgh and Gottenburg, frequently in collaboration across national boundaries. Examples of this technique as applied to educational research (on factors influencing students' learning) are found in Marton and Säljö (1976a, b), Svensson, (1977) Hounsell (1979), Moreira (1980), Marton (1981), Entwistle and Ramsden (1983), Marton et al. (1984) and Ramsden (1992). Marton himself describes this approach as phenomenographic, which he describes in the following terms (Marton and Booth, 1997):

> In a very important sense, the methods of phenomenographic data collection and data analysis are inseparable. For one thing, during the collection of data, whether through interviews or in some other form, analysis is taking place, and early phases of analysis can influence later data collection. (p. 117)

After describing this more qualitative approach to research on teaching and learning, Ramsden (1992) makes the following statement which indirectly challenges the traditional quantitative methods:

> A recurrent finding of this research into student learning is that we can never assume that the impact of teaching on student learning is what we expect it to be. Students' thoughts and actions are profoundly affected by the educational context or environment in which they learn. They react to the demands of teaching and assessment in ways that are difficult to predict: a lot of their learning is not directly about chemistry or history or economics, but about learning how to please lecturers and gain high marks ... An important part of good teaching is to try to understand these contextual effects and to adapt assessment and teaching strategies accordingly. (p. 6)

Just as a student's learning is affected by influences other than the teaching or assessment methods being used, so may the results of other experiments or measurements in scientific investigations be affected by influences beyond the control of the experimenter. Consequently it is important that when assessing research projects undertaken by students, supervisors and examiners should take into consideration the conditions under which the research was undertaken; in many cases it would be inappropriate to expect a student to rely wholly on quantitative measures.

Originality in a doctoral thesis

It is frequently assumed, if not actually stated in the regulations, that a doctoral thesis should demonstrate originality. Unfortunately for students, supervisors and examiners it is not always clear what is meant by the term 'originality'. Phillips (1993) asked a selection of academic staff what they expected in an original thesis. Their answers included:

- saying something nobody has said before
- carrying out empirical work that hasn't been done before
- making a synthesis that hasn't been made before
- using already known material but with a new interpretation
- trying out something in this country that has previously only been done elsewhere
- taking a particular technique and applying it in a new area
- bringing new evidence to bear on an old issue. (pp. 17–18)

If a list such as the above could be more widely circulated among academic staff and students, many of the worries experienced by students in selecting an 'original' topic to investigate would be dispersed. In their preliminary consultations it would be helpful if each student and supervisor (or supervisory panel) could discuss which of the above definitions of originality were most appropriate to the proposed investigation (it is very likely that more than one definition would be applicable).

Composition of the assessment panel

Whenever an institution requires masters or doctoral candidates to undertake course work *and* submit a thesis, there is a general assumption that the course work will be examined and graded within the institution (sometimes under the oversight of external examiners) while the thesis will be assessed by a small panel of experts, preferably recruited from outside the institution where the student is enrolled.

In the series of reports on honours degrees commissioned by the Australian Vice-Chancellors' Committee (AVCC), the question of whether a supervisor should be a member of the assessment panel is discussed. The panel which examined the teaching of psychology at honours level reported differences in practices among major universities in Australia. Members of the panel noted that two primary reasons had been advanced by university teachers for the involvement of the supervisor in the examining procedure. These are reproduced below (AVCC, 1992a):

> The first is that the supervisor usually has a much closer knowledge of both the field of research in which the student has worked and the problems faced than do other members of staff. This knowledge places the supervisor in a strong position to make an informed judgment about the quality of the report and the level of honours that it warrants.
>
> Second, in smaller departments particularly, it is frequently difficult to find examiners with the appropriate background and research experience for a reasoned assessment of the report. (p. 41)

The same panel reported that those departments which specifically prohibited supervisors from assessing students' research reports justified the rule by saying that:

> ... supervisors work closely with students on problems that fall within the area of research interest of the [supervisor] and are not always in a position to render an objective judgment on the quality of the report. Put in its more extreme form, this view holds that such is the input of supervisors into the project and its report that in serving as an assessor they are partly assessing their own work.

The AVCC panel which conducted an overview of physics teaching reported that 'generally the project supervisor has a significant role in assessment'. The panel goes on to say that it 'was very uncomfortable with the rather extreme cases where the whole of the grading exercise was undertaken within the research group relating to the project, or a large component (up to 30 per cent of total assessment) came from the supervisor alone unsupported by written justification' (AVCC, 1990). The report makes the following strong recommendation:

> The panel is strongly of the view that written reports (from the supervisor/examiner) improve the objectivity of assessments and has actively encouraged their adoption. As a further aid to objective assessment some departments use a two-stage process where examiners' reports are compared initially and major variations in grading taken up with the examiners before the grading of the project is finalized.

In any event the project should be assessed against objective criteria taking account of different degrees of challenge inherent in different projects. Examiners should be given clear guidelines as to the nature of their report. The panel believes that examiners' reports should be retained by departments over a period of years to aid consistency in grading. (pp. 48–9)

Publication of thesis research

Whenever the research leading up to the thesis makes a significant contribution to knowledge, it is desirable that an account of this research be published as soon as possible. It is essential that the student and the supervisor come to an early agreement on ways in which all persons responsible for the research should be adequately acknowledged. Frequently this recognition will need to extend beyond the two people most directly involved, first to other members of the research team, if one exists, and then to the wider community of scholars whose work has led the student to the discoveries described in the thesis. The latter are normally identified in the literature search, most of which is reported in the opening chapters of the thesis.

Most people would have heard of cases (not always substantiated) where supervisors or heads of research teams have taken the credit for research done by students in their charge. One must admit that there could be times when all the ideas came from the supervisor and the student acted as a research assistant. If that is the situation we would expect the senior person to take major credit for the research, giving due recognition to the student's contribution in the introduction to the report. Where situations such as this exist the value of the thesis must be questioned and the whole approach to supervision needs to be reviewed.

Under normal circumstances the most appropriate form of publication is for the supervisor and the student to prepare a joint paper, in which due acknowledgements are given to others who have contributed to the research. At a later stage the former student may well undertake further research or discover new applications from the original investigation, in which case sole authorship would be appropriate.

9

Objective tests

Nine out of ten people who change their minds are wrong the
second time too.

(Author unknown)

While the essay, the oral examination or successful completion of
defined practical tasks are probably the oldest forms of examination,
each has problems with time and maintaining equity among
students. Thus there developed within the twentieth century an
approach to examinations which was more suited to large classes
where an emphasis on comparability was desirable. The newer types
of tests were called 'objective' to emphasize their difference from the
older forms of testing which were judged to be too subjective. At
one stage, objective tests of one form or another dominated school
and college examinations, particularly in the United States where
highly sophisticated objective tests were developed by the
Educational Testing Service (ETS), a private organization with its
headquarters in Princeton, New Jersey and branches in a number of
other states.

ETS continues its work in producing and marking tests for a large
range of disciplines at all levels of education from early childhood
through scholastic aptitude tests to postgraduate professional certification. Tests available from ETS for specific use in higher education
include:

- Academic Profile for assessing general education
- Major Field Tests for assessment in the major
- Goals Inventories for institutional planning
- Program Self-assessment Service for program and department
  reviews
- Student Instructional Report for faculty development and
  student evaluation of courses. (ETS, 1991)

In 1990, 16 Major Field Achievement Tests were available, covering the fields of biology, business, chemistry, computer science, economics, education, engineering, geology, history, literature in English, mathematics, music, physics, political science, psychology and sociology (ETS, 1990). These are all objective tests using multiple-choice questions and designed to be completed in two hours and according to ETS 'are valid, reliable measures of student outcomes; have national comparative data for each test, can be administered at the institution's or department's convenience, and can include an option for adding locally written questions for any test' (ETS, 1990). ETS also makes the following claims:

> The content specifications for the Major Field Achievement Tests reflect the basic knowledge and understanding gained in the undergraduate curriculum. The tests have been designed to assess mastery of concepts, principles and knowledge expected of students at the conclusion of a major in specific areas.
>
> In addition to factual knowledge, the tests evaluate students' ability to analyze and solve problems, understand relationships and interpret material. They contain questions that call for information as well as questions that require interpretation of graphs, diagrams and charts based on material related to the field (ETS, 1990, p.3).

An example of the broader purpose of these tests may be seen in the outline for geology (ETS, 1990) where it is stated that:

> The questions are designed to measure important abilities such as:
>
> - ability to analyse geological phenomena using, for example, maps, graphs, cross sections, block diagrams, diagrams resulting from instrumental methods and perceptions in three dimensions
> - ability to comprehend geological processes, including comprehension through the application of physics, chemistry, biology and mathematics
> - ability to demonstrate knowledge of basic geology. (p. 3)

Further information about these tests is readily available from the Educational Testing Service, Princeton, New Jersey 08541 or at <http://etsis1.ets.org/> on the Internet. Another source of information and assistance for designers of multiple-choice questions is a publication of the University of London, *Introduction and Guide to the Use of Multiple-choice Questions in University Examinations* (1976).

There has been a great deal of research on the effects of the type of assessment used in a university course and students' approaches to study in that course. Further reference to this research will be made in Chapter 14 where we discuss the evaluation of assessment procedures. Nevertheless it is important in the context of the present chapter to refer to recent research on the relationship between students' learning strategies and their expectations regarding assessment in an institution where one form of objective test, multiple-choice questions (MCQs), are used as a regular part of assessment. Scouller and Prosser (1994), who conducted the investigation, found that 'students who have a deep general orientation to study make plans to employ [deep] study strategies when preparing for their MCQ examinations', whereas 'students with a surface general orientation to study appear to have no planned strategies for preparing for their examinations and may have incompatible conceptions of the difference between reproduction [of learned material] and understanding'. Strangely enough, when Scouller and Prosser (using Bloom's levels of cognitive objectives) analysed the types of MCQs actually used in the courses being investigated, they found that:

> the majority assessed knowledge of factual information, and those few items identified as assessing higher levels of cognitive processing were categorized at the lowest one of comprehension. No items were classified as assessing such higher levels of cognitive skills as application, analysis, synthesis or evaluation. (Scouller and Prosser, 1994, p. 271)

This incidental finding from the above research does not invalidate the use of MCQs for testing higher order objectives; it merely provides further confirmation that it is much more difficult for examiners to construct such questions. Consequently they tend to limit the use of MCQs to testing recall and comprehension. Application, analysis, synthesis and evaluation are more frequently tested by means of problems or essays. Nevertheless in situations where large numbers of students are being given the same examination, the extra time taken in setting objective questions which measure higher levels of learning pays dividends when marking time is taken into consideration.

Unfortunately, it is possible for educational authorities to err on quite a large scale when too great an emphasis is placed on MCQs for measuring the higher cognitive levels. An investigation by Ferland *et al.* (1987) of final-year medical examinations in three universities in Québec revealed that most of the 540 questions used over the three-year period from 1982 to 1984 were unable to measure traits other than simple memorization in the cognitive domain. Despite these discouraging findings, the investigators were optimistic regarding the future of MCQs provided they are properly designed. The authors state that there is:

> ample evidence of the psychometric qualities of multiple choice items; if they are correctly used, they can be a valid, reliable and objective instrument for the measurement of knowledge. However, given the importance of higher levels of knowledge for clinical competence, efforts should be directed at ensuring that the appropriate levels are evaluated (p. 113).

In the remaining sections of this chapter we shall describe and evaluate some of the varieties of objective tests which are available to examiners and, if possible, give examples of questions from each genre.

Multiple-choice

The general pattern followed by multiple-choice questions is probably well known to readers as many will have experienced them when they were students themselves and some will have used multiple-choice questions for assessing their own students' knowledge and skills. Even so, it is likely that some readers are not familiar with the basic principles underlying the construction of these questions as they have never been responsible for constructing them for use in their own classes. A brief summary of the principles involved is therefore appropriate.

The simplest form of multiple-choice question is probably best suited to testing a student's knowledge of facts. It consists of an incomplete statement, called the *stem*, followed by (typically) five options for completing the statement. One of these options is either the *only* correct response or is the *best* response, the others are termed *distracters*. Tuckman (1975) reminds us that the distracters should all be plausible, preferably using the type of incorrect answers that are often given by students who have an inadequate grasp of the topic.

Some examiners attempt to discourage guessing by deducting marks from the total score of students who select a wrong answer, but the value of this practice is debatable. It is better to spend additional time in setting and evaluating the efficacy of a multiple-choice test in order to ensure that the chance of better students selecting the wrong response is minimized. When a new multiple-choice test is being evaluated it is common to conduct a simple statistical analysis of the distribution of students' choice of responses for each question in the test. Students' responses to each item are compared with their scores in the test as a whole, it being expected that every question in the test will discriminate between 'good' and 'bad' students. An example of a table showing this comparison between answers to an individual question and answers to the test as a whole is given in Table 9.1 (modified from ETS, 1963).

Table 9.1 *Students classified by total test score*

Responses	Lowest Fifth	Next Lowest Fifth	Middle Fifth	Next Highest Fifth	Highest Fifth	Totals
Omit	32	22	15	16	4	89
A	5	6	2	1	0	14
B	15	13	22	10	9	69
C	7	10	13	12	16	58
D	8	8	9	8	4	37
E*	6	15	13	27	41	102
Totals	73	74	74	74	74	369

*= Correct response
Per cent of total group of 369 students answering correctly 28%
Correlation between success on this question and total score on test 0.47
(Discrepancies in total numbers in each fifth are caused by drop-out of students not completing the test.)

Without even seeing the question which gave rise to the results in Table 9.1 it should be clear that it was a reasonably difficult one. The degree of difficulty is indicated by the low correlation coefficient and by the number of students either omitting this question or selecting distracters B and C. It should also be noted that 28 students (or 7.6 per cent) who selected C as the correct answer came from the top 40 per cent of the class as measured by this test as a whole. One possible explanation of a result such as this is that distracter C might be the correct response under certain conditions, and that this was recognized by some of the better students in the class but presumably overlooked by the person who constructed the test.

A multiple-choice item which tests higher level objectives, such as ability to analyse information or evaluate alternative hypotheses, commences with some data, a question on the data and a series of possible responses to the question. For example, the above responses were to a question in an economic history examination developed by the Educational Testing Service. The first part of the question consisted of a seven- to eight-line extract from an article or book on economic history which was probably unfamiliar to most, if not all, students taking the examination. They were then asked to select from a list of five people the one who was most likely to have written the passage. The writers of the handbook from which this question was taken point out that students 'are *not* asked to, or expected to, recognize the statement from memory'. Instead they are expected 'to evaluate it in terms of their knowledge and under-standing of American intellectual history, and then to select from the five names listed the person to whom the statement might most reasonably be attributed' (Tuckman, 1975). The writers go on to describe why some students might choose each of the distracters and particularly why none of the best chose response A, whereas a number of good ones selected C. It is relatively easy to see how questions such as this could be used in examinations in philosophy, literature or a number of the social sciences.

Another question from the same source using a very similar format was the provision of a map of a mythical country, showing locations of various cities, transport systems and natural resources. Students were then asked to select which of the cities listed would be most suitable for establishing a steel mill. The problem with this specific question is that there is an example from recent history where similar criteria led to the establishment of steel mills near the ancient Polish city of Gdansk, as a result of which much of the beauty of the old town was spoilt, even destroyed, by the increased population and traffic and fumes from the factory. This particular example illustrates the difficulty encountered by very good students in answering multiple-choice questions. Students who know much more than is expected may find that the additional knowledge inter-feres with their ability to select the most likely answer to such a question.

True-false

The form of objective test which is apparently the simplest to answer and is certainly easy to mark is the type where students are confronted with a series of statements, each of which must be designated by the student as either true or false. These tests are particularly well suited for use when the tests are being marked by the students themselves immediately after taking the test and the test scores are not being counted towards the final grade. Results from these tests can give an indication to students where their own weaknesses lie and to the teacher where the class as a whole needs more teaching or revision on a topic.

The most obvious difficulty in designing true-false tests is in making all the statements *appear* to be correct without resorting to any trick phraseology. Thus statements made by students, either verbally in answer to a teacher's questions to the class or in their written essays, provide a good source of items for true-false tests. As with multiple-choice questions, there is a danger that better students will perceive difficulties with every statement and tend to label each one as false even though the teacher has assumed that approximately half the statements are true and the remainder are false. (There is, by the way, no logical reason why an examiner should set a test in which the proportion of true to false statements is approximately equal. It would, however, be undesirable for all, or almost all the statements to be of the one type.)

In designing a true-false test it is necessary to avoid statements which are controversial such as:

> The downfall of Richard Nixon as President of the United States began with the break-in at Watergate.
>
> Huldrych Zwingli was the most important reformer in the Swiss Protestant Reformation.

Completion

Another form of objective test is one in which students are asked to complete a sentence, preferably with only one or two words, or the labelling of a diagram. Generally speaking, these questions are testing students' ability to recall terminology and recognize the context within which particular terms are used. They are not particularly useful for testing higher order objectives. The simplest form of an incomplete sentence is one in which a definition is given but the key word is omitted, as in the following examples from biology:

> .... is the name given to the type of cell division which results in the number of chromosomes being halved. In the

process of cell division the stage when chromosomes line up on the equator of the spindle is called ....

The stage in the cycle of respiration when ATP is converted to ADP is ....

Diagrams or photographs with labels missing allow a speedy assessment of students' knowledge of nomenclature without requiring them to spend time on the drawing itself. The structures to be identified should be indicated by arrows, otherwise students will not know how many features to label.

Multiple grid system

A variation on the two previous forms of questions is particularly useful when students' knowledge of sequences is being tested. Multiple grid systems may be used in subjects where a logical sequence is being sought, such as philosophy or mathematics, a chronological sequence, such as in history or embryology, or a chain of chemical reactions. In some of these questions it is useful to include distracters, ie responses which do not fit the series and must not be chosen by students. The following, purely hypothetical, question illustrates the approach used in a multiple grid which contains distracters.

The following grid contains a number of statements, some of which apply to the steps which must be followed in order to produce an alphabetical sequence. Write down in the correct sequence the steps which are relevant ....

1. DDD	2. AAA	3. $\mathcal{LLL}$	4. BBB	5. 333
6. %%%	7. EEE	8. ★★★	9. CCC	10. ABC

Multiple completion

This is a more complex version of the familiar multiple-choice item. It is more suitable for testing high order objectives and is thus a more demanding test of students' abilities. As the following example from the University of Lancaster (quoted by Mathews, 1977) shows, it is important to allow students sufficient reading time when questions of this length are included in a test even though the student has to check five boxes.

ALL FIVE of the alternative answers require a response. For those choices judged to be TRUE (CORRECT) check the box in the T column. For those choices judged to be FALSE (INCORRECT) check the box in the F column.

T   F   Myoglobin

           a) contains a high proportion of a-helix

           b) is monomeric

           c) consists of a number of sub-units

           d) has a sigmoid oxygen-binding curve

           e) has a hyperbolic oxygen-binding curve.

Matching

Another variation on the multiple-choice theme is for students to be presented with two lists, their task being to match the most appropriate item in the second list with each item in the first. Although some matching questions have an equal number of items in the two lists, it is better to have more items in the second than in the first, thus reducing the chance of students obtaining the correct answer by a process of elimination. It is possible to construct matching tests which measure higher order objectives, but unfortunately the most common use appears to be for testing students' recall and recognition of subject matter. The following question is an example where a student would only need to be certain of the answers to five of the items to get the sixth one right, but it does suggest one way of setting out these questions.

The following terms are related to disease in humans. The left-hand column contains a numbered list of phrases, each of which is applicable to one of the medical conditions in the centre column. In the right-hand column place the number of each phrase opposite the term it identifies.

Identifying Phrases	Condition	Number
1. Disease of mouth and teeth	auto-intoxication	
2. Inflammation of large intestine	pyorrhoea	
3. Intestinal disease caused by bacteria	colitis	
4. Related to impure water supply	haemorrhoids	
5. Swellings in region of rectum	dysentery	
6. Caused by absorption of poisons	typhoid fever	

As the example shows, it is essential that each item in one column is specific to its corresponding item in the other column. Thus if we wished to improve the question by adding *either* more 'Identifying Phrases' or more 'Conditions', we would need to avoid two types of error. If, for example, we decided to add two more medical conditions to our list, we would first seek to avoid the error of including a condition that obviously has no relationship to any of the identifying phrases, such as 'varicose veins' or 'brain tumour'. The other danger would be to include another intestinal disease caused by bacteria (or any of the others listed among the 'Identifying Phrases') such as salmonella, unless, of course, we also changed *one* to *one or more* in the instructions for this question.

Relationship analysis

Here we have a type of question which tests students' factual knowledge and their reasoning ability. Because the directions are more complex than in most other objective questions, students must be given sufficient reading time and preferably some practice in answering this type of question. The example given is from Mathews (1997).

The following question consists of an assertion (statement) in the left-hand column and a reason in the right-hand column. On the appropriate line of the answer sheet mark:

- if both assertion and reason are true and the reason is a correct explanation of the assertion
- if both reason and assertion are true but the reason is NOT a correct explanation of the assertion
- if the assertion is true but the reason is a false statement
- if the assertion is false but the reason is a true statement
- if both assertion and reason are false statements.

Assertion		Reason
The blood sugar level falls precipitously after hepactectomy.	BECAUSE	The glycogen of the liver is the principal source of blood sugar.

Definitions and diagrams

These are not really objective questions as some subjectivity is usually possible in the marking. They are really examples of short-answer questions and are included in the present chapter among other questions which are *relatively* easy to mark. Unlike objective questions, these are very easy to set, but a little more difficult to mark. The examiner needs to determine the criteria which will be used for allocating marks, especially as it possible for a student to be partly right, either in the definition or the drawing or diagram.

Define the following quantities and state their SI units:
a) Force
b) Boltzmann's constant
c) Electrostatic capacitance.
   Draw carefully annotated diagrams or graphs to illustrate:
d) the forces on two bodies of unequal mass which are connected by a string which passes over a smooth peg
e) the electrostatic field lines between the plates of a parallel plate capacitor
f) the variation with temperature of the resistance of copper and of carbon, near room temperature
g) the variation of pressure with depth in a liquid
h) the variation with height of the pressure of the atmosphere.

Compare and contrast

As with the previous type of question, 'compare and contrast' problems are not strictly objective. As with the definitions and diagrams there is an element of subjectivity in marking; more than one answer could be acceptable. It may be that from the examiner's viewpoint certain answers are preferable to others and therefore deserve higher marks, in which case the amount of subjectivity in marking is greater than for definitions and diagrams. The following illustrates this type of question.

Give two similarities and two differences between each of the following pairs:

1. value parameter   var parameter
2. formal parameter   actual parameter
3. EoLn   EoF

4. local variable   global variable
5. recursion   looping
6. array   record.

Reviewing objective items

In his booklet on objective tests, Mathews (1977) devotes a section to the need for careful scrutiny of test items before they are used for the first time. Because good objective tests are difficult to construct, there is a tendency for examiners to use some items on more than one occasion. Under these circumstances the examiner has the opportunity of using data from analyses of students' responses to the same questions when used in earlier examinations or progress tests. A relatively simple analytical procedure for use with multiple-choice questions was described earlier in this chapter, ie comparing each student's response to a particular item with their performance on the test as a whole. A similar operation could be used for most other types of objective questions and the comparison need not be limited to students' scores in the same test. The validity of any one item (or test) may be checked by comparing performance in one type of test with each student's performance in other components of the overall assessment plan.

Mathews provides a checklist which examiners are encouraged to use *before* administering the test to students. The following is an abridged, and slightly modified version of his original suggestions:

1. Read and answer the question.
   - Is there more than one correct response?
   - Is there an ambiguity in the question or response(s)?
   - Can it be read and answered in the brief time available?
2. Check the stem.
   - Is the question important enough to be asked?
   - Is there sufficient information provided in the stem to answer it?
   - Is it precise, concise and grammatically correct?
   - If the statement is negative, is the negative highlighted?
3. Check the responses.
   - Have all got some plausibility?
   - Does the correct response contain a superficial clue?
   - Are all responses about the same length?
   - Do they all contain a repetitive phrase which could better be included in the stem?
   - Is each response grammatically consistent with the stem?

4. Check the format.
   - Does each item have the same number of responses?
   - Is the lettering or numbering of items and responses consistent?
   - Does each response begin on a new line?
   - Alternatively, if all responses are brief, are they on the one line?
   - Are directions for each question, stems and responses all on the same page?
   - If responses are numerical, are they arranged sequentially with the smallest first?
5. Classify the item.
   - What kind of learning does the item test?
   - What area of subject matter does it test?
   - At what level would you estimate the difficulty of this item?
6. Provisional judgement of the item
   - Acceptable as it stands
   - Acceptable with some minor alterations
   - Needs major reconstruction
   - Item should be rejected.

Marking objective tests

Provided the number of students taking a test is high enough to justify the expense, most objective tests – excluding the short-answer questions described earlier – are admirably suitable for machine-marking. In addition to the question sheet, students are issued an answer sheet which is specially designed for the questions being used in a particular test together with a soft pencil fitted with an eraser. When the questions are relatively brief, it is possible to use the same sheet of paper for both questions and answers. Students are required to darken the appropriate cells on an answer grid similar to that in Figure 9.1.

A bundle of answer sheets can be processed by an optical mark reading (OMR) scanner in a few minutes. According to Singer (1990), the Chinese are making extensive use of OMR answer sheets and scanners at many levels of education and across a range of subjects. Because the automatic feed scanners can process from 3,000 to 10,000 forms per hour (depending on the type of machine and the quality of paper used), it is possible to make widespread use of standardized tests for determining fitness for university entrance. They are seen to fulfil a need when students from large numbers of secondary schools are competing for the limited number of places

Question	Response				
Number	A	B	C	D	E
1	■				
2					■
3		■			
4					■
5				■	

Figure 9.1

available in higher education. In those provinces which have used the system on a trial basis, educational administrators have reported substantial savings in cost compared with similar examinations marked by hand. Despite Singer's enthusiastic support for the use of OMR technology in processing examination results, it is important to recognize that the type of tests which can be machine-marked have their limitations as we have discussed earlier; for the measurement of certain objectives, completely different types of tests must be used.

At the institutional level, or even within a university department with large numbers enrolled in first-year programs, OMR processing of progress tests can be very useful. When the scanner is linked to a computer, as is normally the case, examiners are able to obtain scores for each student and an analysis of results for the class, which may include comparisons between tutorial groups or cross correlations with other sets of scores. In Chapter 13 of this book Kevin Cox describes how all types of examination results are fed directly into the central records of the City University of Hong Kong.

A more sophisticated measure of performance in multiple-choice tests has been developed by Jody Paul of the Department of Computer Science and Engineering in the University of Colorado at Denver, Colorado. The test can only be administered by computer, as students have to respond to questions by using the mouse to point to the region in a diagram on the screen which best indicates how confident the student is that a particular answer is the correct (or best) one. As Paul points out (1994), when three possible answers are listed, a student may think 'I strongly believe B to be correct' or 'I believe C to be incorrect but can't distinguish between A and B' or 'From what I know, each alternative seems equally likely to be correct'. With traditional multiple-choice testing methods there is no way of telling whether a student really knows the right answer or has guessed it. Using the method devised by Paul it is possible for a teacher to measure the confidence levels for each student in a class and, if necessary, plan further remedial work.

The technique described by Paul is designed for use with MCQs which, as noted above, have three possible answers. While the computer programs could be fairly easily modified to cope with four or five answers, she cites 'educational and psychological literature indicating greater efficacy of using three options rather than a higher or lower number of alternatives'.

Pollard (1989) has also addressed the limitations imposed through the use of simple marking systems for MCQs. He acknowledges a need for rewarding students who are able to identify *incorrect* responses in addition to those who identify the *correct* ones. Students are invited to place a tick next to any answer which they know to be right and a cross next to any answer(s) which they know to be wrong. Students receive positive marks for ticks or crosses which are appropriately placed and negative marks when the response is inappropriate.

Computer-managed assessment

Computer-managed assessment (CMA) may involve any of the following uses of computers in assessment:

1. generation of data for items involving calculations
2. random selection of questions from an item bank
3. on-screen presentation of items in a test
4. acceptance of students' responses using a keyboard, mouse or touch-sensitive screen
5. keeping records of individual responses to each question and, if relevant, the time taken by each student on each item in the test
6. analyses of item validity, individual performances and class records.

Some comments on the above list may be helpful. Many university subjects require students to carry out calculations, sometimes in association with laboratory, workshop or field work that has been undertaken by the students themselves. It is not always feasible to organize formal examinations of the practical work, particularly when classes are very large. Under these conditions the course coordinator may decide to use computer-generated data – possibly from a bank of items – which are administered through the university computer network or even on students' home computers when they are undertaking course work in a distance education program. Because each student has a different set of questions, but of comparable difficulty, it is not possible for any student to copy the answer from another person. There is, however, no simple way of preventing students from asking a friend to solve the problem for them except when the computer-managed assessment is administered under formal examination conditions in computer laboratories which are strictly supervised. It is therefore preferable for this type of CMA to be restricted to diagnostic and formative tests.

Pudlowski and Rados (1987), working in the University of Sydney, Australia, describe how they found CMA effective in testing students' aptitude for undertaking studies in electrical engineering. They developed tests which presented students with diagrams of incomplete electrical circuits and up to six possible ways of completing the circuit in order to satisfy a given equation. Further standardization of these tests was done in co-operation with a group of labour psychologists from the Institute of Psychology at the Jagiellonian University in Cracow, Poland – an interesting case of inter-disciplinary and international co-operative research. Pudlowski and Rados list a number of features which they were aiming to include in the final version of these tests. Although their field is electrical engineering, the list, with minor modifications, could be used as standard for other forms of CMA:

- presentation of electrical circuits on the screen
- display of instructions
- selection of answers by simple key strokes
- imposition of time constraints on individual parts of the test
- time performance record
- both quantitative and qualitative analysis of student achievements including individual problems, if necessary
- printed diagnosis of student aptitude for an individual student which includes the level of performance as well as the assessment of the student's weaknesses and strengths

- easy access to student records as well as group performance records
- imposition of different grades of performance according to student's age.

It is clear that a strong link exists between computer-managed assessment (CMA) and computer-assisted instruction (CAI) even though the emphasis of each is distinct. One project in which the two uses of computers in teaching and assessment were brought together is described by Bailey *et al.* (1987). A team of CAI specialists and physics teachers was recruited from five institutions teaching introductory physics courses at the tertiary level and from high schools where teachers of physics could contribute from their expertise. The aim of the project was 'to produce a series of seven CAI programs appropriate to the needs of students who are commencing tertiary Physics courses and who possess little or no background knowledge of Physics'. Diagnostic tests administered by CMA can be used to direct students into the instructional programs (delivered by CAI) most suited to their immediate needs. Where necessary a student can work through a series of related problems, but with varying data, until they grasp the concept being taught.

10

Assessing group projects

It's hard to work in groups when you're omnipotent.
(Q, in *Star Trek, The Next Generation*)

Much has been said about the desirability of reducing the competitive element in assessment tasks. Over the years students have developed ways of circumventing this competitive component. Some of these techniques are normally regarded as cheating, others as co-operation. What is the difference?

Co-operative learning

An over-simplified distinction between cheating and co-operation could be to ask whether a student who is engaging in this non-competitive activity is profiting from the activity without making any contribution to the success of others in the group. If the answer is 'yes' it is cheating; if 'no' it is co-operation. Thus students who copy the work of others and submit the copied material as their own are clearly guilty of cheating or plagiarism, which we shall describe in Chapter 15 under the heading of 'Academic (dis)honesty'. They should be heavily penalized, provided that the teacher (and the institution) has made it clear from the beginning of the course that such actions are unacceptable. This over-simplified solution is difficult to apply in a situation where students are expected to reproduce either the lecturer's arguments or sections of their textbooks. In these instances a student is regarded as cheating when the material is directly (and usually surreptitiously) copied from written notes or photocopies of the book; however it is regarded as legitimate for the student to commit the material to memory and later recall that memory under examination conditions. Educational disadvantages of questions which demand only reproduction or recall were discussed earlier in the first part of Chapter 3.

Team work or syndicates

From time to time the course coordinator may wish to encourage small teams of students to work together on a project. The advantages of such projects are obvious:

1. students gain experience in working in teams, which is likely to be the norm in their future employment
2. the project is normally larger and more complex than any which could be handled by a student working alone
3. by allocating different, but related projects to each team in a particular class and requiring each group to report to the whole class, the teacher provides an opportunity for a major area of subject matter to be discussed by each student
4. material learned by these methods is more likely to be retained by students once the course is finished, provided that each group has adequate opportunities for interacting with other groups, not only when reports are being presented but during the research phase of the project
5. students generally enjoy such projects and report that their learning is more effective than for other forms of learning such as lectures.

The last point in the above list was confirmed in a survey of students in an optometry course at the Hong Kong Polytechnic reported by Conway *et al.* (1993) who added that 'the only significant negative elements of the student feedback concerned the fairness of the assessment'.

While the concept of team projects is educationally sound, there is a practical difficulty when it comes to assessing the contributions of individual students to a group project. The basic question which needs to be answered is whether each team should be awarded a mark or grade for its work and all students in that team receive the same mark, or whether it is possible to recognize the worth of each member's contributions to a project and reward each one appropriately? Several students in the survey conducted by Conway commented upon the equity of awarding all group members the same mark. Typical comments were as follows:

> During the group work, if members of a group are not co-operative, the workload of one of the students may be too great to support.
>
> Preparation of these projects takes time and requires compromise between group-mates. Especially when there is a test or assignment, one group member may think that it is not worth taking so much

time when they think the topic is not very relevant to their own interest. (pp. 45–6)

In order to overcome the difficulties identified by the students, the coordinators of the optometry course introduced two forms of peer assessment.

Firstly, each *group's* presentation was assessed by the remaining members of the class. Secondly, students assessed the contribution of their fellow group members to the work of the project. The aim was to award *each student* a mark for the project work which was a reflection of the individual student's contribution to the project. (p. 46)

Different approaches to the use of self- and peer assessment in group projects will be described in the final sections of the present chapter.

Examples of group projects

Small teams of students may be formed to undertake many different types of projects which will contribute to their learning and their general understanding of the discipline. The following list illustrates the broad scope of topics which might be investigated by small groups or syndicates:

1. preparing a report resulting from field work in history, politics, earth science, social science or biological science
2. writing a script for a film in one of the humanities or in a social science
3. presenting arguments for and against some theory in philosophy or religion
4. designing and building a model of a structure in architecture or engineering
5. suggesting a series of diagnostic tests followed by treatment for a patient with specified symptoms in medicine. (Miller, 1987, p. 43)

Garvin *et al.* (1995) developed a challenging set of group projects for first-year students in the School of Biology and Biochemistry at the Queen's University of Belfast. The projects, which had to be completed over a two-week period about eight weeks into first term,

were specifically designed to mimic, as far as possible, situations which typically arise in the world of business or industry, and to raise students' awareness of the application of biological principles to industrial and commercial problems. The overall aim was therefore to simulate situations which require solutions by small research teams. (p. 274)

Each team consisted of four students, each of whom was following a different specialization in the biological sciences, eg molecular biology, biochemistry, microbiology, genetics or one of the biological sciences. In this way the course coordinators sought to encourage maximum interaction and involvement by team members, thus emphasizing the cross-curricular nature of the projects. According to Garvin,

> Three research areas were identified and project packages were designed around:
> 1. plant-microbial interactions – where the effects of growth inhibiting compounds (from a fungus) on seedling development were investigated
> 2. citric acid production – where a comparison had to be made between extraction from citrus fruits and production by a fungus
> 3. whey treatment – where the waste from cheese production had to be converted into high value-added product.
> … Group members were expected to decide what to do, how to do it and how to manage the project in a given time. The groups had finally to present their findings in the form of a poster which formed a major part of the assessment. (p. 274)

The two features of this group project which the students liked best were 'the opportunity for team work' (36.7 per cent of respondents) and 'the freedom to think for themselves' (25.0 per cent). The most negative feature was 'limitation of time' (20.7 per cent).

In many ways the type of group project just described suggests a pattern for group projects in many disciplinary areas. Successful group projects are likely to have the following qualities:

1. the problem to be solved is an example of the type of problems found in the community, in industry or in commerce
2. solution of the problem requires the use of knowledge, skills and attitudes which are part of the students' curriculum
3. the problem can be solved by a small team of students, none of whom possess the necessary knowledge or skills to solve the problem alone, yet each member is able to contribute to the solution

4. decisions regarding investigative methods and the respective tasks for each team member are the responsibility of the group rather than being decided by the teacher
5. the final report needs to be brief and suitable for presentation to an audience (of other class members)
6. it should be possible to judge the relative value of each student's contribution to the project
7. assessment procedures should be such that they will be accepted by students and faculty as valid and reliable.

Collier (1985, p. 5) discusses the value of syndicate-based courses in which part or all of the course consists of a 'series of assignments carried out on a co-operative basis by the syndicates (each of which consists of 4–8 students) working as teams, for much of the time in the absence of a tutor'. He lists three distinctive features of this approach to learning, namely:

1. the small-group work is central to the academic study
2. the assignments are designed to draw on a variety of selected sources as well as on the students' first-hand experience
3. there is some alternation between student-led syndicates and the tutor-led plenary sessions of the whole class for consolidation of the conceptual structure as it emerges.

He adds that 'the heart of the technique is the intensive debate within the syndicates, which by no means prevents individuals from developing their own opinions'. Collier (1985 p. 9) cites many investigations which support his contention that *successful* syndicate work leads to a number of desirable outcomes, a summary of which follows:

1. Heightened motivation of the students, as shown by:
    – the amount of extra time and energy they put into their work
    – better attendance at timetabled sessions
    – greater job satisfaction
    – a stronger sense of mutual obligation among members of a syndicate
    – an active search for information and wider reading in the field studied
    – a greater willingness of students to attend carefully to one another.
2. Development of higher order skills, as shown by:
    – a better capacity for applying learned concepts in new situations

 – an improved capacity for interpreting the evidence and analysing concepts
 – a more sophisticated and systematic approach to problem solving
 – a more critical approach to reading
 – an enhanced sense of the personal meaningfulness of the material
 – a fuller appreciation of the rich variety of opinion and experience
 – a keener appreciation of the provisional nature of the current state of knowledge.

In designing an assessment scheme which is suitable for a course based mainly on syndicate work, the course team may well seek to devise measures of the extent to which each of the above outcomes may be observed in each syndicate group and in individual students.

Project assessment

While student projects occur in a wide range of disciplines and include a diverse range of activities, the nature of project work is summed up by Adderley *et al*. (1975): 'Projects are meant both to teach certain skills and at the same time to provide a basis for testing the students' acquisition of such skills.'

For project and self-assessment, THESYS (Gentle, 1995) has been designed as a computer-based, expert system. THESYS is not specific to any academic discipline and is particularly useful in providing an impartial means of maintaining quality. We shall discuss THESYS in more detail in Chapter 16. The program has proved valuable in:

1. giving students a clear statement on assessment criteria, advice on how to plan and execute the project, and information on how to write the thesis (or dissertation)
2. giving new staff information, and reminding old hands, of the assessment criteria, how to run a typical project and cope with problems, and how to produce an objective final mark
3. ensuring a reasonable degree of commonality of standards across different assessors and providing arbitration advice in any disagreements between examiners.

In all of these studies of self- and peer assessment, there is the risk of reinvention and redundant repetition. There are also issues relating to terminology. It is obvious that each year there will be many new assessment practitioners and, of course, the 'old' practitioners may wish to be involved in an appropriate form of continuing professional development.

One of the authors participated in the opportunity provided by a world-wide, distributed electronic conference (EECAE, 1995) that focussed on issues of importance to assessment and evaluation related to learning and instruction. One of the conference topics was 'Self- and Co-assessment' and two invited papers (Trevitt and Pettigrove, 1995, and Hall, 1995) provided the basis for discussion. It was reported that over 500 people from 38 countries joined the 'Econference'. It is worth noting that Hall emphasized the importance of a shared vocabulary and that assessment should always be fit for its (stated) purpose. In regard to vocabulary he uses 'co-assessment' (Bloch, 1977) to 'refer to a situation where student and teacher participate in assessment as a joint effort'.

The comparative worth of individual contributions

The easiest approach and, in some respects, the most desirable when comparing a university class with the ideal situation in industry is for all members to share the mark or grade allocated to their team. If this convention is explained to the class and accepted by them when projects are allocated it may be the best and simplest procedure to adopt for that component of the total assessment. However, because one of the functions of assessment is to measure the capabilities of each student, it is essential that marks for group projects should be supplemented by marks for a student's own work.

Conway *et al.* (1993, p. 46) refer to earlier work by Gibbs *et al.* (1986) who identified some more fundamental issues relating to the assessment of group projects. These issues would be most relevant when the group project forms a major part of the summative assessment and there is also an attempt for this part of the assessment to be 'norm referenced' rather than 'criterion referenced'. Gibbs and his colleagues remind us that students undertaking group projects are usually very enthusiastic and highly motivated; consequently they tend to score well in these projects. It is therefore difficult to distinguish between the performance of different students, a problem which is exacerbated by the disparate nature of the group projects.

'Norm referencing' refers to a test design which allows students to be compared with others in the class, as would be the case when an order of merit has to be produced as part of a mechanism, for example, of determining those best suited for entry to a competitive higher level program. With norm referencing it is desirable to have a test which separates out students' marks as widely as possible so that there are few ambiguities as to which students should be admitted to the higher program and which should be refused entrance.

'Criterion referencing', on the other hand, refers to a test design which measures the extent to which each student has achieved pre-determined criteria for performance, regardless of others in the class. Thus there is no reason why all students taking a criterion-referenced test should not have the same (usually high) marks.

If, in the initial discussion of the projects, it becomes clear that there is considerable opposition to the idea of all students in a parti-cular group receiving the same mark or grade, a mechanism will need to be evolved to allocate marks fairly, that is in proportion to the work put into the project by individual members and to the value of each person's contributions to the total project. Some teachers have given the team members the responsibility of allo-cating marks to individual members, the justification being that team members know best how much their colleagues have contributed to a project. This would appear to be an abrogation of a teacher's responsibility as it asks students to evaluate the quality, as well as the quantity of work done by their peers. Despite this objection, a strong case has been made for self- and peer assessment, as we shall see in the next section.

The importance of assessing the value of individual contributions is not limited to group projects. Where an important component of a course is participation in discussion sessions, faculty may deem it appropriate to include a mark for participation in determining the final grade for the unit of study. This has been a difficult procedure for many tutors and teaching assistants, some of whom lack the necessary training or skills for making such judgements. In a study of assessment practices funded in Australia by the Committee for the Advancement of University Teaching, Nightingale identified a number of teaching programs where the development of discussion skills was deemed to be important (Nightingale *et al.,* 1996). She describes the rationale, abilities assessed and criteria for assessment and discusses some of the problems which might be encountered in assessing class participation. While the example is from a school of law, the principles have a much broader application.

Self-assessment

Recent literature dealing with assessment in higher education strongly supports the use of both self- and peer assessment as essential components of students' learning. For example, Woods *et al.* (1988), describing the use of self-assessment in chemical engineering at McMaster University in Canada, open their report with the following definition which is followed by some more general statements concerning the nature of assessment. These could be extended to all types of assessment:

> Self-assessment is the ability of a person to accurately evaluate or assess his/her performance, and his/her strengths and weaknesses ... Mature self-assessment recognizes that evaluation concerns the *performance* and not the *person*. When an assessment is made, the judgment is not whether the student is 'good' or 'bad'; rather it is whether the *performance* of a task was 'good' or 'poor'. To emphasize this point, self-assessment might be renamed 'self performance assessment'. Likewise, self-assessment is not 'self-marking' or guessing the grade that a teacher will assign. (p.107)

From the above quotation one could infer that, even in those institutions or teaching programs where the assessment is completely under the control of the faculty, an essential element of student learning is that students should be able to evaluate their own progress. This was the main point which we emphasized in our discussion of formative assessment in Chapter 2 of the present book. Other authors have also stressed the importance of self-evaluation. For example, Brown and Knight (1994) remind their readers that:

> students will be expected to practise self-evaluation in every area of their lives on graduation and it is a good exercise in self-development to ensure that these abilities are extended. In many of the types of assessment that students undertake, they are expected to assess the *process* as well as the *product*, and while the assessment of product is very often best undertaken by a third person, assessment of process necessarily involves those involved in that process. Where, for example, students are being assessed in groups, it is essential that if the process of group working is to be assessed, the participants themselves should be involved in so doing. (p. 51)

Brown and Knight also make the case that self- and peer assessment give learners a greater ownership of the learning they are undertaking. They add:

> Assessment is not then a process done to them, but is a participative process in which they are themselves involved. This in turn tends to motivate students, who feel they have a greater investment in what they are doing. Using self and peer assessment makes the process much more one of learning because learners are able to share with one another the experiences they have undertaken. (p. 52)

A useful source of information on self-assessment is provided by Boud (1995) in his book on enhancing learning through staff assessment, described as 'an important new book' (*PS News*, 1996). There is a chapter on the use of self-assessment for marking and grading but the principal message is to develop self-assessment as a transferable skill and as part of the student learning experience. It is perhaps worth noting that Boud (1989) discussed the role of self-assessment in student grading. There are many other such studies, one being an analysis of student grade expectations and marker consistency conducted by Penny and Grover (1996) who reported that there was a poor match between self-assessment and tutor grades. Their research suggested that the grading by tutors had inherent and dubious assumptions of norm referencing whereas clear criteria (and standards) for self-referencing are necessary for the enhancement of learning.

Another excellent review of the literature on self-assessment is provided by Toohey (1996). Citing research by Falchikov and Boud (1989), Boud and Falchikov (1989), Boud (1989) and Williams (1992), she shows that self-assessment by students is generally trustworthy provided that criteria have been made explicit, students have had opportunities to practise assessment skills, the rating instruments are simple and a second marker is used to moderate individual self-assessments.

In effect, if the student as learner understands the learning requirements and if the academic as teacher initiates and manages the learning diagnostically and with feedback, the outcomes are likely to be positive for all concerned. In this regard here are two generalizations that emphasize the relationship between learning and assessment with reference to the learner.

> It is fitting that I learned from EL Thorndike's grandson, Robert M Thorndike, what I regard as the best generalization we can currently

make. He suggests that knowledge of results eventuates an improved performance when the learner is motivated, when the knowledge of results is informative and when the learner knows or is told what to do to correct errors. (McKeachie, 1975, p. 47)

A second generalization is offered by Ausubel (1968):

If I had to reduce all of educational psychology to just one principle, I would say this: The most important single factor influencing learning is what the learner already knows. Ascertain this and teach accordingly. (p. iv)

Peer assessment

Peer assessment is clearly a variation on self-assessment with the potential to add value in the following ways:

1. Two students sharing each other's assessment can be more objective when basing the assessment on a shared set of criteria and assessment schedule.
2. The active and interactive experience can develop insights and enhance understanding through the process of articulating assessment comments (discourse).
3. The peer experience of shared assessment can encourage shared study and teamwork thus developing a related transferable skill.
4. Peer assessment can contribute to group or team assessment (eg Lejk, 1994) and is likely to be used when two or more students are involved in project work which is intended to develop co-operative learning and team skills. Project supervisors can then use peer assessment as an input to the final individual assessment if the mark or grade is not to be the same for each member of the team.

Earl (1986) reports an early approach to the assessment of group work in a mathematical modelling program at the Robert Gordon Institute of Technology (RGIT) in Aberdeen, Scotland. In this case there are two major components to be assessed when teams present their reports. Each team is judged on the quality of its mathematical modelling and also on its communication skills. Equal weighting is given to the scores given each team by lecturers from the departments of mathematical sciences and communication studies. These scores then form the 'base mark' for each member of the team, with all members of the one team receiving the same base mark. To this is added a peer mark derived in the following way:

> Peer marks, equal in weighting to Base marks in Group Activity, are submitted by each student in the group for all other members. Students do not submit a mark for themselves and students are not given precise criteria. (p. 65)

Although, as the author says, students are not given precise criteria for assessing the contribution of their peers, she adds that students are reminded that they should take into account any work on the project which has been completed outside class contact hours and the extent to which each team member contributed to, or hindered, the group's task. It is clear from the remainder of her paper that faculty in the RGIT were well aware of experimentation with peer assessment in other institutions in the United Kingdom, Australia and the United States and it is likely that, given the lapse of time since this study was reported and changes in higher education in the UK, further modifications have been made to the assessment scheme described in Earl's original paper.

A strong case for peer assessment of group projects is made by Rafiq and Fullerton (1996) who have used this approach with civil engineering classes in the University of Plymouth, England. They point out that most civil engineering projects require team work, so that industry looks for graduates who are able to make continuous assessments of each stage in their own contributions to a project as well as the work of other team members.

> Continuous project meetings, consultations and project coordination are an essential part of the stage of design. Generally the success or the failure of a project depends on the coherence of the design team's activities. Every member of the team monitors, discusses, assesses and criticizes the activities of the others throughout all stages of the design process. This is how a real life project develops from initial thoughts and ideas. (p. 70)

Rafiq and Fullerton adapted a plan of peer assessment originally suggested by Goldfinch and Raeside (1990) which had two components, the first being related to the skills exhibited by each group member (other than the one making the assessments) in completing each of the tasks which were essential to the project. Part 2 was based on the rater's perception of each of the other students' contributions to the group discussion and decision making. In an appendix to their article, Rafiq and Fullerton provide a sample of a questionnaire used in the School of Civil and Structural Engineering at the University of Plymouth. Items listed in Part 2 were:

- overall level of participation
- understanding what was required
- suggesting ideas
- extracting something useful from ideas
- performing routine tasks
- drawing things together (consolidation)
- keeping the group going in difficult patches
- sorting out problems. (pp. 80–1)

Readers will readily see how the above criteria could easily be applied to the student ratings of peer performance in any group which relies strongly on discussion for the solution of problems. Naturally most of the Part 1 segment of the questionnaire used in the above course is subject specific. There is, however, a general question which precedes the specific ones. It asks each student to rate his or her peers on the others' contributions to planning and distribution of responsibilities, suggestions about assumptions and preliminary design ideas, and the compilation and writing up of the final report.

We strongly support the above views regarding the value of self- and peer assessment and would urge all university teachers to ensure that their students practise these at some stage in their studies. Nevertheless, before making a decision to use these forms of assessment, teachers and course coordinators need to be aware of potential complications which may be introduced. Leaving aside the more obvious problems of students who may be tempted to base their judgements on their feelings about the person being graded (a problem not confined to students!) or their desire to award themselves higher marks than they deserve, there is the dilemma about grading students who contribute unequally – either in quality or in time spent on the project – to a group project. At the end of the previous section we noted that some teachers attempt to overcome this problem by awarding the group a mark and then leaving members of the group to share that mark in whatever way they think is reasonable.

As an example of ways in which this form of peer assessment can be unfair one might consider a case in which one student volunteers to type the full report for the group and prepare a high quality print-out, another volunteers to do the illustrations while the other three members of the team undertake the basic research for the project. The first member may be an expert typist but has made no contribution to the academic aspects of the project and may not have understood what was being typed! The one who provided the illustrations may be a good artist or photographer and may or may not have learned from the project, depending on the extent to which accurate illustrations were an intrinsic part of the project. The three who undertook the basic research may have inadvertently divided the work unevenly or the quality of their individual contributions may be quite varied.

It is the teacher's responsibility to stress at the outset that each team member must make a significant contribution to the team's project and that each person's contributions will be graded accordingly. It is not expected that all members will make equal contributions as it is likely that there would be varying levels of ability, interest and application in every group. Consequently the teacher will either need to question team members separately about their contributions to the team project or find some other method of assessing the quality of each individual's contributions to the task. If class numbers are too great to allow teachers to evaluate the contributions of team members on the basis of personal interviews, the simplest option for ensuring that group members are rewarded appropriately is for the group work to be supplemented by a written examination in which students are asked to describe the significance of the project as a whole and of their own contributions to the project. The final grade for the project would then be determined on the basis of the value of the project as a whole together with the teacher's assessment of each student's contribution to that project as revealed in the interview or the relevant examination question. Difficulties in assessing group work will again be considered in Chapter 13 when the problems of combining marks from different learning activities is discussed.

Freeman (1995) describes an approach designed to improve both the reliability and the quality of group presentations by final-year business students at the University of Technology, Sydney, Australia. The class of 210 was divided into 41 teams, each of which was required to work together for a team presentation worth 25 per cent of the final mark. Each team was given a choice concerning the allocation of the remaining 75 per cent. The alternative choices are shown in Table 10.1.

All but one of the teams chose assessment package B where marks other than for the presentation were derived from an individual quiz worth 30 per cent, a team quiz worth 20 per cent and an examination worth 25 per cent. The members of each team worked together throughout the course. Freeman describes the procedures used to improve the reliability of assessment and quality of team presentations in the following passage.

Table 10.1 *Choice of weightings for a final grade*

Choice	A	B
Group Presentation	25%	25%
Examination	55%	25%
Individual Quiz	10%	30%
Team Quiz	10%	20%

Each student was given the presentation checklist/marking and feedback sheet in week 1. This was provided to encourage a high level of performance in the presentations, to make students more comfortable with the process and to ensure greater equity in peer scoring. Other aids included a video of clips from all the presentations from the previous year, various videos and articles on how to optimize a presentation. This checklist specifies eight items relating to content (eg originality, argument and structure) and 14 items relating to the presentation (eg personal style, presentation mechanics and media including handouts). After each presentation, each team, except the one presenting, spent about five or six minutes discussing the presentation and providing feedback under the 22 items on the checklist before allocating a mark out of 100 for the content and presentation components. Staff (faculty) also used the same checklist/marking guideline as a team. To ensure students were mindful of the learning objectives of the subject and not over-focussed on entertainment of their peers, the content and presentation components were weighted by 60 per cent and 40 per cent respectively. (p. 293)

Readers who intend using group presentations as an integral part of coursework may wish to develop similar briefing sessions and checklists to those described by Freeman. A copy of his checklist/marking and feedback sheet is included as an appendix to his original article. Another checklist, used by Goldfinch (1994), has two parts: the first being task related while the second seeks ratings of group functions. According to Goldfinch, the checklist was developed over a three-year period at the Napier University in Edinburgh, Scotland and the Hong Kong Polytechnic (see also Goldfinch and Raeside, 1990, and Conway *et al.*, 1993.) Students who use her checklists are asked to rate themselves and each of the other members of their team, using a four- or five-point scale. The criteria for marking task related items are:

- 3 for a 'major contributor'
- 2 for an 'average contributor'
- 1 for a 'below average contributor'
- 0 for no contribution to this task.

(NB: 'average' here meaning 'much the same as the rest of the group')

An optional five-point scale is available for assessing group functions, namely:

- 3 for 'better than most of the group in this respect'
- 2 for 'about average for this group in this respect'
- 1 for 'not as good as most of the group in this respect'
- 0 for 'no help at all in this respect'.

If necessary, you can award:

- –1 for 'a hindrance to the group in this respect'.

A formula is used for converting self- and peer ratings to marks, applying appropriate weightings for each task in the total assessment pattern. Goldfinch makes two important observations about her procedures in using this system. First, peer ratings submitted by students who have missed most of the group meetings are ignored when marks are calculated; and second, students see and discuss the rating forms and the criteria used *before* they commence their project.

11

Practical skills and field work

The essence of intelligence is skill in extracting meaning from everyday experience.

(Author unknown)

Importance of practical experience in professional studies

As laboratory and field work are integral components of many university courses it is essential that students' performance in these activities be assessed and given adequate weighting in the determination of final grades. In this chapter we shall not limit our discussion to traditional laboratory classes in the sciences and science-based professional programs nor to the field trips associated with these. Field work may also include experience in commerce or industry, sometimes for a whole semester or academic year. How may this work be assessed?

Before discussing the assessment of practical skills and field experiences we need to emphasize the importance of these activities in most disciplines taught in universities. Readers are well aware of the importance of laboratory work in the physical and natural sciences and of field experience in professional programs. Any study of a science that is based entirely on lectures and reading lacks an essential ingredient: the challenge of direct observation of natural phenomena and an opportunity for critical investigation of changes which occur as a result of the addition of new forces, chemicals, or human intervention.

Similarly, one expects that trainees for professions will be required to spend part of their time as an undergraduate observing and participating in an appropriate workplace such as a clinic, factory, hospital, industrial laboratory, orchestra, school, studio or workshop. Students of languages, including their own language, are often encouraged to participate in drama or to write poetry or prose; if the language being studied is regularly spoken in another country or in a tribal community, students may live in the community for a period which is long enough for them to absorb some of the culture. Opportunities for direct experience of other cultures may also be provided for students of anthropology, sociology and history. If the above activities are regarded as an essential component of students' learning experiences, one would expect that their contribution to each student's learning would be assessed in an appropriate manner.

The weighting given to this assessment of practical experiences will vary, depending on the importance attached to the activities by the educational institution and the course coordinator. In some cases, the only grades available are 'Satisfactory' or 'Unsatisfactory' and any students who are rated 'Unsatisfactory' are deemed to have failed in the whole program. An example of such a rule is in some faculties of education where students preparing to be school teachers must obtain a 'Satisfactory' grading for practice teaching. While one might find some justification for this rule, it is hardly satisfactory from the student's point of view. Each student needs to have an indication of their strengths and weaknesses in classroom management and all the skills which make up the action we call 'teaching'. For example, some education students may have an excellent rapport with their pupils, but be severely lacking in their ability to communicate the details of subject content. We shall discuss some of the criteria which may be used for grading professional experiences in the final section of this chapter.

One likely explanation for course designers' reluctance to use more than a two-point scale (Pass/Fail or Satisfactory/Unsatisfactory) for grading practical experience is that they perceive serious difficulties with the reliability and, to a lesser extent, the validity of these measures. For ratings of a task to be *reliable* it is important for students to be tested under virtually identical conditions, yet in a field experience program no two students work under exactly the same conditions, nor even in the same workplaces. Unless the class is a small one, it is impossible for all students to be observed and assessed by the one member of faculty; what is more likely is that students undertaking work experience will be supervised by a senior person in the workplace and there is a strong possibility that standards will vary from one supervisor to another. A difficulty faced by some supervisors is that they may expect certain problems to be solved in ways that they themselves have found to be successful, yet there may be other ways which are either just as successful or even more efficient.

The Fieldwork Handbook (DSS, 1995) for the Diploma in Social Work at City University of Hong Kong, is the thirteenth edition (63 pages) and provides clear details of assessment for students and staff – in particular the field work supervisors. For field work placement, the assessment areas or categories are knowledge (25 per cent); skills (40 per cent); values, attitudes and professional development (35 per cent). These categories are subdivided into criteria (expected behaviour/attitude) used in conjunction with a six-grade scheme : A = Excellent; B = Good; C = Fair; D = Pass; F = Fail; G = Badly fail.

The Handbook includes a reference guide, 'What to look for in grading students in placement'. For each grade, the guide sets out four categories of performance descriptors with reference to: competence, initiative, task completion, understanding. The *Handbook* represents years of accumulated experience complemented by other sources of experience, such as external examiners.

We might also question the *validity* of some field experience programs. For example, how close to 'real life' is the field experience program? Do students (interns) have the same responsibilities as qualified practitioners? As the answer to each of the above questions is clearly in the negative we must accept the situation that students' success in field work can only be *indicators* of their likely success as graduates.

In his discussion of the validity of assessment at the workplace, Benett (1993) refers to the need for distinguishing between interns' *experiences* in a field program and their *learning*. From this we deduce that a student's diary, or even a video-recording of their actions, is not a valid measure of their learning. At some stage the faculty member responsible for assessing the value of the field program must determine the most effective way of measuring the amount and quality of learning that has occurred for each student, and in the program as a whole.

Assessing routine laboratory and studio work

An essential component of courses in the natural and physical sciences is the practical work consisting of detailed observations and experiments usually conducted in university laboratories or on planned excursions to places of geological or biological interest.

Students in computing and engineering have their workshops; in the visual and performing arts, students are provided with opportunities for painting, drama, ballet, playing instruments and singing, and all these activities need to be assessed. We may summarize the qualities to be assessed under the headings of identification of specimens; practical skills; aptitudes and attitudes, and actual performance.

While a debate exists as to the precise definition of a performance test, the term is used here to describe those testing situations that call for students to demonstrate their ability in a task or situation calling for the use of knowledge, practical skills, aptitudes and attitudes. Within such a description would fit the following.

Identification tests

– testing the ability to identify specific items from a collection of diverse items, to identify the state of repair for items and to identify specific behaviours and/or situations. Part (a) of the question which follows illustrates one form of identification test.

Practical tests

– testing specific practical skills such as using drawing instruments, drills, special test equipment, etc (see Part (b) of the same question).

Aptitude tests

– testing the development of specific aptitudes such as hearing, sight, dexterity, etc.

Actual performance tests

– the testing of a specific process, its product or both. The testing takes place in a realistic setting and requires a completion of a real task. Actual performance tests can be grouped as work tests, work-sample tests and situational tests. An example of requirements for the assessment of laboratory records is given below.

Artistic accomplishments tests

– opportunities for demonstrating one's level of attainment in the visual and performing arts.

If one of the aims of a teaching program is to give students an opportunity to practise and experiment with techniques and equipment, then assessment for grading should not begin too early in the program. Premature assessment may inhibit students from practising, as they wish to avoid making mistakes and receiving a low grade. (We should remember that mistakes are part of the learning process and therefore merit feedback.) Whenever a performance test is held at the end of a course, the examiner should make allowances for the large amounts of space and equipment that will be required if all students are to be examined at the same time.

Sample question

1. The drawing shows a section through a typical helicopter tail rotor gearbox. State the following:
   (a) (i) Location and type of adjustment for the axial location of the input shaft and gear (item 22).
   (ii) The item which sets the 'pre-load' of the input shaft support bearing.
   (iii) Location and type of adjustment for the axial location of the output gear.
   (b) Using the collection of components which is supplied, actually set up this bearing/gear assembly, including setting and checking the backlash between the input and output gears. Sketch the tooth pattern you have aimed for.

Laboratory Records
2. Experimental work only will be assessed. Drawings and accompanying notes will not be marked, but work of an adequate standard will be considered as part of the requirement for terms. Experimental work will be assessed by grades (A-E) under the following headings:

		Grade
GENERAL	(a) Scientific approach	( )
	(b) Team work in joint experiment	( )
	(c) Presentation	( )
QUALITY OF	(d) Originality	( )
DISCUSSION	(e) Interpretation of results	( )
AND	(f) Consultation of literature	( )
CONCLUSIONS	(g) Organization and clarity	( )
	(h) Linking of theory to practical	( )
	(i) Suggestions for improvement or extension of the experiment	( )

While practical performance is an integral part of many courses, the weight attributed to such performance in the final course is usually low. The role of practical performance in a course needs to be clearly defined so that appropriate weight can be given to the performance assessment. For example, the performance component may be used for any or all of the following:

1. to stimulate interest in the subject
2. to integrate various parts of the syllabus
3. to develop essential skills.

Where several staff are responsible for the marking of performance, inconsistencies in marking are common. If, however, the objectives and outcomes of performance have been defined clearly, and a marking schedule prepared, this will minimize marking inconsistencies. Too often, assessment is based entirely on a written report and not on direct observation of students' performance; there is a mismatch between the stated objectives and the focus of assessment. Burns *et al.* (1979) provide a possible solution to this problem in the following report on the practical component of a first-year chemistry course:

> Each year the Stage I Chemistry course, CHEM 101, has an enrolment of approximately 300 students. Practical work (three hours/week) is considered to be an essential part of such a course, and its assessment contributes a proportion of 20 per cent of the student's grade for the course. The practical work program has been planned to run throughout the year in parallel with theoretical developments of organic, inorganic and physical chemistry. The laboratory experiments are self-sufficient in terms of theoretical principles, references and instructions, which are presented in the Laboratory Manual.
>
> In the past, each laboratory experiment was assessed using guidelines which included aspects of student performance, but the main emphasis was on the written report – each laboratory experiment mark (20 experiments) contributing equally to the grade contribution of the practical work program. There was no guarantee of level of competence or mastery of the skills which were considered essential for the would-be chemist.
>
> The current program incorporates a different procedure. Every fifth week each student repeats one of the experiments performed during the previous four weeks. The performance of this repeat experiment is scrutinized much more closely, with questioning by the demonstrator, and the assessment focus is moved from the written report. In this case the practical work and the report can be completed in the three hours timetabled. For assessment for grading, each repeat experiment is weighted at four times the normal weekly experiment.

It is often difficult to assess student performance ability because poor performance may be attributed to inappropriate teaching methods, to faulty or inadequate equipment or to poor supervision. If the ability to perform is an important part of the course and if students are to be assessed on their practical performance, staff should ensure that the equipment is available in a good working condition so that students are not penalized for events beyond their control.

Classroom theory and performance should be closely coordinated if it is intended that one should relate to the other in the course. If not, the performance program should *complement* the other activities of a course and be perceived as independent by the students.

Resources and facilities

In the next chapter we shall look at the need for specifying what resources and facilities are required for staging major examinations. Our emphasis in the present chapter is on the requirements for the assessment for laboratory, workshop or field work. In a module on the assessment of practical work, Hall and Imrie (1994) stress a need for identifying those tasks which are regarded as highly desirable or essential in the performance of various trades and professions. Before students' performance of the tasks can be assessed, it is necessary to break up each major task into a number of sub-tasks which the authors define as 'an activity or group of connected activities which must be done as a step on the way to completing a task (cg attaching the wires to their terminals is a sub-task of wiring a three-pin plug)'.

The next step is task analysis which they describe as 'a method of determining exactly what a person must do to carry out a task'. Hall and Imrie continue:

The analysis should identify:

- the steps, essential knowledge, skills and attitudes in the task
- the important cues that tell students when an action is needed and the feedback that tells them how the action went
- the resources and equipment needed
- the conditions under which students must do the task
- and the standards students must reach when they are assessed.

Once the above procedures have been followed, it is easier for the examiner to see exactly what type of equipment and materials will be needed by candidates in the examination and to decide whether these should be provided by the candidates or by the institution. Where the equipment is normally provided by the institution for use in class (eg computer terminals, microscopes, video cameras and recorder, heavy engineering machinery) it is the responsibility of the examiner to ensure that each item of equipment is in good working order and that no student will be disadvantaged by faults in the equipment. If students have to bring particular items of equipment to the examination (eg calculator, dissection kit, stethoscope, pencils or brushes for drawing or painting) they should be given clear instructions early in the semester as to what is needed and what is allowed.

Frequently in practical examinations, students will be asked to identify specimens, follow a set of procedures, or make further investigations. Again it is important that the examiner (or a qualified technician) has checked that the quality of materials provided to the students is consistent. If these checks are not made the reliability, and ultimately the validity, of the examination will suffer.

Problem-based learning

Boud (1988), in his guest editorial to an issue of *Assessment and Evaluation in Higher Education*, defines problem-based learning (PBL) as 'a number of different approaches to teaching and learning in which the prime focus is on a problem or problems rather than a discipline or body of knowledge'. He describes three basic components of assessment which have been emphasized in PBL, namely:

1. the importance of careful specification of learning objectives and criteria for assessment
2. assessment as a process rather than a measurement activity
3. assessment is for the benefit of student learning. (pp. 88-9)

The article which follows Boud's introduction illustrates each of the above features in a legal workshop at the Australian National University. Hort and Hogan (1988) write:

> Following Mager (1975), the statement of objectives for each subject in the Legal Workshop includes three things:
>
> 1. What the students should be able to do at the end of the instruction that they were not able to do, or to do at the required standard, at the beginning of it (the task);
> 2. Under what circumstances or with what resources they will be expected to perform 'the task' (the conditions); and
> 3. To what standard they will be required to perform the task, and what observable evidence will be accepted as demonstrating that they have attained the standard of competence required (the

standards). (p. 93 – for a later version of Mager's work, readers should consult Mager, 1991)

The above authors give examples of typical projects which are undertaken by students in the legal workshop, each project being a simulation of challenges which could be met in a typical legal practice. In each case they set out clearly the *task*, the *conditions* under which they might encounter such a task and *standards* which will be used in assessing their handling of this task. The two tasks described in some detail deal with issues in basic book-keeping and legal ethics. They also describe (Hort and Hogan, 1988) a marking procedure for assessment of a student's performance in a moot court in which students learn about criminal procedure. Each student is awarded a grade on a five-point scale for six aspects of deportment, these grades being determined as a result of consultation between lecturer and student after they have seen a video replay of the court. In addition, the lecturer awards grades (on the same five-point scale) for seven aspects of presentation.

In the previous chapter, within the context of our discussion of self-assessment, we referred to an article by Woods *et al.* (1988) strongly supporting this practice. The major portion of that article describes an integral component of the four-year degree in chemical engineering entitled the 'McMaster Problem Solving Program' which is described as a 'collection of experiential activities to develop, and integrate, about 35 component skills which are taught as stand-alone units', usually in tutorials. The units include the following topics:

1. Awareness of the process used to solve problems
2. Using a strategy
3. Analysis
4. Creativity
5. Group skills
6. Chairperson skills
7. Listening skills
8. Stress management
9. Defining problems
10. Drawing diagrams.

The authors add:

Although the courses appear to be separate courses in Problem Solving, care has been taken to bridge and embed the application of the skills to solve Chemical Engineering problems. The major goals of this entire course sequence include 'to develop Problem Solving,

Interpersonal and Communication Skills' and be able to apply these general skills in the context of professional problems, ordinary home-work problems and everyday problems.

Feletti (1993) describes the essential features of problem-based learning (PBL) as used in nursing and medical education and then compares it with inquiry-based learning (IBL) in the same fields.

> The essential stages ... are as follows: a small group of students meet to discuss a clinical patient problem they have not seen before. They initially get limited data on a real or simulated patient, and are encouraged to use analytical skills (eg hypothetico-deductive reasoning) and occasional guiding questions from their tutor to diagnose and/or manage the patient's condition. Paper cases are typically used, being carefully crafted to help students focus on a well-defined or at least well-structured problem. Cases contain multidisciplinary learning objectives which emerge from the wording and sequence of case-related information. The student group also identifies relevant topics or questions they need to study, and divide these learning tasks between them at the end of the session. They pursue independent studies, generally using textual resources, between sessions. For first year medical students a paper case is typically designed to require two or three sessions several days apart, and to be completed within a week. At the end of each session, and when 'closing the case', students and tutor review their personal contributions to the group's learning process in terms of efficiency and cooperation.

From the above description we see that PBL commences with a cross-disciplinary 'case study' (usually simulated) which determines the problem to be solved by the tutorial group, and the tutor plays a key part in facilitating discussion (but not in providing information). Although Feletti's example is from the medical field, almost everything he says in the above paragraph could apply to other professional studies.

By way of contrast, IBL commences with students' clinical experiences or personal encounters on which they reflect and out of which questions may arise (Feletti, 1993). Further reflection on the questions may stimulate the students to undertake investigations, working alone or in small groups, as a result of which they may be able to draw conclusions, not only about whether they have found satisfactory solutions but also about the effectiveness of the learning procedures they have used.

In the quotation which follows we have emphasized words or phrases which we regard as key components of IBL. Feletti refers to developments in the School of Nursing in the University of Hawaii where, in 1992, the Faculty defined IBL as:

> an orientation towards learning that is *flexible* and open and draws upon the *varied skills and resources of faculty and students*. Faculty are *co-learners* who guide and facilitate the *student-driven* learning experience to achieve goals of nursing practice. This includes an *inter-disciplinary* approach to learning and problem solving, critical thinking and *assumption of responsibility* for their own learning. (p. 146)

Interactions with clients

Many professional courses are designed to prepare future graduates for work which involves regular interaction with clients, with para-professionals and other support staff. Obvious examples include accountancy, agriculture, dentistry, divinity, engineering, law, medicine, teacher education and veterinary science. For many years now some of these courses have included a compulsory component in which students are introduced to the problems of professional practice and frequently required to undertake duties associated with their vocation under supervision of experienced practitioners. Thus pre-service programs in teacher education would include visits to schools where it is possible to observe high quality teaching in appropriate disciplines or educational levels. This should be followed by extended periods of 'practice teaching' during which the education students are given responsibility for preparing and conducting lessons or parts of lessons. These lessons would be super-vised by the normal teacher for the class and occasionally observed by a staff member of the university or college which accredits the program. Sometimes the only requirement is that the student teacher's work should be 'Satisfactory'. In other cases a grade would be awarded and would contribute to the final award as do the grades from any other unit in the curriculum.

For many years it has also been assumed that future workers in the health sciences – dentists, doctors, nurses, physiotherapists and veterinarians – require practical experience in hospitals or with qual-ified private practitioners before they can be allowed to practise without supervision. For potential specialist medical practitioners there are long periods of internship and further theoretical and practical examinations continuing well after the acquisition of the original medical degree. It is essential that during this internship the future medical specialists be given many opportunities for interacting with patients.

One institution which has taken seriously the challenge of preparing its students for careers where they will need to interact with clients is Alverno College in Midwestern United States. Loacker and Jensen (1988) describe how the faculty and administration of this liberal arts college for women adopted a new approach to the curricula in 1973 in order to meet the needs of their students. The college identified eight specific abilities which all students should acquire, regardless of the discipline in which they were majoring, namely:

1. communication
2. analysis
3. problem solving
4. valuing in decision making
5. interaction
6. taking environmental responsibility
7. effective citizenship
8. aesthetic response. (p. 129)

Loacker and Jensen claim that assessment is at the heart of the educational process at Alverno and give examples of the applicability of the above skills to some of the careers for which their students are preparing. A mix of self-assessment and faculty designed assessment is facilitated by specifying well-publicized criteria which are used for determining whether students have reached the designated levels of performance for each of the above abilities. For example, they have identified six levels of problem solving, with appropriate criteria for measuring each. These are:

1. Articulates and evaluates own problem-solving process
2. Defines problems or designs strategies to solve problems using discipline-related frameworks
3. Selects or designs appropriate frameworks and strategies to solve problems
4. Implements and evaluates solution and the problem-solving process
5. Uses problem-solving strategies in a broad variety of professional situations
6. Approaches problems and issues with a problem-solving attitude. (p. 131)

Criteria for grading professional experience

Benett (1993) refers to a 'considerable reluctance' towards adopting formal assessment of learning and describes some of the reasons why educators perceive difficulties in 'achieving valid, reliable and comparable assessments, given the complex interactions of human, social, technical and practical processes at the workplace'. He lists as some of the hindrances to assessment 'the variability of students' placements in industry, commerce and the public sector, the differing quality of learning opportunities and the diverse approaches to the supervision of students'.

Brown and Knight (1994) also describe difficulties encountered in assessing learning which occurs during work placements. They refer to the situation that previously existed in the United Kingdom:

> In the past, placements often were not assessed; learning was often assumed to have taken place but not specifically accredited. It was often assumed that although this was the most important part of the course, other than a work diary or a log, there was normally little in the way of assessment of the learning involved. (p. 89)

The introduction of competency-based learning, they claim, has altered this unsatisfactory situation, at least in the Universities of Portsmouth and Northumbria, whose programs they describe. In these two British universities (and in many others, according to Brown and Knight) the problem of assessing work experience is addressed through the use of *learning contracts* in which they identify four basic stages. These are:

1. a skills, knowledge and understanding profile
2. a needs analysis
3. action planning and activity
4. evaluation. (p. 90)

It would be useful to consider what is required in the first stage of a learning contract, as this sets the scene for the whole contract and strongly influences what happens in the last three stages, which do not need further elaboration here. Before students commence their work experience programs it is important that they, with the help of their tutors, identify 'what skills, knowledge and abilities they already have' (Brown and Knight, 1994). One would assume that unless a placement in industry, commerce, a hospital or school is going to provide new experiences and add to the student's learning, it will be a waste of time and effort. For example, if medical practitioners are undertaking further postgraduate studies to qualify for a higher degree or admission to one of the professional associations, it would be pointless arranging for further experience in clinical procedures with which they are quite familiar. Similarly, if industrial experience is being planned as part of an undergraduate program leading to a degree in engineering, one would need to ensure that the students are provided with opportunities for learning new techniques which have been described in their lectures, are not available in university laboratories but which may now be experienced in industry as they observe the theories being translated into practice.

Trowler (1996) describes recent approaches in British universities to the accreditation of prior experiences that are deemed to be relevant to university courses. He commences his paper with a quotation from Evans (1987):

> Hidden within all students ... lies a mass of knowledge and skills acquired in a wide variety of ways and distributed between heart, head and hands. Some are significant; some insignificant. The task of both student and teacher is to bring this mass out into the open, to identify it through appropriate assessment, to record it as evidence on paper, on tape, or by artefact and put it to use. (p. 11)

While accepting the views expressed above by Evans, Trowler refers to two models of accredited prior experiential learning (APEL) which he prefers to describe as 'twin poles on a continuum' rather than the 'irreconcilable opposites' which is the way some teachers view them (Trowler, 1996). APEL is the process by which an institution recognizes its students' prior work experiences as fulfilling part of the requirements for the award of a degree. The two models have been designated by Butterworth (1992) as the *credit exchange model* and the *developmental model*. The first of these models, according to Trowler, has been used in many institutions in the United States for many years. Prospective students are exempted from certain units of study on the grounds that they have already acquired the expected knowledge and skills through their experiences in the workplace. Thus they are granted *credit* for their earlier learning and exchange this for a release from any requirement to undertake further work in that aspect of their university studies.

By way of contrast, the *developmental model* recognizes that students' work experiences can make a valid contribution to their university studies, but only when each student is provided with an opportunity to reflect on those experiences and integrate their experiential learning with the more theoretical studies at university (Trowler, 1996). Later in the same article, Trowler emphasizes a need for strong involvement by tutors in assisting their students to make the connections between work experiences and formal studies at the university or college. He also draws attention to the challenges inherent in assessing such work. Wisker (1997) reports that students in a writing course at Anglia can submit a variety of creative and reflective work when claiming accreditation for prior learning. She is also examining ways of taking into account students' prior work experience when they enrol in management courses.

A good example of the developmental model at the level of post-graduate education is seen in a recent news item from the University of New England, Australia, concerning its doctorate in education (UNE, 1996):

> UNE's Doctor of Education Program is a 'professional' doctorate and currently has approximately 60 senior professionals enrolled since accepting its first cohort in 1994. They have responded positively to the opportunity for professional interaction on theoretical and practical concerns at unit residential schools. The first graduates are expected in 1997 having completed 25 per cent by coursework and 75 per cent by research.

Winter (1994) discusses the problems of assuring the quality of work-based learning in sandwich courses and short-term placements in the workplace. This powerful educational model is more widely known as *cooperative education*, with considerable development of assessment strategies and techniques. The World Association for Cooperative Education fosters this type of experiential learning which includes socialization in the workplace.

Winter takes a definition of 'quality' which is used to describe manufactured products and applies it to the processes of vocational education, arguing that the industrial measures of 'fitness for purpose' and 'meeting customer expectations' are quite suitable for assessing the value of work-based learning, provided certain assumptions are made. Thus 'fitness for purpose' refers to the educational outcomes expected from the work experience program and the 'customers' would include students, their educational institutions, potential employers, professional associations and the providers or monitors of educational funding (usually a government department of education or agencies such as, in Britain, the National Council for Vocational Qualifications).

In the above paper Winter also refers to the importance of 'good' practice. If an institution wished to use 'benchmarking' as a process of quality enhancement, then the work of Coates and Wright (1991) might be considered. Their *Guidelines for Good Practice on the Integration of Work-based Learning with Academic Assessment* sets out clearly the issues and implications. The factors which should be assessed are summarized as: knowledge, skills, behaviour, and achievements. Coates and Wright draw attention to the importance of moderation to cope with the wide range of experiences encountered in this type of learning.

In his discussion of 'fitness for purpose', Winter (1994) reviews some of the difficulties in specifying purposes or desirable educational outcomes from work-based learning:

> To begin with, statements of specified required competences need to be exhaustively checked, to ensure that they are both realistic (rather than mere evocations of an ideal), general (rather than a contingent feature of a particular context), and that they embody the requirements of good practice (rather than actual practice). This involves negotiating between practitioners, their managers, professional bodies and academic professional theory ... Even after such negotiations have apparently been carried out successfully, further adjustments need to be made.

The author goes on to emphasize a need for regular staff seminars which are 'devoted to the comparison of a tutor's responses to students' files of evidence' and adds:

> The point is that when explicit statements of required outcomes are made publicly available, as the basis for assessment decisions, much more effort needs to go into creating the staff consensus on which the justice of those decisions depends, if the assessment process is to survive its exposure to public scrutiny, by students as well as by quality auditors. (p. 250)

In the report, *Higher Education in the Learning Society*, Dearing (1997) notes that 'employers place high value on new recruits having had work experience' and recommends that 'all undergraduate programmes ... offer students an option of a year-long work placement'. The report goes on to make the following suggestion for consideration by the government of the United Kingdom.

> The Government and other bodies might consider the following options:
> - the use of intermediary agencies (such as Chambers of Commerce and trade associations) to identify opportunities for work placements
> - tax incentives to encourage small enterprises to employ students, by covering part of the cost of managing such programmes
> - an extension of the STEP scheme by which major employers provide students with short periods of work experience
> - institutions working actively with local employment agencies to identify opportunities for student employment
> - encouragement of public sector employers by the Government to expand placements, especially for vacation work. (Section 9.36)

The STEP (Shell Technology Enterprise Programme) scheme mentioned in the above quotation has evidently been most successful in providing opportunities for undergraduates to gain work experience. Students are placed in small and medium-sized enterprises for eight weeks during the summer vacation, generally at the end of their second year of studies, and a majority of students so placed reported that the experience 'had satisfied or exceeded their expectations' and that 'their academic work had benefited from the skills learnt on the programme' (Dearing, 1997).

In its description of STEP, the Dearing Report does not refer to any direct measure of students' success in their work experience, only the indirect effect of the experience on their formal university studies and their personal development. Later in the same chapter, however, the Committee discusses the need for improvements in assessment procedures in higher education and an urgent need for closer links between program or module design and assessment. By implication this link should also apply to work experience programs whenever these are deemed to be an essential (or even an optional but important) component of undergraduate education.

The key to reliable and valid measures of the quality of work-based learning lies in ensuring that each planned work experience is complementary to a student's formal education at the university and is designed as a 'value-added' exercise. As a result of their placements in a situation for which they are undergoing training, students should return to their university studies with new perceptions of their chosen professions and with a demonstrably better integration of theory and practice. Those who are responsible for assessing the level of attainment of students in a practicum or professional place-ment need to be aware of the expectations and standards of the educational institution and the industry or profession, together with the expectations and abilities of the students themselves.

Judging creative performance

Successful performances or exhibitions in the creative arts are an essential component of summative assessment in schools of music, drama, art and architecture, yet the criteria by which these perfor-mances or exhibitions are judged are not always made clear to students. It is possible that members of faculty who have the respon-sibility of assessing the value of each student's work have not clari-fied in their own minds those features of a musical, stage or artistic presentation which are essential, which ones are merely desirable or how one presentation might be compared with another. Most of us have experienced cases of highly idiosyncratic (or perhaps just fashionable) judgements and awards at art shows, musical competitions, drama festivals or design competitions for new cities or buildings.

There has been considerable research in recent years on the assessment of students' performance in the creative arts, recognizing that in some cases it is a solo performance which has to be judged, but on many occasions a judgement has to be made concerning the performance of a group (eg an orchestra, choir or cast of a play) and the contributions made by individual members of that group. Nightingale *et al*. (1996) describe a number of case studies in Australian, US and Scottish universities where satisfactory criteria have been developed, validated and used in such diverse fields as architecture, mechanical engineering, media art, dance, visual arts and music. For example, in a case study from music, contributed by David Lockett of the University of Adelaide, students are judged on technical proficiency, musicianship, musical character/temperament and overall impact. Each of the first three items is further divided into sub-categories, thus providing a useful checklist for those responsible for judging the performance. The Conservatorium of Music has also developed a clear set of criteria for differentiating between levels of performance, in this case, High Distinction, Distinction, Credit, Pass Division 1, Pass Division 2 and Fail (Nightingale *et al*, 1996).

12

Designing a final examination

If you want to test your memory, try to recall what you were worrying about one year ago today.

(Rotarian)

Given the range of assessment tasks that can be used for judging students' levels of performance by the end of a unit of study, it is not surprising that there are many combinations of tasks which a teacher may choose to use in a final examination. There are also other decisions which must be made before the most suitable examination for a particular unit is finally designed. Some of these issues will be discussed in the present chapter. We do not propose to reiterate the arguments for and against objective tests, which were canvassed in Chapter 9, nor a description of the many types of essay questions, described in Chapter 7; in the present chapter the focus is on the type of final examination in which students are required to attempt a relatively small number of questions, each of which will take about thirty minutes to answer. Two other types of final examination are not discussed in the present chapter as they have been dealt with earlier: dissertations or theses were described in Chapter 8 and the testing of laboratory, studio or workshop skills was in Chapter 11.

Relation to objectives

In Chapter 3 we provided brief descriptions of selected classification systems for cognitive objectives and included a number of test questions which illustrate the different categories and levels of objectives. Table 3.2 demonstrated how one might achieve a balance between the various levels of objectives and important subdivisions of subject matter. The same table indicates how a teacher or examiner might

193

allocate the proportion of marks that may be earned from each combination of objectives and subject content.

If a mark in a final examination is only one of a number of contributors to a final grade, the examiner may feel that it is not necessary to test every level of objective in that examination. Under these circumstances, the final examination would normally be designed to measure the achievement of higher order objectives such as the ability to analyse problems and to suggest constructive solutions, particularly in science- and mathematics-based disciplines or professions. In the humanities a final examination may focus on students' ability to demonstrate a thorough understanding of the field of study by selecting appropriate references, presenting the student's own interpretation of a situation and arguing for that viewpoint.

Time allowed for the final examination

The time allowed for taking the final examination will be determined by such factors as the length and number of questions in the paper, their degree of difficulty, the percentage of the total course which needs to be examined using this format and what is regarded as a reasonable concentration span for students. In exceptional circumstances the examination may extend over a whole day, in which case arrangements will have to be made for candidates to have access to food and toilet facilities without compromising security. The most common period of time for a final examination appears to be about three hours; if a long period is required the examination is divided into a number of sections, each of which deals with a different aspect of the subject. At the more senior levels of university study there is no good reason why the whole of the three-hour period should not be devoted to answering just one question provided, of course, the question is sufficiently demanding to require such an extended treatment. It would be rare, in such circumstances, for students to be given no choice; much more common would be the instruction:

Candidates should attempt only ONE of the following questions.

More will be said on the topic of choice in a later section of the present chapter.

Meanwhile we would argue against the inclusion of too many short questions in a final examination; these are better suited to progress tests. When a final examination consists of more than about five questions, some of which require a shorter time to answer than others, candidates can become quite confused about the allocation of time and effort and will not perform to the best of their ability. We commend the practice of designing a final examination in which students are required to attempt five questions of approximately equal levels of difficulty during a three-hour period.

Facilities and resources

An essential prerequisite in planning any major examination is for the teacher or course coordinator to list the facilities and resources needed for students to undertake the examination and perform under optimal conditions. Need for this is most obvious with practical examinations where one must provide adequate laboratory facilities, scientific instruments, chemicals and sometimes specimens. Reference was made to this need in the previous chapter when we discussed practical examinations.

Hall and Imrie (1994) pose a series of questions about resources and facilities on a series of floppy discs originally prepared for the in-service training of technical institute tutors in New Zealand in the techniques of assessment and now available from Professional Development and Quality Services, City University of Hong Kong. The authors have kindly given us permission to reproduce these questions in the current chapter. The wording of the instructions has been changed slightly to fit the format of the present book.

A. Rooms
1. Will you need a specialist room, such as a laboratory or work-shop?
2. Will you need to book rooms in advance?
3. Will the rooms be big enough?
4. Will desks be sufficiently spaced out to prevent students reading other students' answers?

B. Equipment and materials
1. Will you need to provide special equipment, such as machinery, tools, computer hardware, typewriters, safety glasses, etc? Specify.
2. Will you need to provide materials, such as chemicals, specimens, wood, writing paper etc? Specify.
3. Will you need to provide resource books and documents, such as statistical tables, workshop manuals, legal regulations, etc? Specify.

4. Will students need to provide equipment (eg tools, calculators) and materials (eg cloth, art materials)? Specify.

C. Library resources
1. Are there sufficient copies of key texts in the library?
2. Should library copies of books be put on restricted loan (eg three-day loan)?

D. People
1. Will you need help in supervising tests and examinations?
2. Will you need secretarial help in preparing tests and examinations?
3. Will you need help in marking students' answers?

E. Other (specify)
Now go through the list of resources you have just compiled and write down any constraints which might restrict your assessment programme. For example, consider:
A. Whether your institute has sufficient equipment, materials, library resources, personnel back-up, etc.
B. Your own workload (eg how long will it take to prepare and mark each assessment? How many answers will you have to mark?).
C. The workload of your students.
D. Deadlines for returning marks to the registry or an examining authority.
E. The type of course you are teaching (eg block versus full-year course).
Finally revise your original list of resources to take account of the constraints identified above.

One additional resource which would not have been readily available when the above list was first compiled is the personal computer. Now that most students in developed countries prepare their assignments on computers (their own or equipment available within the university or hall of residence), it may seem reasonable to allow them to use personal computers for writing essays in formal examinations. Computers have, of course, been used for some time in those examinations where computing skills are being assessed, such as programming and accountancy or in the administration of objective tests as part of a computer-based learning program. Some institutions also allow students with particular disabilities to use a lap-top computer in a formal examination when the student is incapable of writing but has the necessary keyboard skills. Others are experimenting with ways of delivering whole courses using the Internet and how best to examine their students using this medium (Hill, 1997).

There are still some critical issues which need resolution before a personal computer can be used as a normal writing tool under examination conditions. Students with superior keyboard skills would have a marked advantage over others; probably more so than currently exists between students with different levels of manual dexterity. For some universities the cost of providing sufficient personal computers would still be regarded as too high, although the price of suitable equipment continues to fall as reliability improves. If students are allowed to use a computer supplied by the university for writing essays in examinations it is essential that there be no difference in the performance of the equipment. Allowing students to bring their own lap-top computers into the examination room creates a further problem, namely that it is virtually impossible to prevent students bringing in unauthorized material. Superficially this may be similar to an open-book examination (to be discussed later in the present chapter); in practice students could bring sample answers, prepared by other people, which they could then use as their own.

Amount of choice allowed to students

Students generally expect to have some choice of questions which they must answer in a major examination. Provision of choice helps to overcome the element of luck (or success in sampling) where some students may have spent more time studying the topic or topics for an exam in which all questions are compulsory. In cases where students from different lecture, tutorial or laboratory groups are sitting for the same examination, the quality of teaching may have varied, thus providing advantages for some students or putting others at a disadvantage. If the purpose of the examination is to provide an opportunity for students to demonstrate how well they can reason, then one would advocate giving the students as wide a choice of questions as is possible. In determining the amount of choice to be given, examiners need to take into account the amount of reading time students require before they start to answer any questions. The major part of this reading time should be spent in thinking about the implications of the chosen examination questions; only a small proportion of the time should be spent in deciding which questions will be attempted.

There are, however, two strong arguments against the practice of allowing students some choice in a major examination. First, the examiner may well decide that certain topics are so important that every student should be required to demonstrate an ability to answer questions on each of these topics at a satisfactory level. In cases where the examiner judges all topics to be essential and equally important, it would be reasonable to make all questions compulsory. If, however, there are only a few topics of such importance, it is preferable for the examination paper to consist of two parts: Part A in which ALL questions are compulsory, and Part B in which students must attempt x of y questions. The values of x and y will largely be determined by the number of questions in Part A and the total number one wishes to include in the paper. If, for example, the examiner has decided that the final examination paper should contain five questions of equal value and only one of these is to be compulsory, then Part B will consist of between about six and ten questions, from which students will be expected to attempt four.

A second argument against allowing students some choice of questions in a major examination is related to the *validity* of the test questions. We shall be discussing the issues of validity and reliability in more detail in Chapter 14. At this stage, the following simple definitions for these statistical terms will suffice.

> An item in an assessment program (eg an examination question or a task which students must perform) is *valid* to the extent that it actually measures the type of learning for which the item was designed.
>
> A test, or any one item in that test, is *reliable* only to the extent that, if the same test or item is repeated, marks given for similar levels of performance will be consistent.

The following example illustrates the problems that arise with validity when each candidate in a competition has to perform a different task. The Australian Broadcasting Commission organizes an annual event entitled 'The Young Performer of the Year Awards'. As in athletics, successful players from the heats and semi-finals eventually compete against each other in a public concert, in association with a symphony orchestra from one of the state capitals. This concert is both televised and broadcast throughout the country. In the 1996 concert the competitors were a pianist, a mezzo-soprano, a flautist and a violinist. One may well ask how these four musicians can be compared. We would expect that the criteria on which they are judged will, as far as is possible, be the same for each musician yet the very nature of their instruments (including vocal cords) prevents them from playing (or singing) the same piece of music. It would not even be desirable to require them all to choose the same composer or the same period (eg baroque, classical, romantic, etc).

In a contest where the candidates are performing different but related tasks, the criteria used to judge the best performer might be: choice of (musical) work, difficulty of chosen work, interpretation, expression, accuracy.

'Open-book' and similar examinations

In an 'open-book examination' students are allowed to take into the examination room books or other resource material which they may need for the examination. This type of examination is particularly suitable when the emphasis is more on the ability to select appropriate data and interpret that data rather than on the memorization, recall and repetition of facts. In fact an open-book examination is entirely inappropriate when one wishes to test memory skills. Clift and Imrie (1994) claim that this type of examination is best suited for measuring skills of problem solving, interpretation, critical evaluation, appreciation and/or application necessitating the use of references.

Clift and Imrie also list a number of criticisms of open-book examinations. These include a false sense of security which discourages revision, a temptation to take too many references into the examination room (a practice which is liable to increase students' tension), and a belief that students who can gain access to the most books will have an unfair advantage. Most of these difficulties may be overcome through prior discussions with students about the purpose and special nature of open-book examinations and a restriction of the amount of material they are allowed to bring to the exam. It is also helpful to give students practice with this type of examination, possibly as part of the formative assessment which takes place in the early stages of a teaching program. As with assignments, there should be penalties for uncritical copying from resource material into a student's examination paper.

Pre-published examinations

Another modification to end-of-course examinations, namely the pre-publication of the exam paper or of major questions, is sometimes justified on the grounds that it helps reduce examination stress. One purpose of this strategy is to ensure that all students have had adequate time to undertake the research necessary for answering these questions, thus avoiding superficial answers. There may be some value in this approach, provided it is not combined with an unrestricted open-book policy, a combination which could lead to widespread plagiarism. A satisfactory compromise could be to allow students to bring into the examination room a very limited amount of written materials if they are taking pre-published examinations.

In some cases the notice given out before the examination does not contain precise details of the final questions; it merely gives an indication of the breadth and depth expected or the range of topics to be tested. It might, for example, refer to a specific theory or an article which students are expected to have studied in some detail and which they might be expected to analyse. On other occasions the examiner may list a number of questions, only some of which will be in the final examination paper. The danger with this approach is that students may be even more prone to guessing the most likely questions and concentrating on these than they do for normal examinations. The following examples from Clift and Imrie (1994) give students an indication of the type of examination to be expected without including the actual questions in their final form.

Only in exceptional cases would we recommend the pre-publication of examination papers; our preference is to provide fairly detailed information about the type of examination to be used and the scope of topics to be covered and retain both the 'open-book' and 'pre-published questions' approaches for essays to be written during term.

Examples of modified pre-published examination

(1)   For this examination you will be required to answer three (3) compulsory questions.

Question 1 (worth 40 marks)
You will be given one of the following articles and asked to write a critical review of it:

Beach, L. R. 'Sociability and academic achievement in various types of learning situations', *Journal of Educational Psychology*, 1960, 51, 4, 208–212.

Palmer, R. E. and Verner, C. 'A comparison of three instruction techniques', *Adult Education*, Summer 1959, 232–238.

Question 2 (worth 40 marks)
You will be asked to answer a number of short answer questions about the following article:

Aiken, L. R. and Dreger, R. M. 'The effect of attitudes on performance in mathematics', *Journal of Educational Psychology*, 1961, 52, 1, 19–24.

Question 3 (worth 20 marks)
You will be given an article and asked to list the points you would discuss in providing a critical assessment of it.

(2) The examination paper is set out as follows:

Question 1 consists of two alternatives, each worth 40 marks.

Either: You are given 20 concepts drawn from every part of the course. These are set out in pairs and you are asked to define and compare the terms in each pair.
N.B. Answers will have to be succinct and to the point – no room for waffle.

Or: You are to compare two of the four types of societies discussed at the beginning of the course (bands, tribes, peasants, states) and to discuss where and how well a particular society from your ethnographies fits into this typology.

Questions 2–8 You have to do only two questions out of seven, and there is a choice built into most of them. Every question requires you to illustrate your answer with reference to one or more of the societies in your prescribed books – but leaves the choice to you.

Part 3

Examining assessment

13

Reporting on assessment

I think the world is run by 'C' students.

(Al McGuire)

In this chapter we describe the requirements of an assessment reporting system, the purposes it has to serve, the operational requirements and the way it can help students, staff and administration. We illustrate the ideas by describing one of many possible ways of recording assessment. The tools and techniques are common, simple and available in all institutions of higher education. While many of these tools are frequently used, the full potential and value of assessment recording are sometimes not realized. It is the purpose of this chapter to provide some ideas on how to improve assessment with common computing tools.

While we concentrate on the statistical adjustment and reporting of scores, this is not the only benefit that comes from using computers in recording and reporting assessment. The use of computers reduces much of the clerical load on assessors. The simple procedure of the assessor entering marks directly into a machine-readable form as soon as possible reduces the likelihood of transcription errors. Adding up all the scores with a calculator and checking against the machine-computed total of all the entered scores is an easy way to verify that data was entered correctly into the computer system. Moving data such as student names and identification from other computer systems is normally simple. It is possible to print out reports for tutors and students as well as have a reliable way of providing results to administrative systems.

The chapter is structured by first outlining the overall reasons for recording assessment. We then describe operational requirements of a reporting system and finally provide descriptions of some typical reporting and recording systems.

The purposes

Reporting on assessment has many roles. While there is the obvious one of acting as part of the institutional memory of student performance, the other roles are in many ways of equal importance and relate to the progress of a student. These include:

- feedback to a student
- administration of classes
- feedback to assessors
- performance monitoring of students and staff involved in assessment
- prediction of the future and comparisons with the past
- moderation across modules.

Institutional memory and style

It is a requirement of all institutions to report on and record the performance of students. The most common output is the student transcript of results. The form of a student transcript tells much about an institution and in many ways reflects the approach to education of the institution. It is the institution's surrogate for its most important output, namely its students. It tells the world how the institution evaluated the student. For students it is their evidence of work done, knowledge gained and performance attained. It becomes their passport to another life and remains an important indicator and measure throughout their entire life. The student transcript is a major link between an institution and the rest of society as it tells society about the education of its students.

It is difficult to overemphasize the importance of a student record to both the student and the institution because it is on this record that many judgements and decisions are made. Because of its importance, the control and security of student records is a major preoccupation of all institutions. The form of record is an initial major decision for most new institutions, but once established the form rarely changes or is rarely reviewed. The form of record is an important factor in the continuity of an institution. Typically changes only occur when there are major institutional adjustments.

The student record is also an important defining aspect for many individuals. The record is permanent and does not change. It gives a snapshot of a person at a particular time and summarizes the student's performance and history at an institution. No matter what graduates do in later life, their first class or third class honours results have important social and economic implications. Tables 13.1 to 13.5 show the style of typical transcripts from England, Hong Kong, Australia, Canada and the USA .

Table 13.1 *Style of a transcript from England*

Module Code	Module Name	Course Work	Examination	Result
BUS123	Economic Modelling	13	15	PASS
COM116	Micro-Computer Systems I	16	13	PASS
COM118	Introduction to SE	18	20	MERIT

Table 13.2 *Style of a transcript from Hong Kong*

Module	Grade/ Code	Remarks
Quantitative Analysis	C	
Computer Systems IV	B	
Data Management III	D	

Table 13.3 *Style of a transcript from Australia*

Unit Name	Level	CR PT	Grade
Computers and Computing	1	3	P
Basic Design I	1	3	CR
Financial Accounting I	1	3	W

Table 13.4 *Style of a transcript from Canada*

Area	Code	Name	Weight	Mark	Grade
Psychology	281	Stats for Psychology	1.0	082	A
French	002	Intensive French	1.0	067	C
Music	050B	Studies in Theory I	0.5	092	A+

Table 13.5 *Style of transcript from the USA*

Code	Name	Att Name	GR	Earn	Q Pt
BMGT 380	Business Law I	03	A	03	12
BMGT 110	Business Enterprise	03	B	03	09
HUMN 310	Bus & Prof Ethics	06	A	06	24

The student transcript reflects the institutional policy on assessment. If the institution has a format of transcript in which grades are allocated and the results are norm referenced, this will influence teaching as compared to an institution that records results as criterion-referenced assessment. In practice almost all higher education institutions use a norm–referenced method of grade allocation and it is this approach that is emphasized in this chapter. It is not the place of this chapter to argue for or against norm-referenced methods but to indicate how we can make the system better achieve its objectives. A summary of the relative advantages of norm- and criterion-referenced assessment is provided in Chapter 2.

Even though different universities use similar approaches to assessment, the ways they record the results of assessment vary considerably. There is no consistent definition of any of the components recorded, let alone any consistency in the meaning of different measures. Often the abbreviations used are not defined on the transcript. In the transcripts reproduced in Tables 13.1 to 13.5 some of the abbreviations are obscure and, unless the reader has a good knowledge of the institution, then the transcripts become almost meaningless.

Student feedback

In most institutions the institutional record is a summative record made by the institution and has little formative feedback value to the student. A student receives a grade or mark which is of little use in directly helping a student in the learning process. Formative influences might come indirectly as a result of students wishing to get higher grades and perform better.

For assessment to be useful to students as part of the learning process, the assessment must be visible and related to the learning goals of the participants. Not only must assessment be visible but students must understand it and, if possible, accept and agree with its relevance and applicability. By knowing how assessments are made, students can work towards achieving good results. Most rational adults will act this way. It is, of course, important that we do not frustrate the students and their intentions in the way we process and report assessments. Other chapters have addressed the problems of how to assess and how to assign marks and grades to pieces of work. What we do here is to discuss how we can record these results and how we can analyse the results to check for internal validity. While we have stated that the reporting of results has little direct feedback effect on students' learning, the procedures adopted to ensure the validity of results influence *perception* of the quality of students' awards.

Class administration

Lecturers in most institutions are required to report and record assessments for their students. Most will have class lists and have a formalized method of reporting results. Again most institutions will have class lists in a machine-readable form either as text files or as subsets of larger databases. Some institutions have an institution-wide system that handles most of the regular data processing needs for recording and analysing marks. However, most will not have a complete system that is suitable for all assessors. Some systems provide no assistance for recording marks or for grade manipulation and analysis. Either way there is often a need for an assessor to do some calculation or analysis that the institution's system does not handle. Frequently the system will only allow the final grade to be entered and will not allow any recording of the results for each individual question, yet an assessor may wish to analyse the marks for individual pieces of assessment as well as look at the total scores.

It is important that whenever components are combined to arrive at an overall ranking or grading then it is done in a rational manner. The tools that an institution provides its assessors should give this assistance. However, if this is not done assessors can use spreadsheets as these are simple and widely available. The following examples make use of spreadsheets, but we stress that the ideas expressed here should be built into the institution's own recording systems. There is a considerable amount of effort involved in recording and analysing marks and it is desirable that assessors get full value for their time and effort. They should not be required to duplicate their efforts by transcribing, separately for the institution, students' marks for further analysis (see also Cox, 1993).

In general, the more data we enter (ie record), the more information we can obtain and the more informed will be our ensuing judgements. For example, more information can be obtained by entering all the marks for all questions in an examination rather than simply entering the total. If it is planned properly, the work to enter all marks for all questions requires no more effort. For example, entering examination question marks is no more effort than entering the marks into a calculator for addition. The advantage of using a computer system rather than using a calculator or adding mentally is that once entered the numbers can be manipulated further and transcription errors are eliminated.

A case study

As an illustration of the procedures recommended above we shall take a set of results from a real test. The analyses are typical of those used to aid an assessor.

Table 13.6 gives the raw results of a class of students who sat a test in which each test question was marked out of 10. The data were entered by the assessor directly from the test scripts. The data took 15 minutes to enter into the spreadsheet. This is no longer than it would take to add up the marks for each student. However, once the marks are in the computer we can immediately calculate several simple statistics that give us extra information about the assessment.

For each component of the test an average and a standard deviation has been calculated. The high average score for Question 2 indicates that most students found this question relatively easy, while the low average for Question 4 suggests that it was difficult. This information should alert the assessor to possible problems with these questions. The assessor should therefore seek reasons for the

Table 13.6 *Raw scores and simple statistics*

Student	Group	Questions				Total
		1	2	3	4	
1	1	8	5	10	0	23
2	1	8	10	10	10	38
3	1	6	10	5	3	24
4	1	7	10	10	0	27
5	1	10	10	10	8	38
6	1	6	10	10	5	31
7	1	3	10	10	3	26
8	1	7	10	4	5	26
9	1	8	10	8	3	29
10	1	0	10	0	0	10
Nos 11–27 omitted.						
28	2	10	10	10	6	36
29	2	9	10	10	7	36
30	2	3	10	10	0	23
31	2	7	10	6	7	30
32	2	2	10	5	5	22
33	2	8	10	4	1	23
34	2	8	10	10	5	33
35	2	7	10	0	0	17
36	2	10	10	10	10	40
37	2	8	10	3	0	21
Average		6.59	8.78	6.84	3.68	25.89
Intended Contribution		25%	25%	25%	25%	
Standard Deviation (sd)		2.91	2.64	3.75	3.00	[1] 8.85
Correlation (r) with Total		0.72	0.43	0.86	0.81	
Contribution (r × sd)		2.09	1.12	3.22	2.42	8.85
Actual Contribution		24%	13%	36%	27%	

[1] Note the sum of the individual standard deviations is 12.3 which is different from the standard deviation of the totals. The sum of the contributions is the same as the standard deviation of the total.

differences and consider whether they influence the overall assessment. Possible explanations for the results could be that the way Question 4 was written led to misinterpretation by students, or it may be that the question covered material that students did not generally know. Question 2 on the other hand may be too easy or perhaps students could guess the answer with a high probability of being correct. These are only some possible reasons; there could be many more. The point is that a simple, easily obtained analysis of the numbers indicates areas that are worth investigating.

We can continue our analysis and examine questions to see which have the most influence on the final ranking of the students. When we use normative assessment we try to discriminate between students. We often believe that some items of assessment have more influence on the relative ranking of students than other items. We know that if all students received exactly the same mark on a partic- ular question, that question would have no influence on the relative rank of students. We can easily discover the importance of each question on the ranking of students through the use of the correla- tion between the question and the total of all questions. In Table 13.6 we show the correlation coefficient and we show the intended 'contribution' of each question to the overall standard deviation and ranking of the total score.

Questions which have a high correlation and a large standard deviation contribute more to the overall variation or standard devia- tion of the total than questions with a low correlation and a small standard deviation. If we multiply the correlation coefficient by the standard deviation then we get the contribution to the total standard deviation. We can then express this as a percentage. For the ques- tions in this test we find that Question 3 was the best discriminator between students and was three times as effective as Question 2.

It is worthwhile for the assessor to try to understand why this may have occurred. What is it about Question 3 that makes it so impor- tant in discriminating among students? Was this expected? In this particular case the assessor believed that students had to exercise higher level conceptualizations to answer Question 3 than were necessary to answer Question 2. This gave the assessor confidence that indeed the questions were appropriate for discriminating between students in an appropriate manner. From the examiner's viewpoint Question 2 was still valuable in that it allowed students to show their knowledge, even though as a discriminator it was rela- tively unimportant. Unless they have been advised to the contrary, students tend to assume that questions carrying the same marks will contribute the same weighting to the total outcome.

The relatively simple type of analysis illustrated above is useful for assessors in devising appropriate questions for different tasks and then being able to check that the questions are indeed fulfilling their purpose. In cases where there are unintended outcomes, having the data in the computer makes it easier for the assessor to make appropriate rational adjustments. It is interesting that a superficial examination of the means and standard deviations would not give a clear indication of the value of the questions for ranking students. Superficially it would appear that Question 2 may have more of an influence because the average was higher and the standard deviation did not appear to be very different. However, the difference arose from the higher correlation between Question 3 and the total score. The students who did well on the whole test did well on Question 3 and those who did poorly on Question 3 did poorly overall. In this particular case such a result was quite acceptable to the assessor because of the nature of the assessment. However, there are other situations described below where a result similar to the above may not be acceptable and where the examiner expects all items of assessment to contribute equally or in some defined proportion to the overall result. The 'contribution' calculation shown in the last row of Table 13.6 is an important method for discovering this information.

Another unexpected piece of information in the data is the large number of zeros (in the original data) for Question 4. One possible explanation could be that, due to time constraints, many students were unable to finish the test. In this particular case, however, the zeros indicate a total lack of knowledge on that topic as there were no time constraints and all questions had been attempted.

As mentioned earlier, the correlation of the individual scores with the overall result is helpful in estimating the importance of the contribution each question makes to the distribution of total scores. Similarly we can use the correlations between questions to indicate possible overlaps. Table 13.7 shows the cross-correlations between questions and the total. This again points out the difference between Question 2 and the other questions. The very low correlation between Question 2 and the other three questions suggests that it was measuring something quite different from the others. Again, it would be worthwhile examining Question 2 and trying to understand what is the basis of the difference.

We may also be concerned about differences between groups of students. The students who took the test described in Table 13.6 came from two tutorial classes, shown as Groups 1 and 2. If we wish to ascertain whether the students had received equivalent assessment we will need to check whether there is any difference between the students in the groups. To do this we can use many different statistics. A common one is to use a t-test. This statistic gives an estimate

Table 13.7 *Correlations between questions and total score*

	Question 1	Question 2	Question 3	Question 4	Total
Question 1	1.00				
Question 2	−0.11	1.00			
Question 3	0.59	0.19	1.00		
Question 4	0.51	0.24	0.54	1.00	
Total	0.72	0.43	0.86	0.81	1.00

of whether two sets of numbers come from the same population. If there is a difference between the groups then we require some estimate on whether the difference could have arisen by chance. If the t–test statistic shows a value of 1 per cent we can be reasonably sure that there is a significant difference between the two sets of numbers. It is not our purpose here to define the meaning and interpretation of statistics. Typical sources are standard texts on statistics (eg Thorndike and Hagen, 1977; Winer *et al.*, 1991) or specialized books on student assessment (Lacey and Lawton, 1983; Gronlund, 1985; Brown and Knight, 1994; Pole, 1993).

Graphical representations

Another simple tool available to assessors is a graphical representation of data. Not all information is suited to a graph format, which is best used for seeing patterns in data or for observing 'the big picture'. The simple histogram reproduced in Figure 13.1 indicates the numbers of students whose marks fell within specified ranges in the test described earlier. The chart shows that the numbers were spread over most of the range of marks with a peak towards the higher marks. This is a typical graph for the type of test described above. If the histogram were different then we would be seeking an explanation. For example, if there were two distinct groups at the top and the bottom then we might look to see why the class was divided in that way. If the results were bunched around a small range of marks we would probably assume that the test was a poor discriminator of student performance.

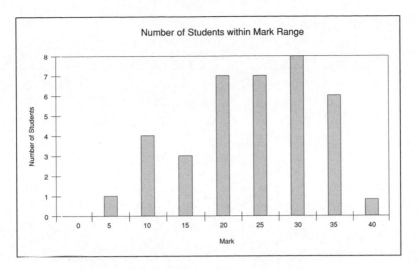

Figure 13.1   Distribution of performance

Adjusting marks

To interpret marks from different questions or assessment tasks they must be comparable. To illustrate this point let us assume that a student has been awarded 40 marks for two pieces of work. Such a mark is meaningless unless we know whether the test was marked out of 50, 100 or some other figure! Assuming that the first task was marked out of 50 and the second was out of 100, it is obvious that two scores of 40 represent quite different levels of performance. Whenever we wish to compare or combine marks from different types of assessment we will therefore need to adjust them in some way. In the above case we could convert all marks so that the maximum score for each test was 100; the individual marks would then be scaled linearly so that a mark of 40 out of 50 becomes 80 out of 100.

With the notable exception of the Educational Testing Service (ETS), there are few standard tests in higher education of competency for different subjects and so there are few norms or reference scores we can use in the same way as the reading and comprehension tests used widely in primary and secondary education. (For further details concerning the work of ETS, the reader should consult Chapter 9. The ETS page on the Internet should also examined.) Most of the adjustments we make to student scores are to enable us to compare results between different years and between different

Table 13.8 *Simulated case study*

Item No.	Typical	Even	Opposite	Low std	Random	Average	Rank
1	53	50	95	70	89	71.4	5
2	54	55	90	70	76	69.0	6
3	55	60	85	71	56	65.4	10
4	61	65	80	71	61	67.6	8
5	62	70	75	72	88	73.4	2
6	63	75	70	72	53	66.6	9
7	64	80	65	72	77	71.6	4
8	72	85	60	73	53	68.6	7
9	73	90	55	73	71	72.4	3
10	80	95	50	74	78	75.4	1
Average	63.7	72.5	72.5	71.8	70.2	70.14	
Standard Deviation	8.92	15.14	15.14	1.32	13.70	3.20	
Correlation	0.53	0.46	−0.46	0.48	0.77	1.00	
Contribution	4.76	7.03	−7.03	0.63	10.62	3.20	

modules, units or courses. We also make adjustments to make assessments internally consistent.

Let us first consider a simulated case study showing the variations which can be obtained with marks and the ways in which we combine them. Table 13.8 shows a set of marks which might represent the results in an examination, marks for various items of assessment within a module or marks representing performance across different modules. The principles and problems remain the same.

Table 13.8 lists five contrasting sets of marks. The first set follows a normal distribution; the second has an even distribution; the third has a negative correlation with (or is opposite to) the second set; the fourth has a low standard deviation, and the fifth is composed of a set of marks which are randomly allocated between 50 and 90. The marks are averaged and shown in the final column. The average, standard deviation, correlation of the column to the total and the contribution of the column to the standard deviation of the total have all been calculated and displayed in the bottom four rows.

The first difficulty is with the negatively correlated marks. A negative correlation probably means that the particular piece of assessment is measuring something quite different from that which gave rise to the other marks. If this is the case then it is undesirable for us to combine the one set of marks with the other because they are probably measuring different abilities. Under such circumstances we would need to reconsider the system of assessment and our reasons for trying to combine the marks. Perhaps one piece of assessment is measuring scholastic ability and the other is measuring athletic prowess or even attendance!

The set of marks which has a low standard deviation also creates some difficulties. Although the correlation between individual marks and the average score is quite acceptable, this test does not discriminate well between students. For the purposes of discrimination there is little point in including this mark in the overall combination. Removal of this question from the test would make little difference to the overall ranking. *If it is our intention that all components should rank equally in determining the overall rank then the contributions of the marks should be similar.* For this to happen the marks for individual pieces of assessment have to be adjusted in some way, such as by requiring the piece of assessment to fit a common distribution. This is the point behind the standardization of marks which is designed to ensure that each component of the assessment is more likely to contribute equally to the overall mark. However, we must be confident that this is our intention and that we really want each item of assessment to have the same weight.

There are some situations, however, when our intention is to exclude a particular component of the assessment procedures from the ranking of students. In situations where we are unsure of who does the work, such as in a group project, we would probably not want this assessment to contribute to the overall ranking, although we may well decide that it should contribute to the overall mark for other reasons, such as motivation. Another situation might occur when some examination items must be answered by all students as minimum competency tests whereas other items test higher level skills. We expect these more challenging questions to discriminate between students. In such cases we would not wish to adjust the marks.

The case of the random allocation of marks is interesting. When we include the negatively correlated marks we find the random allocation has the greatest contribution to the overall ranking. However, from the cross-correlations (Table 13.9) between assessments we can see that the random marks are different from the others.

Again the negative correlations should alert us to discrepancies in our measurements. When this occurs we should consider other evidence or other approaches. We could simply eliminate the marks

Table 13.9   *Cross tabulations*

	Typical	Even	Opposite	Low sd	Random	Average
Typical	1.00					
Even	0.97	1.00				
Opposite	−0.97	−1.00	1.00			
Low sd	0.97	0.98	−0.98	1.00		
Random	−0.12	−0.18	0.18	−0.16	1.00	
Average	0.53	0.46	−0.46	0.48	0.77	1.00

that give negative correlations on the assumption that they are measuring different things but, before doing so, we need to remember that any decision about the retention or removal of particular items is a matter of professional judgement.

Another method, while it has significant theoretical problems (Vassiloglou and French, 1982), is easier to justify in practice. Here we simply ignore the marks and only consider the relative ranking of students in each of the different pieces of assessment. We then do a straight addition of the individual rankings to come up with an overall ranking.

Table 13.10 shows the rankings for the simulated case study which was first shown in Table 13.8. The column headed 'Rank 1' is the ranking of averages from the data in Table 13.8, while 'Rank 2' is the rank order from the average of the rankings in Table

Table 13.10   *Combining rank orders*

Item	Typical	Even	Opposite	Low sd	Random	Average	Rank 1	Rank 2
1	1	1	10	1	6	3.8	5	10
2	2	2	9	2	8	4.6	6	7
3	3	3	8	3	3	4.0	10	9
4	4	4	7	4	4	4.6	8	7
5	5	5	6	5	9	6.0	2	5
6	6	6	5	6	2	5.0	9	6
7	7	7	4	7	7	6.4	4	3
8	8	8	3	8	10	7.4	7	1
9	9	9	2	9	5	6.8	3	2
10	10	10	1	10	1	6.4	1	3

13.10. In effect if we turn our scores into ranks we eliminate the strengths of the individual assessments. We find that this method, notwithstanding its theoretical problems, often gives a good indication of the assessor's intentions. It can often be used in situations where we have not standardized the individual components yet we want all of them to have an equal effect on the overall ranking. If we have negative correlations it is probably the best method to use because our marks are measuring different things and adding them is *not* a rational thing to do. However, the rank of rankings can be compared to a voting system where we are scoring some 'average' judgement of many assessors.

Another way of adjusting marks is to change the marks so that the average contribution for each component is about the same. We can do this by an iterative process. Table 13.11 shows a set of marks in which there is a wide variation in the contribution made by each component even though they were intended to be of equal weight. We can adjust these preliminary results by changing each mark in a component in a linear fashion so that we reduce or increase the mark depending on how close it is to the average. This does not change the relative rankings within a component but changes the standard deviation.

Table 13.11   *Unadjusted marks*

Item	Test 1	Ass 1	Test 2	Ass 2	Total
1	5.75	10	5.6	8.67	30.02
2	9.5	8	6	6.67	30.17
3	6	10	6	8.67	30.67
4	6.75	9	3.4	8.67	27.82
5	9.5	10	10	6.67	36.17
6	7.75	9	6.2	8.67	31.62
7	6.5	10	4.6	6.67	27.77
8	6.5	10	2.8	6.67	25.97
9	7.25	8	4	6.67	25.92
10	2.5	9	5	6.67	23.17
Average	6.80	9.30	5.36	7.47	28.93
Standard Deviation	2.00	0.82	2.00	1.03	3.64
Correlation	0.73	0.29	0.84	0.26	1.00
Contribution	1.46	0.24	1.68	0.27	3.64
Expected Contribution	.91	.91	.91	.91	
Factor	1.60	0.26	1.84	0.30	

Table 13.12 *Adjusted figures*

Item No.	Test 1	Ass 1	Test 2	Ass 2	Total
1	4.58	12.78	5.78	12.52	35.65
2	12.52	2.84	6.48	4.10	25.93
3	5.11	12.78	6.48	12.52	36.88
4	6.69	7.81	1.94	12.52	28.96
5	12.52	12.78	13.45	4.10	42.85
6	8.81	7.81	6.82	12.52	35.96
7	6.16	12.78	4.03	4.10	27.08
8	6.16	12.78	0.90	4.10	23.94
9	7.75	2.84	2.99	4.10	17.68
10	−2.31	7.81	4.73	4.10	14.33
Average	6.80	9.30	5.36	7.47	28.93
Standard Deviation	4.24	4.09	3.49	4.35	9.00
Correlation	0.51	0.54	0.68	0.52	1.00
Contribution	2.16	2.21	2.37	2.26	9.00
Expected	2.25	2.25	2.25	2.25	
Expected	0.96	0.98	1.05	1.01	

The factor shown in the last row of Table 13.11 is obtained by several iterations of dividing the contribution by the total standard deviation multiplied by the expected contribution, ie factor = (contribution ÷ total standard deviation) × expected contribution.

If we keep doing this we gradually converge on a solution providing that there are no negative correlations between any of the components and the total. A closer solution is given in Table 13.12.

As can be seen this makes a large difference in the final rankings and scores of the students. The marks have to be changed a great deal to make the contributions equal *if this is what the examiner intended*. A further example and discussion of this problem can be found in the 'Hardgrind' case study (Imrie, 1981 and 1993).

Assessor feedback

In this chapter we have described processes for analysing marks after they have been obtained. Assessors should, however, try to predict the marks they expect before assigning them. Do they expect students to do well on a test? Are some questions more difficult than others? If these questions are asked before marks are allocated then discrepancies between the predicted and the actual can provide useful information.

One of the simple checks we can make is to compare previous year's results with the current year. Tests are often similar in format and difficulty. If we have been able to improve teaching and assessment procedures then we would expect an improvement in results. Longitudinal evaluation gives us a way of checking if the changes we make in teaching and assessment actually lead to improvements in learning outcomes.

Implementing systems on an institution-wide basis

So far this chapter has described how spreadsheets can be used to record and analyse assessment. Spreadsheets are a valuable tool and are a simple and easy way for individuals to record and analyse their marks. However, they are not the best way. It is better to have simple tools available to all members of staff throughout the institution and integrated with other administrative systems. Here we describe why an institutional system is desirable, what functions it should perform and we shall highlight some of the administrative issues involved in implementing such a system.

An institutional system is desirable because:

- It gives consistency (ie improved quality assurance) to the recording and analysis of marks throughout the institution and makes assessment reports easier for students to understand.
- It makes good assessment recording practices readily accessible to all staff (provided, of course, that adequate password protection is available). The ideas we described earlier in this chapter can be easily used by any member of staff. They do not have to learn how to use a sophisticated spreadsheet software tool before being able to record and analyse marks.
- It provides continuity in recording and reporting practices and acts as an important part of the institutional memory.
- It makes the administrative work of handling marks easier, with less need for checking and with a higher degree of reliability. It can fit seamlessly into other recording systems such as enrolments, examination processing and class lists.

- It makes comparisons across modules, departments and faculties easier and makes a whole new dimension of management statistics available to the teachers and assessors.
- It encourages more effective accountability.

The functions that the system should carry out are those described previously. In summary, the system should allow for recording of marks for all components of assessment and at several levels. We can represent this by the structure shown in Table 13.13.

Table 13.13   *Overall mark for a module*

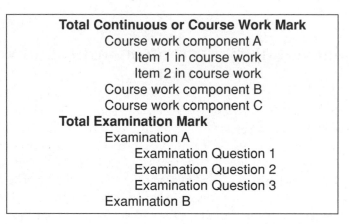

Total Continuous or Course Work Mark
Course work component A
Item 1 in course work
Item 2 in course work
Course work component B
Course work component C
Total Examination Mark
Examination A
Examination Question 1
Examination Question 2
Examination Question 3
Examination B

Computation and data entry facilities

The following list is not exhaustive but is the minimum required for a comprehensive system.

- Each line in Table 13.13 contributes a percentage to the overall mark and each component has a maximum possible mark. The system should allow the entry of marks as letter grades, with number equivalents, or as numbers. The system should provide for analysis of each component and should allow adjustment of any component by one or more methods.
- Data entry should be permitted in various ways. For example, data may be imported from other systems, data may be entered by a student identification number, or by student name or in different tutorial or laboratory groups.
- Simple statistics such as averages, standard deviations, median, maximum, minimum and percentages, should be available on each component.

- Contribution analysis and correlations should be available between components and totals.
- Marks should be able to be arranged by tutorial classes or by other categories such as age and gender, and analyses such as ANOVA should be available to check the variation across categories.
- Simple histogram graphs should be available on all components and totals.
- A variety of reports in different sorting orders should be available.

Institutional integration

In many ways the computational and calculation aspects of the system are less difficult than the administrative requirements of such a system. Once it is decided to establish an institutional system, it must be designed to fit in with the rest of the institution's computing systems. For example, should the system be a centralized one or should it use some form of distributed control? We would suggest a distributed system in which the central administration is given only the data needed for the institution's records. This normally consists of a final mark or grade for each module for each student. All the details are not needed by the central administration and should remain the property of the individual module examiner.

The mechanics of doing this may vary but in a modern system we would suggest that the campus network be used for data transmission and that each administrative unit such as an academic department have its own computer system for assessment records with detailed information about each of the department's modules.

This is preferable to individual lecturers having their own copies of the programs and the system as it reduces the total cost but still does not suffer from the problems of excessive centralization. (In modern computing terminology it is a good candidate for a client/server implementation.)

A system using most of the above ideas has been implemented at City University of Hong Kong. It is used by most lecturers across all faculties. In the first year of operation most lecturers used the system to enter their final coursework and examination marks. It is expected that faculty will use more of the facilities as the system becomes more familiar and trusted. Reference manuals for the system called MPS (Marks Processing System) are available from the Computing Services Centre, City University of Hong Kong.

Problems of authority and access

It is to be expected that different groups of people will be responsible for maintaining the data to which they need regular access but that appropriate procedures will be established to transfer data between groups and to ensure that security is not breached. For example, we may have an individual tutor or teaching assistant attached to a group of students and responsible for recording the coursework marks for the group. Once the tutor is satisfied with the marks, these are passed to the module examiner who is then responsible for the marks from all groups in the module. Once the module examiner has completed the marks analysis and is satisfied with the marks they are passed to the central administration where they are recorded and owned by the institution. Checks and procedures are necessary at each step. Authority access procedures are necessary for all phases of marks analysis. These are non-trivial problems to overcome.

All this processing would be relatively easy if we were dealing simply with batches of students progressing through modules in regular ways. Unfortunately real systems are much more complicated and these complications will vary from institution to institution and within a particular institution. For example, students often have to repeat assessments. Sometimes assessments are deferred. Sometimes extra criteria are established for awarding grades, sometimes the institution wishes to impose limits on the number of grades of particular standing to award. All these problems have to be dealt with and the system must be flexible enough, or incorporate manual systems, to cope with the variations.

14

Evaluation of assessment procedures

Do not condemn the judgement of another because it differs from your own. You may both be wrong.

(Dandemis)

Introduction

Throughout this book we have stressed the importance of assessment as an integral part of teaching and learning, with an emphasis on assisting students to learn more efficiently. We have also flagged the need for universities and colleges to ensure that when they award grades for students' work, these grades should reflect as accurately as possible each student's level of performance and equivalent grades should be comparable from one unit of study to another or even from one institution to another. A possible approach for ensuring intra-institutional compatibility was suggested in the previous chapter and attempts to improve inter-institutional compatibility were described in Chapter 8.

In the present chapter we shall describe some of the factors which affect students' performance in assessment tasks so that we might evaluate the quality of different types of assessment more accurately.

Effects of assessment on learning styles and strategies

As we have seen in the earlier chapters, students' progress in, and satisfactory completion of, a course is almost always measured by some form of assessment which frequently takes the form of a final examination, the marks for which may be combined with marks from progress tests, essays or other assignments. If the final examination is the only form of assessment, it is possible for students to spread their work throughout the period of the course in any way that suits the student – in some cases leaving the major learning tasks to the period immediately preceding the examination. Any misjudgement regarding the amount or type of learning required can have disastrous results for the learner!

During the late 1960s and early 1970s students in institutions where performance was assessed by the one final examination protested about the injustices of this system. They sought and obtained a system of 'continuous assessment' which changed the emphasis from performance in the final examination to include work completed during the course. Sometimes the final examination was abolished or merely retained for those students who wished to improve on their score. Fortunately there appears to have been a healthy reaction to this practice so that institutions and individual examiners are seeking for the best balance between the two forms of assessment. For example, in a recent survey of undergraduates at Loughborough University in the United Kingdom, Kniveton (1996, p. 236) found that there is considerable support for a balanced program of assessment, which combines continuous and end-of-term measures. Students in the survey reported that 'they regard continuous assessment as a fairer process, as a better judge of their ability and as providing more opportunity for them to organize their own work programs'. Kniveton goes on to say:

> It should be emphasized that this finding is based on opinions of the merits of each type of assessment and should not be interpreted as a preference for one type of preference over another. Indeed, if one examines the question which asks them to specify how much of their overall grade should be based on continuous assessment, the average for the whole sample is 51.95 per cent. This certainly does not indicate a total rejection of the idea of examinations nor overwhelming endorsement of continuous assessment. (p. 234)

Those who enthusiastically adopted continuous assessment overlooked the fact that assessment fills many different functions. Feletti (1980), for example, has listed eight different functions for continuous assessment in medical studies. These included giving students opportunities to demonstrate application of knowledge, skills and attitudes; diagnosing particular strengths and weaknesses so that some students may take elective studies while others do remedial work; and assisting students to judge the quality of their own work. Clift and Imrie (1981) and Harris and Bell (1986) refer to links between the assessment of students and the evaluation of courses and teaching, the latter authors reminding us that teachers often use the results of a test to guide them when planning changes to their courses.

With assessment procedures being expected to fulfil such widely differing functions, it is no wonder that teachers and students become confused! The distinction between the 'formative' and 'summative' functions of assessment (see Chapter 2) is not always recognized by those who advocate or practise continuous assessment. Tests, which should be used for the sole purpose of providing feedback to students and teachers on students' progress, are seen as heavy *millstones*, rather than important *milestones*, and have adverse effects on students' learning. Research on student learning, such as that described in Chapter 3, shows that students are more likely to adopt 'surface' learning strategies when the workload is excessive or inappropriate forms of assessment are used (Ramsden, 1984).

The literature on student learning includes many other research studies which examine the effects of assessment procedures on students' study habits and the type of learning which ensues. The influence of assessment on students' perceptions of the curriculum is well illustrated by Bowden *et al.* (1987) who showed that the type of influence varied between faculties and also between subjects within the same faculty. A worrying aspect of their findings was that students in those faculties which require high tertiary entrance scores are more likely to believe that a superficial approach to learning will give them a greater chance of success in their university assignments and examinations.

Given that the type of assessment used may affect the learning strategies adopted by students, there is a danger in assuming that 'the quickest way to change student learning is to change the assessment system', as was tentatively suggested by Elton and Laurillard (1979). Biggs (1996a) questions the validity of this assumption and continues with a discussion of what he calls the 'backwash' effects of examinations:

> The characteristics of the test, and the context in which it is given, may provide the objective basis for backwash effects, but it is the student's perception of the test, and of the demands that it is seen to make, that generate the effects of backwash. Students differ greatly in their ability to read the cues provided, cue seekers being very alert to what will tell them how best to prepare for the test, and go out of their way to optimise, while the cue deaf seem unaffected by backwash (Miller and Parlett, 1974). Further, students' perceptions of what is required, and teachers' own intentions, may be very different. (p. 8)

A compelling point made by Biggs is the difference between the *quantitative* and the *qualitative* traditions in learning and the implications of these for assessment. In the former, learning is perceived as an 'aggregation of content', including facts, skills and competencies. Thus a quantitative view of learning leads to many discrete items of assessment and, even when an essay is being graded, the examiner tends to give a mark for each relevant point made.

By way of contrast, Biggs describes the qualitative tradition as one in which 'students are assumed to learn cumulatively, interpreting and incorporating new material with what they already know, their understanding progressively changing as they learn'. He says that 'the teacher's task is not to transmit correct understanding, but to help students construct understandings that are progressively more mature and congruent with accepted thinking, recognizing that in many subjects students' everyday experiences have helped them to construct alternative frameworks for construing reality'.

If qualitative learning is to be assessed, one must be able to 'discover where students are in the development of understanding or competence in the concept or skill in question'; one also needs to be assured that the student can 'solve a problem involving instructed knowledge in a real context' (Biggs, 1996a). The first of these two features of assessment of qualitative learning would appear to be one of the main functions of 'formative assessment' (Chapter 2) and the second is that which we hope to achieve when assessing students' ability to apply their knowledge and skills in the workplace (Chapter 11) or when we set an examination question which presents a problem in the context of a 'real life' situation.

The present authors have worked with university and college teachers in a number of different countries and cultures over many years, during which time they have observed the development and fairly wide acceptance of those newer theories of learning which Biggs includes in 'the qualitative tradition'. We have observed that even when academics give verbal assent to this developmental theory of learning, there are still many who, in their assessment practices and in the way they teach, regard their task as giving students as many bundles of knowledge or skills as possible in the time allowed. If our observations and assumptions are correct, then it is conceivable that a change in assessment techniques could, after all, bring about changes in students' approaches to learning.

Rather a different approach to the interaction between assessment and approaches to learning has been taken by Docking (1987) who uses the analogy of non-destructive testing of materials in industry in

Table 14.1 *Influences of assessment on student feelings and motivation*

DESTRUCTIVE	CONSTRUCTIVE
Effects on Feelings	
Coerced	Co-operative
Helpless	Adequate
Alienated	Involved
Classified	Self-determined
Demeaned	Encouraged
Stress and anxiety	Excitement and challenge

Effects on Motivation	
Extrinsic motivation	Intrinsic motivation
Competitive	Co-operative
Crammed study	Sustained study
Faking/cheating	Reality/honesty

his description of a system of 'criterion-referenced' tests which are designed to provide precise information to teachers and students on the extent of students' learning without destroying students' incentives to engage in higher levels of learning. He contrasts the effects of 'destructive' versus 'constructive' assessment on students' learning behaviour, feelings, and motivation and on their teachers' behaviour and attitudes. Table 14.1, which is an extract from his larger list of comparisons, focuses on students' feelings and motivation.

Faculty who believe that students respond well to challenge will initially be reassured by the findings of Kings (1987), who conducted a survey of students enrolled in postgraduate diploma courses (excluding the diploma in education). The survey revealed that courses which were more difficult and had higher work demands were more likely to benefit students; they attracted more enrolments and had higher retention and pass rates than courses which students perceived as less demanding. It is important to note that most of the students surveyed were 'mature-age' and had experience in the workforce; and the courses tended to be vocationally oriented. Kings makes the point that 'it is not the amount of work or the level of difficulty *per se* that can result in students acquiring knowledge, skills and abilities but rather the answer lies in the appropriateness of the work'. In other words, it is most important that students see and accept that the assessment tasks are directly related to the requirements of their chosen occupation – that they have 'face validity', an issue which we shall discuss in more detail towards the end of this chapter.

Cue-consciousness

Research conducted by Miller and Parlett (1974) cast further light on ways in which students' perceptions of assessment techniques affect their approaches to study. After a series of interviews of staff and students in the Departments of Law, History and Physics in the University of Edinburgh, the researchers identified three quite distinctive approaches to assessment. They describe their three types of students as being 'cue-deaf', 'cue-conscious' or 'cue-seekers', depending on the extent to which the students are aware of cues concerning what is expected of them in a coming exam and the extent to which they actively seek this information. We shall describe the three categories in reverse order.

Cue-seekers appear to be aware of the way the examination system works; they recognize any problems they may still have in knowing how to perform well, and they deliberately set about solving these problems. Miller and Parlett claim that these students, who are also the best performers, are not just 'playing the system'. They really study hard and are most likely to engage in informal discussions with faculty, these discussions being part of the cue-seeking process. University and college teachers who have made their course objectives clear to students may well wish to encourage more students to adopt an active cue-seeking approach.

The *cue-conscious*, as their name implies, are generally able to recognize cues given by their teachers as to what is required in an examination and will modify their study procedures accordingly, but they do not engage in active cue-seeking.

Cue-deaf students appear to be unable to recognize cues when these are given by teachers; their preparation for assessment is not influenced by anything the teacher says or does.

In describing the above three categories, the present authors do not wish to give the impression that the categories are immutable; in fact from our own experience, both as students and teachers, we have formed the opinion that students who are 'seekers' in one situation may be 'deaf' in another and vice versa. While some students, such as Perry's dualistic thinkers (see Chapter 5 and Perry, 1970 and 1981), are more likely to be cue-deaf, under different circumstances and with a more challenging teacher, they could develop the skills of cue-consciousness or cue-seeking. Over time, maturation should result in more students becoming cue-sensitive.

Double marking of students' work

It is generally acknowledged that it is more difficult for examiners to agree on an appropriate mark or grade for some pieces of students' work than others; this is one of the arguments advanced for a greater use of 'objective tests' similar to those we described in Chapter 9. In order to ensure the fair marking of relatively subjective material, such as essays, sculptures or paintings, musical or dramatic performance, the practice of double (or even triple) marking has been adopted. Some of the complications associated with double marking are identified in a short discussion paper by Partington (1994) who refers to two strong reasons for adopting this practice. The first is to ensure 'that students' results should not be unduly influenced by the personal predilections of the marker', and the second is to provide support for the examiner, and the institution, should there be an appeal by a student. Partington argues that for each of these aims to be achieved it is essential that the second examiner should be unaware of the mark given by the first but that there is, however, a need for the two (or more) markers to agree on the criteria which will be used in assessing students' responses to each examination task. As noted by Kniveton (1996), there is also a need for anonymous work to be marked/double marked to avoid biases related to the marker's preconceptions regarding the student's gender (for example). For more ideas about double marking the reader should consult Chapter 7, where we dealt with the matter in more detail.

External pressures on assessment procedures

Any evaluation of the assessment program in an institution or in particular courses should not overlook the strong possibility that students' performance in examinations or in completing other assessment tasks will be influenced by external factors. These generally fall into one of two categories which we could describe as either natural or institutional. *Natural* factors, such as weather, road accidents and disease, affect the population at large while the *institutional* factors are aspects of the academic or professional world which influence the quality of learning in a university and the success of its students.

Both natural and institutional factors may operate at the personal or the community level, that is they could affect the assessment of individual students or of a whole cohort of students.

The extent to which examiners or institutions are able to take these factors into consideration when planning tests and timetables, or when awarding grades, is debatable. Clearly when there is some major disaster which affects all students, such as earthquake, flood or fire, one would normally postpone examinations or due dates for assignments. The problem really arises when only a few students are affected, perhaps only a single student. Most institutions have provisions for 'special examinations' under such circumstances but there are times when, in an effort to cater for one student with illness or some other unforeseen problem, other students are inadvertently penalized. Some of those who did not apply for special treatment may have had difficulties in their personal circumstances which were as disruptive to study as were those experienced by the student who was granted a deferral. It is therefore essential for each institution to have clearly stated and well-publicized regulations so that all students know the conditions under which extended time or special examinations will be granted.

Many of the external conditions which influence assessment procedures are ephemeral except, perhaps, where they lead to a change in procedures for granting students the right to take special examinations. Balla and Boyle (1994) list a number of factors which may influence assessment practice. Where these forces result in changes for the better, we may regard them as evolutionary – new and more efficient methods of assessment are developed to suit the changing needs of students and the society as a whole. Consistent with this theme of evolutionary change, the authors state that 'pressures have been brought to bear consistently on institutions and units within institutions to critically review and improve practice in assessment of student performance'.

External pressures identified by Balla and Boyle were: external examiners; employers and professional bodies; international developments, and quality or performance indicators. We shall refer briefly to some of these in a later section of this chapter. *Internal* pressures arise when faculty 'evaluate practice within their own institution, department or discipline' (Balla and Boyle, 1994). Indicators of quality and performance are linked with a need to ensure that the assessment has high validity and reliability, two issues which we shall consider in more detail in the next two sections of this chapter.

Ramsden (1982), in reporting on a series of learning research projects in Lancaster (UK), Gothenburg (Sweden) and Newcastle (Australia), noted that two main types of departmental context can be identified, irrespective of discipline. The first he called *control centred*. These were departments which 'combine a heavy pressure to fulfil curricular and assessment demands with a lack of freedom in choosing content and method of study'. The other type he called *student centred*. These are departments where 'there is perceived freedom in learning and good teaching'.

Regardless of discipline, the latter departments were 'more likely to develop an orientation towards meaning' (ie a deeper approach to learning) whereas in the control-centred departments 'students respond by adopting reproducing strategies' (ie a superficial approach to learning with an emphasis on memorization). A more detailed analysis of this research is given by Ramsden and Entwistle (1981).

When we consider the research reported by Ramsden in the light of other research on learning and assessment it is easy to see that there is a possibility for confusion among students if the learning context of the department, its stated objectives and the type of assessment used is in conflict.

Validity

A test is said to be valid when it measures the extent to which the objectives of a teaching program have been achieved. Thus in clinical medicine, one of the objectives could be that students must be able to recognize a particular disease or condition, distinguish it from other conditions with similar symptoms, and prescribe a suitable course of treatment. One test of this subject matter which would *not* meet the criterion of validity would be to ask students to describe the symptoms of this disease and the recommended procedures for treatment. While the second part of the question meets the objectives, the best way to ensure that students can recognize this particular disease from the symptoms is to present them with an actual patient who is suffering from the disease. A reasonable compromise might be for students to be shown photographs, or preferably a video-recording of a number of patients with similar symptoms. The first patient shown could be the one who has the disease or condition; students are asked to identify what is wrong with the patient; what treatment they would prescribe and whether any of the other patients pictured are suffering from the same condition.

A further complexity which might well influence the validity of the above test is that a qualified medical practitioner should know that not all patients can be given the same treatment for a given disease or condition. One needs to take into consideration such matters as the patient's blood pressure, general state of health and other medication being followed. Consequently students must be given the opportunity to seek information on these matters before they prescribe treatment. This is where computer-managed tests are invaluable, particularly now that multi-media packages are available which include video clips or can supply further data on demand. A student who did not seek the additional information about the patient's health or medication would not score as highly as a student who took these other factors into consideration. It is not difficult to imagine similar complex problems in architecture, engineering and ecological management.

Among the many references in the literature to the need for tests which are valid are a number which attempt to distinguish between different types of validity. For example, Benett (1993), while focussing on the need for validity and reliability in the assessment of work-based learning, reviews some of the more general principles. He describes five different types of validity: *face, content, predictive, criterion related* and *construct*. We shall concentrate on the first four types as they are likely to be of greater interest and relevance for our readers. In his paper Benett acknowledges a number of sources for these concepts. The descriptions which follow are based on those given by Benett.

An assessment task is said to have *face validity* if a number of judges – ranging from experts in the field to students – agree that the test item is valid. Wagner (1996) emphasizes the need for taking the student's point of view into consideration when judging the validity of an assessment task and says that this is particularly important in a climate of increasing accountability in the higher education sector.

Content validity is high if a test samples students' learning in a representative range of course content and low if only a small proportion of the course is being tested. As there is no way that a traditional examination can measure the successful achievement of all aspects of a course, there is always some compromise in deter-mining the level of content validity that is acceptable.

According to Benett (1993), *predictive validity* is a measure of the extent to which an assessment scheme is able to 'predict accurately the performance of students in their subsequent professional careers'. We could safely extend this definition to cover the extent to which performance in an introductory course or an entrance examination is able to predict a student's performance in more advanced studies.

Criterion-related validity takes into account independent assessments of students' achievements by such people as experts in the workplace. When these 'experts' are directly responsible for supervising the work of specific students they may be in a good position to judge whether a student's acquisition of particular skills has reached a level which will allow that student to perform adequately tasks which are an essential component of their chosen occupation. It is then appropriate to use the supervisor's report as a major factor in determining the grade a student is to receive for a work experience program. Even so, as the final responsibility for awarding the degree or diploma belongs to the educational institution, it is essential that the institution retains control over the award of grades for each component of the degree program.

Benett (1993) emphasizes the need for regular discussions between students and the workplace supervisors in order that a student's self-assessment meets the necessary criteria. We would add that it is equally important for there to be a continuing dialogue between faculty in professional programs and workplace supervisors so that each group might understand what the other is attempting to achieve. There is a danger that practitioners may be unaware of the broader aims of a university program or of recent research and, on the other hand, academics may have outmoded ideas of what happens in factories, hospitals or other workplaces. A further difficulty arises with this measure of validity when professional organizations attempt to control the criteria for graduates to enter their profession. Again we stress the need for regular consultations between faculty and profession (or industry) when new learning programs are being developed and the criteria for satisfactory performance are being determined.

Reliability

To what extent can one depend on the accuracy of examination marks or grades? Is it possible to say with confidence that a superior mark in a test indicates that a student has performed better (is more knowledgeable) that one who did not score as highly? The following example from Hall and Imrie (1994) illustrates the dilemma encountered when an employer (or, for that matter, an educational institution) attempts to discriminate between applicants on the basis of a fairly small discrepancy in their test scores.

> Imagine that you are an employer looking at the credentials of two job applicants, Bill and Mary. You note that although their background and qualifications are similar, Mary scored 50 in communications skills but Bill managed only 48. Which of these two would get the job? Usually, you would be able to draw upon further information to help you choose but if you haven't, you might pick Mary and reject Bill on the basis of his failure, even though narrow. After all, isn't the magic figure of 50 per cent supposed to be the critical point on the yardstick which measures a person's ability?
>
> At this point, think about this example and list your doubts about the decision to select Mary. You might even want to question the conventional figure of 50 per cent as the pass/fail cut-off point. Why not 70 per cent or 80 per cent?
>
> We recently gave the Bill and Mary example to a group of education students studying test construction. Here are some of the more relevant thoughts of the group.
>
> Is Mary really better than Bill? Just how accurate are the marks awarded to students?
>
> Maybe Bill did pass. Was he scaled down? Did he have a tough marker?
>
> Why was Bill classified as a failure? A mark of 50 or 48 tells you nothing about the skills that Bill and Mary have picked up. Isn't that what employers want?
>
> Did Bill and Mary sit the same examination? How do you know that the exams were of the same difficulty?
>
> Did Bill and Mary attend the same college? If not, can you fairly compare their scores?

Questions such as the above are illustrations of the concept of *reliability* which is defined by Anastasi (1976) in the following terms:

> Reliability refers to the consistency of marks obtained by the same individuals, when re-examined with the same test, on different occasions, or with different sets of equivalent test items, or under other variable assessment conditions. (quoted by Benett, 1993, p. 89)

It will be clear from the above definition, and the questions which preceded it, that there is a close association between the reliability of examinations and the maintenance of standards. Although Anastasi's definition refers to a 'consistency of marks obtained by the same individuals', in practice we are more concerned with maintaining a consistency of grades for *different* individuals who have reached the *same* levels of achievement. It would be rare to use exactly the same measures from one year to another, consequently the items which make up the total assessment must be at similar levels of difficulty. Given these conditions, we must assume that it is unrealistic to expect to achieve 100 per cent reliability; we just aim to make our tests as reliable as is possible.

A lack of attention to reliability leads to situations where standards vary from year to year, or even from one class to another in the same year. For this reason organizations that are responsible for designing tests which are used nationally take great care to minimize any possibility of unreliability. Use of the same test items year after year is clearly undesirable as it would lead to students learning only those items which would be tested and neglecting other sections of the course. Benett (1993) points out that over-concentration on a limited section of the course would reduce the level of *content validity*. He goes on to say that the problem may be overcome by basing assessment on 'a set of tasks which, although not identical, are nonetheless consistent with respect to the key features of interest as far as the assessment is concerned'. He adds:

> Put differently, if there is a certain amount of commonality in the variety of tasks assessed (such as a common theme, purpose, theory or procedure), the common factor which runs through these diverse tasks is likely to bring about some convergence, and hence some consistency in the assessments. (p. 90)

The importance of evaluating assessment procedures

Why should we attempt to evaluate our assessment procedures? We may as well ask why governments inspect instruments which measure the weight or volume of goods which we purchase. The type of assessment used in a university is not only a measure of performance of its graduates; it is indirectly a measure of the success and quality of the university. If the assessment procedures are faulty we can no longer rely on using a student's grades to predict the potential of a graduate in employment (or, at an earlier level, the performance of a student in higher level courses).

Any evaluation of a university course is incomplete unless it takes into consideration the type of assessment used; its validity and relia-bility; the relative time given to teaching, individual learning and assessment of progress, and the effects (if any) of the assessment on the students' learning strategies. The following procedures have been used for evaluating the assessment component of university course or learning programs.

External examiners

External examiners have traditionally been used in British universities as a means of ensuring that standards are upheld and that the formal examinations at least have face and content validity. In most cases the external examiner is supplied with a course outline or syllabus and copies of any relevant examination papers, together with marked answers from a representative range of students. One benefit of this system is that university teachers feel they need to explain why particular assessment tasks have been set; they must also justify the criteria used for grading their students' work. Even though the system of using external examiners has served the British system well in the past, some doubt has been thrown on their continued usefulness in the Dearing Report on higher education in the UK.

Student committees

Student committees may be set up to comment upon, or give approval to, the pattern of assessment for all courses in a particular faculty. For example, they could be asked to approve a pattern which includes three major essays at various stages during the year, with each essay contributing 20 per cent towards the final score and an end-of-year written examination which contributes the remaining 40 per cent. In another situation the student committee might consider the relative weightings to be given to field experience, group projects and a major essay. The major value of such committees is that students are given a say in the type of assessment which will be used. Although these committees cannot be shown advance copies of examination papers, they may express views on the degree of difficulty or fairness of previous papers.

Colleagues

Colleagues are more readily available and allow for a more informal review of an assessment plan than external examiners or student committees. This lack of formality may create difficulties if a suggested plan is thought to be unfair or even unusual. Some university departments attempt to overcome these difficulties by making it a regular practice that every assignment task must be approved by another member of faculty who signs a statement to that effect. One fringe benefit of using colleagues to moderate assessment tasks is that new ideas are shared, the department as a whole tends to take responsibility for all assignments and examinations, and the head of department is in a better position to justify both the procedures and the outcomes.

Student surveys

Student surveys are a regular feature of course evaluations and in some universities are used regularly to rate the quality of teaching. It is relatively easy to include questions seeking students' views on assessment but, as most surveys are conducted before the final exams, they do not provide an opportunity for students to comment on the fairness of questions in these examinations. Imrie (1982) has demonstrated how this can be done and how useful the information can be. Some lecturers attempt to overcome this problem by providing students with an opportunity to complete a questionnaire (or, perhaps, to write some general comments) after they have finished their examination, but response rates under such conditions are likely to be low and therefore unreliable. Questioning second-year students about their exams at the end of the previous year provides responses from a biased sample – only those who have passed and have decided to enrol in the second year of the subject.

Departmental reviews

Departmental reviews have been introduced into some universities as part of a quality assurance or control program. Their function is to ensure that the department or centre being reviewed is functioning as well as it might, given the resources available. The review committee may consist of academics in a similar field (possibly from another institution), teachers and administrators from other parts of the same institution, and representatives of academics, general staff and students from within the department being reviewed. As part of the review, the committee may also seek information about failure rates for each course taught within the department or it may attempt to assess the quality of its graduates by looking at their destinations.

In a similar manner, reviews by *professional bodies* will consider whether the assessment procedures are appropriate – including the assumptions and procedures for grading or for honours classification.

Accreditation agencies

Accreditation agencies, such as the former Council for National Academic Awards in the United Kingdom, were a regular part of the review process for polytechnics and similar colleges prior to 1990 when most of these institutions either became universities or were absorbed into existing universities. Such agencies try to ensure that standards are maintained across the institutions for which they are responsible, but there is a danger that in gathering information about teaching programs and assessment they will pay more attention to the processes than to the quality of assessment.

While each of the above procedures has its place in ensuring that assessment standards are maintained and improved, probably the most effective influence on the quality of assessment is the individual university teacher. Every teacher has countless opportunities for examining critically the value of the tests and assignments which are set for his or her own students. A wealth of data is already available or may be readily obtained concerning the performance of different categories of students or the time each student takes to complete particular tasks. These data may be correlated with other data describing students' characteristics or their performance in other tests and thus form the basis of a research project. If the assessment of students' performance in higher education is to be improved it is essential that university teachers should respond to the challenge that research into teaching and learning is as legitimate and as necessary as research into the subject discipline. Pedagogical research is a valid part of the scholarship that should characterize the professional academic.

15

Academic (dis)honesty

The best measure of a man's honesty isn't his income tax return. It's
the zero adjust on his bathroom scale.

(Arthur C Clarke)

Copy from one, it's plagiarism; copy from two, it's research.

(Wilson Mizner [1876–1933])

Introduction

Academic honesty is essential to the academic life of the university.
Thus, academic dishonesty, such as cheating or plagiarism, is a basis
for disciplinary action. (Smith, 1995)

We are indebted to Kandis Smith, University of Missouri, for the
above succinct statement of university policy. We also acknowledge
the contributions of other colleagues who courteously responded to
a request for information on policy and practice relating to plagiarism or academic dishonesty, sent to the HEPROC-L (1995) list on
the Internet. For example, Roger Landbeck (1995), University of
the South Pacific, sent us USP information and kindly copied to me
a similar e-mail request to another listserver by Stuart Marks, School
of Information Systems, Kingston University, England. In turn,
Marks generously sent the paper he had prepared for consideration
by a board of studies (Marks, 1995).

From the University of Hong Kong, David Gardner arranged for
us to receive a copy of his booklet, *PLAGIARISM and How to Avoid
It* (Gardner, 1995) produced by the School of Research Studies, the
English Centre, and the School of Professional and Continuing
Education, to address the needs of an increasingly diverse student
population. This chapter, then, draws upon a wide sample of international experience to address issues and implications of academic
dishonesty for both staff and students.

In particular, for coherence, there is continuing reference to the clear and comprehensive information on academic dishonesty from McMaster University sent by Mary Keyes (1995), Assistant Provost (Student Affairs). The following policy preamble statement is unambiguous:

> Cheating, in whatever form, is ultimately destructive of the values of the university: it is furthermore unfair and discouraging to those students who pursue their studies honestly. This University thus states unequivocally that it demands scholarly integrity from all its members and that it will impose sanctions on those who directly or indirectly contribute to the weakening of this integrity. (p. 1)

Academic honesty or integrity is the academic business of all members of the university – an individual as well as a collective responsibility. While this chapter is primarily about students, faculty have even greater professional responsibilities to be good role models, ie to practise what is preached about academic honesty and to monitor peer and student performance. Values are also emphasized in the following statement of academic honesty policy sent by Betsy Whittaker (Whittier, 1995), Office of Communications, Whittier College, California. Appropriately, the statement appears immediately after the section referring to the Code of Students' Rights and Responsibilities — published annually in the Student Handbook: 'Acts of academic dishonesty are lies. They degrade our shared search for understanding as a community of scholars, and they undermine the integrity of that community by injecting falsehood into our dialogue.'

Issues addressed include definitions, regulations and guidelines, ethics, context, student and staff (faculty) development, and quality assurance. Implications are discussed.

Plagiarism defined

From McMaster University (Keyes, 1995): 'Academic dishonesty is not qualitatively different from other types of dishonesty. It consists of *misrepresentation by deception or by other fraudulent means*.' (emphasis as in the original)

In a university's regulations, a student will probably find a definition for academic dishonesty or plagiarism – a selection of definitions is appended to this chapter for reference. A student might also consult a dictionary but this is unlikely! Such a dictionary definition of *to plagiarize* is: 'to appropriate (ideas, passages, etc) from another (work or author)' (Collins, 1983). Plagiarism is the act of plagiarizing and is attributed to a Latin source: *plagiarus* – plunderer, from *plagium* – kidnapping.

Because it is an act, some universities include intention in an operational definition; this makes the matter much more complex and lends itself readily to a defence by the student. Another related defence is that the student did not know that a particular act was academically dishonest. In both cases, it is the responsibility of the university to provide clear definitions and clear guidelines as part of systematic student development. This will be an important part of the student's induction to the academic culture of the campus. The 'culture' might vary for each faculty but there should be sufficient overlap or commonality with the overall institutional culture.

Some universities focus solely on plagiarism or 'plagiarism and dishonest practice' (USP, 1994). Other universities include plagiarism in a list of definitions of academic dishonesty including cheating which can take various forms or further definitions. Indeed, Franklyn-Stokes and Newstead (1995) list 20 cheating behaviours including different forms of plagiarism. Whittier College lists eight categories to indicate 'the range of conduct which violates academic honesty' (Whittier, 1995):

1. plagiarism
2. submission of same work in two courses
3. unauthorized collaboration
4. cheating (misrepresentation and fraud)
5. misrepresentation of experience or ability
6. falsification of records
7. sabotage
8. complicity in any of the above.

Items 5, 6 and 7 are not directly related to assessment of student performance but represent other aspects of academic dishonesty.

Issues and implications

An issue already mentioned is that of 'intention' in regard to academic dishonesty. One approach is represented by statements in the Hong Kong Polytechnic University's (HKPU, 1996) *Student Handbook* which notes five dictionary definitions of plagiarism and concludes that 'plagiarism involves the idea of intending to plagiarize' and that 'it is important to realize that this dishonest intention will be assumed'. A different approach is suggested by Marks (1995) who notes that intention to deceive may be an additional disciplinary factor in some UK university regulations; he cites the Data Administrator, University of Sussex: '... in every plagiarism case I have been involved in, the student's case is always that there was no deliberate intent' (Richards, 1995).

The following illustration of 'intention' (Charter, 1995) is from a law student's affidavit to the High Court in the UK. She successfully argued against allegations of plagiarism to win a reassessment of her third class degree.

> I was given no advice or guidance about the format and layout of a project of this size and was certainly not told about the need for footnotes or how to refer to source materials used ... I am trying to argue it could not have been plagiarism because I did not intend it and I referenced the book as I had always done.

The first part of the argument deals with the need for student guidelines and development on how to write academically. The second part is the student's perception of both plagiarism and intention.

The issue of intention can be resolved by using the HKPU approach and placing the responsibility clearly with the student. The implications are that the regulations must be clearly stated, with comprehensive definitions, and that this information should be included in the student handbook or catalogue. Further, all such information should be discussed widely throughout the institution – by faculties, student affairs' office, students' union. Guidelines should be prepared and include 'worked examples' (eg CELT, 1994; Gardner, 1995; HKPU, 1996; Reid, 1995; Whittier, 1995). Appropriate programs of student development should be provided – at undergraduate and postgraduate level.

In view of the example of the law student, it is pertinent to note the statement on plagiarism given to postgraduate students on 'How to write a law paper':

> This department views with the gravest concern the action of a student who plagiarizes the work of another person. Plagiarism simply means the taking and using as one's own the thoughts and writings of another. To indulge in literary theft of this kind is highly unethical and ultimately self-defeating. (CityU, 1996)

When Croucher (1996) wrote *Exam Scams*, the back cover of the book stated that he had 'uncovered excuses and cheating techniques used by students around the world to avoid exams, to assist their memories or to explain poor marks'. His book attracted considerable media attention in Australia (including 30 radio and five television interviews). No one, least of all academic managers, should underestimate the amount and range of academic dishonesty in their institutions. In an earlier paper, Croucher (1994) noted that cheating 'seems to have reached epidemic proportions' in some Australian universities; also that, in 1991, he had become aware that it was an international problem. His conclusion is self-evident and should not be ignored: 'One thing is certain, cheating will not disappear if it is ignored.'

In a US Department of Education briefing report *Academic Dishonesty among College Students* (Maramark and Maline, 1993) the question was posed, 'Is there an epidemic of cheating on college campuses?' The answer: 'Today, nearly every published article on academic dishonesty concludes that student cheating on US campuses is both rampant and on the rise.' The report lists 26 examples of cheating activities.

Fishbein (1993) reports an initiative on promoting academic integrity at Rutgers University and the word 'rampant' appears again: 'Students confirmed recent research, telling us that cheating was so rampant that those who might not have cheated in a more honest climate felt compelled to do so to compete and survive.' This is clearly crucial to the concept of a 'campus culture' and the comprehensive recommendations included new and revised procedures for dealing with cheating, also the provision of a non-credit course on academic integrity. As noted by Mark (1995) and others (eg Kibler and Kibler, 1993), 'If we believe in academic integrity, we must teach it.'

Regulations

Statements in regulations should be both clear and comprehensive. These are statements of policy, and there is a professional responsibility to ensure that the policy is implemented. Marks (1995) noted that some universities require all students to sign an agreement. A US example (Fox, 1995) has an agreement relating to withdrawal, dismissal and satisfactory academic progress, that reserves the right to dismiss a student for 'deliberate dishonesty including cheating, plagiarism, giving false information, altering institutional documents'.

McMaster University has a Senate Committee on Academic Dishonesty. The Senate resolutions are comprehensive and set out procedures in cases of academic dishonesty. These include:

- the responsibilities of the instructor, marker, or invigilator, associate dean and the appropriate faculty committee
- the status of the student while under investigation
- the terms of reference of the faculty committee, appeals procedures and the transcript notations.

Of particular interest are the Senate's resolutions on guidelines for reducing opportunities for cheating (Keyes, 1995).

Regulations usually provide for appeals for special consideration of individual cases. Each year when there are examinations or important assessment deadlines, there will be a range of circumstances that will result in a student missing the examination or deadline, or having impaired performance. The main reasons include illness, accident, and family circumstances such as bereavement. For these special circumstances, most universities make provision for special consideration based on written application and supporting evidence, eg doctor's certificate. Falsification of special circumstances is a category of academic dishonesty and incidence rates can be monitored to detect trends. This was the procedure used by Croucher (1995) who noted a 'disturbing increasing trend' of special consideration cases at an Australian university between 1979 and 1993.

Guidelines

There is a case for each academic department or faculty to publish its own guidelines for academic honesty and to use these for student development – ie the development of knowledge, understanding, skills and values – in a discipline context. This is an induction issue – the induction of the student into the culture of the university with variations, as appropriate, at the faculty level. The implications are to ensure that students are involved in the issues and in the related practices. Good practice is illustrated by the following examples.

The first is from Gardner (1995) who, after defining plagiarism, writes to students: 'So, have I got your attention? I hope so because I now want to admit that this booklet is not only about plagiarism. The way to avoid plagiarism is to be a better academic writer.' Gardner goes on to give examples of techniques for avoiding plagiarism, expressing opinions, giving references and using footnotes/endnotes. He then provides examples of 'source texts' together with student texts paraphrasing the sources, and his analysis of the student texts. Finally, and consistent with the aim of student development, the booklet provides details of language enhancement opportunities provided by the English Centre.

The second example is from Northern Illinois University where, as part of the Freshman English Program, all freshmen are required to take a writing class in the first semester during which a *Statement on Plagiarism* (dated 1988) is distributed and discussed in class (Griffin, 1995). The *Undergraduate Catalog* includes the university regulations with the clear statement that 'Students are guilty of plagiarism, intentional or not …' A third example is the document on guidelines on avoiding plagiarism issued by the English Resources Unit (CELT, 1994) of the University of the South Pacific. A final example is from the University of Wyoming: Reid (1995) distributes a handout with examples of good practice when paraphrasing or referring to a source. Reid also makes the point that she has to do more with international students 'since cultural understandings of text ownership vary so widely'. This relates to issues of context.

Context

External to the institutional context, there are the issues of national and international standards or expectations regarding academic dishonesty (staff and students). Internationally, disciplines through their journals and professional bodies set and maintain standards but sanctions are usually the responsibility of the institution.

Within an institution, the Senate and faculty boards have responsibility for policy for academic honesty while faculty have the crucial responsibility for policy implementation or for policing student performance. Perhaps it is more appropriate to discuss this as a stewardship responsibility for the values and standards of academic culture. Presumably, institutional and international norms should have much in common. As mentioned previously, most universities operate in an international setting with significant numbers of students coming from other countries with different 'cultural understandings of text ownership', as noted by Reid (1995). The corollary is the situation of academics working in overseas universities as expatriates with cultural assumptions different because of past experience.

The cultural understanding of academic (dis)honesty needs the awareness of the university (faculty or department). This can only be achieved through informed debate which, in turn, requires research and reflection involving staff and students. Once a methodology is established, trends can be monitored and publicized so that new students and new staff (particularly teaching assistants and part-time staff) clearly understand the issues and the implications. In an important sense, there should be an ongoing strategy of public relations and consciousness-raising with annual reports including cases where formal action has been taken. Academic honesty is a keystone for the reputation of all academic institutions and must be accepted and acted upon as a collective responsibility by staff and students alike – reputations are at stake!

Code of ethics

Some universities have a code of ethics for staff and a charter or code of students' rights and responsibilities. Clearly, academic honesty should be included in such declarations. The process of engaging the members of a university (staff and students) in a debate to develop codes or charters would have considerable intrinsic value for the development of a campus culture. The outcomes would then have value in terms of policy and as the basis for operational guidelines as discussed earlier. There would also be a benefit from a PR point of view in terms of public perception of the university.

An additional operational implication would be for a university to consider establishing an ombudsman — one example being that of Northern Illinois University (Griffin, 1995) which established the Office of the University Ombudsman in 1968. NIU policy now makes the following provision, relevant to cases of academic dishonesty:

> Students who have grievances relating to a denial of freedom, a denial of due process, or inequality of treatment have recourse to the Student Judicial Office, the Ombudsman, or the Student Association for assistance in resolving such grievances.

Student development and perception

Information distributed to students at the commencement of their studies (undergraduate or postgraduate) is essential for student development of academic honesty. As noted previously, such information should include policy, guidelines and worked examples. There should be opportunities for discussion and practice, preferably as part of a credit-bearing program on writing or management of information.

An excellent example of material prepared for students is the student handbook (McNaughton, 1995) written 'to enable students to master the techniques required to produce research papers up to international academic and scholarly standards'. The handbook gives clear examples and also serves the purpose of leaving staff in no doubt about departmental policy and good practice.

The work of Franklyn-Stokes and Newstead (1995) indicates other areas for student development. Their research on cheating not only identified 20 such behaviours but also sought to identify reasons for the behaviour. The main reasons reported were 'time pressure' and 'to increase the mark'. This UK study also reported that North American research indicated stress and pressure for good grades as the main reasons for cheating. There seems to be close correspondence for these research findings, and one implication might be that students would benefit from development programs on time and stress management.

Another UK study (Ashworth *et al.*, 1997) of student perceptions is based on interviews of 19 students, mainly mature students (12) and from one university (11). The findings identify plagiarism as a 'more specific level' of cheating. Student reactions to cheating and their perceptions of the role and responsibilities of their university are discussed. Since cheating and plagiarism are basically moral issues, students, staff and institutional commitment are required.

In themselves, such studies could also provide the basis for student or staff development programs on academic (dis)honesty. It is relevant to note some of the findings of Franklyn-Stokes and Newstead (1995): 'The most commonly reported reason (89 per cent) was "to help a friend" – this in relation to "allowing own coursework to be copied by another student".' Over half of the students sampled by Franklyn-Stokes and Newstead were involved in the following cheating behaviours:

- allowing coursework to be copied
- paraphrasing without acknowledgment
- altering and inventing data
- increasing marks when students mark each other's work
- copying another's work

- fabricating references
- plagiarism from a text. (p. 169)

Franklyn-Stokes and Newstead add:

> Staff (faculty) may well be, at the very least, somewhat naive about the extent and nature of cheating … there may be considerable copying, collusion and plagiarism involved in coursework, and it may be the case that increases in the amount and importance of course-work are actually encouraging students to cheat. (p. 170)

Quality assurance

Quality is an issue when addressing academic dishonesty of students. There are two aspects for consideration. The first is to determine that what is being assessed is the student's own work, ie no copying or collusion involving other students; the second to assess whether there has been any plagiarism. Quality control relates to the detection of academic dishonesty and the consequent actions; quality assurance relates to the procedures used to encourage academic honesty and for its detection.

The National Committee of Inquiry into Higher Education (in the UK) highlighted a need to restore a 'qualified trust' between higher education institutions, students and the public funders of higher education (Dearing, 1997, Section 10.69). Provision is to be made for students, employers or staff who have complaints to take action (Rec. 24).

As noted above, course work is susceptible to academic dishonesty. First-year students are vulnerable for a number of reasons. First, there is an increasing diversity of prior experience of what might be considered (if at all) to be academic honesty. Second, there are usually large numbers of students taking first-year or freshman courses so there is a considerable assessment load. In turn this often requires multiple markers (assessors) thus reducing the likelihood of detecting some forms of academic dishonesty. Fourth, there is now the widespread practice of using postgraduate students (and other part-time staff) as teaching assistants to cope with the assessment load. These teaching assistants require programs to develop an understanding of policy and operational implications as previously discussed. Such programs would form part of their professional induction reinforced on an ongoing basis by the role models of senior faculty acting as supervisors or mentors.

Some definitions

Faculty of Education, The University of Sydney, Australia:

Plagiarism is the verbatim use of another person's work as if it is the student's own work. If students take the writing of a published author and present it as their own, this constitutes plagiarism. Sometimes this is done unintentionally because of poor research habits; sometimes it is quite deliberate. In either case, plagiarism is unacceptable.

Department of History, University of Western Ontario, Canada:

In writing scholarly papers, you must keep firmly in mind the need to avoid plagiarism. Plagiarism is the unacknowledged borrowing of another writer's words or ideas.

Faculty of Technology, Kingston University, England (from the University of Sussex):

Plagiarism is the use, without acknowledgment, of the intellectual work of other people and the act of representing the ideas or discoveries of another as one's own in written work submitted for assessment.

Department of Education and Psychology, The University of the South Pacific, Fiji:

The Department is deeply opposed to plagiarism, which usually takes the form of passing off somebody else's work as one's own, either by copying all or part of somebody else's assignment or by using whole sentences or paragraphs from published work without acknowledgment.

Student Handbook on Writing Research Papers, Department of Chinese, Translation and Linguistics, City University of Hong Kong:

'Plagiarism' can be defined as the attempt to gain advantage for yourself – academic advantage, financial advantage, professional advantage, advantage of publicity – by trying to fool someone, such as a teacher, an editor, an employer, or a reader, into thinking that you wrote something, thought something, or discovered something which, in actual fact, someone else wrote, thought or discovered. Plagiarism is sometimes defined, aphoristically, as 'literary theft'.

Student Handbook, The Hong Kong Polytechnic University:

Plagiarism is defined as the representation of another person's work as the candidate's own, without proper acknowledgment of the source, other than in the case of material that is of common knowledge in the field of concern and therefore needs no citing of authority.

Whittier College, California, USA:

Presenting the words or ideas of another person requires proper acknowledgment; failure to do so is plagiarism. Two examples of plagiarism and an example of proper acknowledgment may be found immediately following these definitions (of other forms of academic dishonesty).

Undergraduate-Graduate-Professional Catalog, University of Missouri – St Louis:

One form of academic dishonesty is plagiarism – the use of an author's ideas, statements, or approaches without crediting the source.

—— 16 ——

Current and future developments

Current and future developments

Education ... has produced a vast population able to read but unable to distinguish what is worth reading.

(GM Trevelyan)

Introduction

In the preceding chapters we have described developments in educational theory and practice which have influenced the methods used for assessing students' performance in higher education. Our surveys of the literature on assessment and descriptions of current practice in innovative institutions suggest some of the directions which one might expect university faculty to follow in developing more effective and relevant methods of assessing their students' performance.

Attempts to predict the future in educational practice are fraught with difficulty as the influences for change are so varied. Internationally, these influences may be economic, political, techno-logical and even philosophical! Even in the same country, different universities, at different times, will engage in 'future developments' in assessment.

Past innovations such as teaching machines and programmed texts have indeed passed out of favour. With the widening availability of computer-based technology, there will be ongoing development of the appropriate use of objective tests, self-paced learning and competency-based assessment, for example. The enduring question for any development in assessment will be, 'Is it fit for its purpose?' Purposes of assessment were discussed in Chapter 1.

For example, there is a need for more consultation with potential employers (not only in the professions) when determining assessment tasks in order that these tasks might be seen as more relevant to the type of work for which a university graduate is supposedly qualified. While developing closer links with industry, commerce and the professions, universities will recognize the dangers of allowing outside organizations to take control of the curriculum. An important overlapping consideration is that professional and employer bodies view the academic/vocational qualification as an *employment qualification* that does not always meet expectations. Purpose of qualification and therefore of assessment must be clearly understood by all concerned.

Teaching and learning quality process review (TLQPR)

During the 1980s and the 1990s, governments (or their agencies) in different countries used various intervention strategies to change practices in universities. The strategies were variously termed 'appraisal', 'audit', 'review', 'assessment', and were linked with 'quality'. This is not the place to discuss these developments, which have significantly changed universities and university systems. TLQPR is selected as a model which has features likely to be developed in the future but with some deficiencies related to student performance, learning and assessment.

In Hong Kong, in March 1994, following the earlier introduction of a research assessment exercise, the University Grants Committee (UGC) sent out a draft consultation paper on their proposed teaching and learning quality assessment exercise (TLQAE). Consultation and reflection resulted in modification of the proposed TLQAE in the form of process audits. This was a good decision and highly significant in that it ensured that there would not be separate quality assessment and quality audit as in the UK. Accordingly, the name was changed to Teaching and Learning Quality Process Audit (TLQPA) and, in 1996, 'audit' was changed to 'review' (without consultation) resulting finally in TLQPR!

The original consultation paper was recast as an information paper, *Assessment of Teaching and Learning Quality* (UPGC, 1994) which set out expectations of a 'quality institution' in the form of principles and also addressed the question, 'How to measure teaching and learning quality?' The subsequent framework document (UGC, 1996) provided 'a way of thinking about teaching and learning quality' and was the common basis for the different HEIs in their preparation for the TLQPR.

The framework also described teaching and learning processes in terms of the following five sub-processes (elements) and institutions were expected to organize their documentation accordingly: curricular design; pedagogical design; implementation quality; outcomes assessment and resource provision. For its TLQPR, City University of Hong Kong added a sixth 'missing' sub-process: 'enhancement of the student experience', on the basis that this should be explicit. In this regard, 'assessment *for* student learning; assessment of performance' should also be made explicit and should be a future development.

A reflective TLQPR seminar was held (UGC, 1997) and there was a strong consensus among the seven participating HEIs that the TLQPR had been successful; also that it should continue and be improved in the light of experience. As has been the experience in other countries with similar exercises, TLQPR had an impact *because* it was an external intervention by a funding body.

Computer-based examination/assessment

Computer-managed learning has been used and available since the early 1960s with projects such as *Plato* (http://www.tro.com). It became more widespread as the cost of computing dropped with the widespread introduction of personal computers from the mid-1980s. The World Wide Web (WWW) is the latest technology which is likely to reduce computing costs by an order of magnitude and has the potential to make the techniques affordable to many users.

The WWW is likely to have a much greater impact than previous technologies because it is cheaper to deliver, cheaper to organize and it is easier to use to disseminate and promulgate techniques. The WWW does not necessarily introduce new techniques; on the contrary it uses the well known and successful. These techniques do not claim to 'teach' so much as to manage learning. In the past the major reasons for the relatively slow adoption of these technologies have been cost and availability. With the reduction in cost and easing of access we can expect the technology of managing learning and assessment to become more pervasive. The key issue is the conceptual shift from *teaching* (the discipline) to *managing* student learning. In itself, the technology is not sufficient;

pedagogical techniques are essential to take full advantage of the techniques.

Examples of how this can be done can be found at the City University of Hong Kong website <http://wwwtools.cityu.edu.hk>. The assessment techniques are well known and are used by millions of teachers throughout the world using manual methods. What is different with the WWW is that the technology is easy to obtain and use. The software and hardware are available to any teacher or student anywhere in the world who has access to the WWW. No special skills are required by teachers or students other than the ability to use the WWW. WWW-based techniques are cost effective, time effective and have the potential to improve feedback and enhance professional judgement.

Examples of some of the tools at http://wwwtools.cityu.edu.hk are Quizzes On-line, Tester and Photo Album (see also CityU, 1997).

Quizzes On-line enables teachers to create on-line quizzes and students to respond on-line. Records are kept of student attempts and reports are created to help students understand how they are progressing *and* to inform the teacher of the learning difficulties of students.

Photo Album is an on-line display of students' portraits, names and e-mail addresses. This helps teachers remember students' names in an environment where much of the contact between teacher and student is through electronic mail. Having students' photographs available is important in assessment as it helps teachers to recall individual students and their difficulties.

Tester is a system for giving assignments and automatically collecting and recording student work. It does not attempt to mark assignments but records the work of students and collects the completed assignments for teachers to mark. Teachers can view the results and then send comments directly to particular students. In an electronic age when students prepare assignments electronically this saves the whole cycle of printing. It also makes it easy for teachers and students to keep a record of student progress.

Although it is prosaic and seemingly simple, the issue of record keeping is crucial in helping manage students' learning. With large numbers of ever-changing students the book-keeping burdens on teachers can be overwhelming. Properly managed electronic communications and record storage have the potential to make management of learning a practical reality rather than an expensive and time-consuming chore.

Teachers and students alike can benefit from electronic record keeping. In the future students will have their own home page on the WWW. Each student will be able to keep a record of his or her work for review and reference. Computer-managed learning in the personal sense will become available to all students. Good record keeping is an aid to individuals in keeping track of their own development and in helping them assess and evaluate their own learning experiences. In effect, individual portfolios can be readily compiled and maintained.

The Curtin University of Technology in Western Australia has been using a learning management system for a number of its courses since 1985 (Curtin University, 1997), a brief description of which may be found on the Internet (www.curtin.edu.au/curtin/dept/cc/academic/cml). The University states that 'the computer provides a feedback function rather than a direct instructional role, and can be used to highlight/manage resources.'

The Department of Anatomy and Human Biology in the University of Western Australia (UWA, 1997) also uses the Internet as an integral part of the delivery and assessment system for its courses. Bunt (1997) reports:

> We use portfolios in assessment in 309 Investigative Human Biology at UWA (a course taken by science students although also open to lawyers, etc; see http://130.95.96.201 for content details). Students are expected to extract information from lectures, TV, media, WWW, references on subjects such as ethics, euthanasia, vivisection, etc. This forms a (small) part of their final assessment.

In the UK, the University of Luton will continue to develop a university-wide computerized assessment system based on 'Question Mark Designer for Windows'. This is an on-line system without paper. Students sit in front of terminals which deliver the examination paper and they respond by keyboard. Management of paper is improved and paper costs are reduced. The problems of handwriting are eliminated or reduced, such as:

- lack of clarity, difficulty of interpretation
- variation in writing speed
- lack of practice – students will use keyboards in the future
- English as a second language.

In 1996–97, approximately 9,000 students sat summative exams (estimated 14,000 in 1997–98); also in 1996–97 1,000 students undertook formative assessments (2,000 estimated for 1997–98). 'It has taken four years of steady growth to achieve university-wide impact.'

Computer Adaptive Testing (CAT) is, as its name implies, administered by a computer in which the difficulty level for each new question is adapted according to a student's response to earlier questions. The Educational Testing Service (ETS) in Princeton, New Jersey, has developed a series of CATs, information about which is obtainable on the Internet at <http://etsis1.ets.org/adap.html>. ETS (1997) gives the following brief description of the nature of CAT:

> Adaptive testing means that the sequence of test questions presented to each student and the questions themselves will vary because they are based on responses to prior test questions. The same student taking the same test twice in succession will almost always receive different questions ... The difficulty of the questions is quickly and automatically adapted to the capability of the individual student. So, challenging tests corresponding to each student's skill level are always provided ... Because of the adaptive nature of the tests, the questions presented on successive tests will vary, which greatly reduces the effects of repeated practice on the tests.

Two institutions where CAT is used and which describe their offerings on the Internet are the Center for Advanced Research on Language Acquisition in the University of Minnesota (CARLA, 1997) and Indiana University – Purdue University Indianapolis (IUPUI, 1997). The former uses CAT in its Center for Advance Research on Language Acquisition; the latter in its placement testing.

Some other developments which are already taking place and are likely to become more widespread in the future include WWW quizzes and provision for 'time to complete' considerations.

Expert system project assessment (THESYS)

THESYS is a computer-based, expert system package to assist with final-year undergraduate project assessment. It is intended for use by assessors and students, and was initially developed for the UK Department of Employment by a team based at Nottingham Trent University (Gentle, 1995). The development involved extensive surveys of the needs of students and staff across many of the more popular disciplines concerning the operation and assessment of final-year degree projects. These results were combined with the findings of a major national survey to produce a list of the main features of project work considered by experienced tutors in assessment. Finally a group of the most experienced tutors ranked these features and weighted them according to how they would take them into account when producing a final assessment.

This information was then installed within an expert system shell as a series of 38 questions, each reinforced by an optional explanatory screen, to which the user responds by moving a cursor over a sliding scale. In this way *a profile of the student's performance* in all aspects of project work is built up and a recommended mark generated, based on historically known statistical distributions, together with advice about what are the best features of the work and where effort could be focussed to improve the assessment.

THESYS is not specific to any academic discipline and the weightings of the various features are fixed. This is specifically because it is not intended to replace the assessor. In using the system the assessor's *judgement remains essential* and irreplaceable. As with any expert system, the purpose is to free the real experts from the mundane tasks which normally prevent them from using their expertise to the full. THESYS is particularly useful in providing *an impartial means of maintaining quality* in what is arguably the single most important assessment of many degree courses. In operation across the UK it has proved valuable in:

- giving students a clear statement on assessment criteria, advice on how to plan and execute the project, and information on how to write the thesis (or dissertation) in order to obtain not just the best mark but also the maximum educational benefit.
- giving new staff information, and reminding old hands, of the assessment criteria, how to run a typical project and cope with problems, and how to produce an objective final mark. In this way it provides an effective mechanism for transmitting recognized best practice.
- ensuring a reasonable degree of commonality of standards across different assessors and providing arbitration advice in any disagreements between examiners.

Student portfolios and student development

It is predicted that there will be continuing development of the student portfolio as a basis for assessment and for career reference. Just as the professional portfolio (or dossier) is well established for career purposes and for continuing professional development so, too, will there be similar expectations for learning and for teaching portfolios.

The student (learning) portfolio will become part of institutional policies for student development which will include training in the skills of being an effective student. Understanding and preparing for assessment should be included in the student development programs provided by any university that cares for the quality of the student experience. Students will receive guidance for preparation of the portfolio. It will have the potential of a 'progress file' to provide a 'means by which students can monitor, build and reflect upon their personal development' (Dearing, 1997 Rec. 20).

Students in the School of Design at the Temasek Polytechnic in Singapore must submit a portfolio as part of their assessment. Koh-Kwok (1997) writes that, across the campus, 'there seems to be a sudden awakening to the immense possibilities and good in using the portfolio as a means of development and assessment'. She adds that another department is planning to use portfolios as an integral part of character education, personal development and career education for its students.

The University of Waikato (New Zealand) is developing a scheme for assessing students' participation in a 12-month work experience program in the School of Science and Technology. Halsey (1997) writes that the present *Industry Report* requires students to describe:

1.   the structure of the organization in which they have worked
2.   their learning objectives
3.   a description of the work they have done
4.   the results of their work.

They also discuss the project as a whole and provide a summary. She goes on to say: 'In the future I hope to enhance the students' workplace experience by asking more of the student in terms of: reflective practice, self-appraisal, solving problems "creatively" and increasing the opportunities to practise communication skills (especially oral).'

Forbes (1997) reports that the building of a portfolio which documents a student's progress in a course is a vital contributor to that student's development. The portfolio, originally called a 'progression document', was one of the requirements for the award of a Diploma in Agribusiness at the Orange Agricultural College, now part of the University of Sydney. The original guidelines on progression documents may be seen on the Internet (OAC, 1997a).

Concurrent with the upgrading of the diploma to a degree course new guidelines were produced for students in the Bachelor of Business (Agricultural Commerce) program. Smith (1997) reports that progression documents have been renamed 'development documents' (OAC, 1997b, c), as it was felt that the latter title more accurately reflects their intent. The preamble to *Development Document A* states:

> Development Documents have been designed to assist students to integrate aspects of their personal and professional development. The process of writing a Development Document will encourage you to think critically about your aspirations and the steps you will need to take towards achieving them.

Another example of portfolio assessment development at the University of Hong Kong (Tang and Biggs, 1997) is described by Tang (1997).

> Portfolio assessment is considered to be a student-centred approach to assessment based on constructivist learning theories which have in common the idea that knowledge is constructed by the *learners* through *learner activities*. In portfolio assessment, the onus is on the students to produce evidence that desirable high quality learning has taken place. A study on portfolio assessment has been successfully conducted in a part-time undergraduate program in education. The concept of portfolio assessment will be extended to postgraduate study, and its effects on teaching and learning at the postgraduate level will be investigated in a sub-project of the UGC funded ESEP Implementation Project. (ESEP, 1997)

In a related project, the notion of student-centred assessment based on the constructivist theory of learning has underpinned development of the assessment of group work for undergraduates (Kuisma, 1997).

> If students construct their learning and knowledge through active involvement in the learning task both through individual and social activity, they should be able to decide what they produce as the evidence of their learning (Biggs, 1996b). It is therefore proposed to implement a portfolio assessment of student learning in the final year group project in the Bachelor of Science in Physiotherapy course at PolyU. This portfolio assessment will replace the supervisors' assessment of student involvement, also self- and peer assessment of contribution. (Kuisma, 1997)

Portfolios do not necessarily have to be presented in hard copy format. Nott (1997) reports that in the Science Mutltimedia

Teaching Unit of the University of Melbourne (SMTU, 1997) 'students will work face to face and on-line in teams. Assessment will be to a large extent based on their individual and group on-line folios ... expressed in the form of words, video, audio, etc ... on the Web.' Further details of this program are available on the Internet at <http://www.science.unimelb.edu.au/SMTU/>. The Web page also provides useful links to on-line courses in other places around the world, classified according to discipline.

Ethics

A judge is a law student who marks his own examination papers.
(HL Mencken [1880–1956])

Professional bodies for practitioners such as accountants, doctors, lawyers and engineers place considerable emphasis on ethics. It is just as appropriate for our teaching professionals in higher education institutions to be concerned with ethics, especially in regard to assessment. This will be an ongoing development for mass higher education as it seeks to provide employment qualifications in part-nership with employer and professional bodies.

For individual ownership of quality assurance, ethical principles (Murray *et al.*, 1996) have a role to play in university teaching. A set of ethical principles has been developed by the Canadian Society for Teaching and Learning in Higher Education (CSTLHE). The five authors are 3M Fellows, ie winners of the national 3M teaching award; the publication is endorsed by 41 other 3M Fellows. These principles are not intended as *prescriptions* but rather as *descriptions* for discussion and adaptation to context ('fit for purpose'). Principle 8, Valid Assessment of Students (see below), reinforces 'the importance of assessment of student performance in university teaching and in students' lives and careers' and the responsibility of teachers.

Quality assurance and assessment expertise

In the very apposite context of guidelines on quality assurance (HEQC, 1996), assessment is considered to be the 'exercise of judgement on the quality of students' work' but emphasizing the 'need to be sensitive to the central role assessment plays in the facilitation of student learning'. There is nothing very new in these

---

Principle 8: CSTLHE Valid Assessment of Students

Given the importance of assessment of student performance in university teaching and in students' lives and careers, instructors are responsible for taking adequate steps to ensure that assessment of students is valid, open, fair, and congruent with course objectives.

This principle means that the teacher is aware of research (including personal or self-reflective research) on the advantages and disadvantages of alternative methods of assessment, and based on this knowledge, the teacher selects assessment techniques that are consistent with the objectives of the course and at the same time are as reliable and valid as possible. Furthermore, assessment procedures and grading standards are communicated clearly to students at the beginning of the course, and except in rare circumstances, there is no deviation from the announced procedures. Student exams, papers, and assignments are graded carefully and fairly through the use of a rational marking system that can be communicated to students. By means appropriate for the size of the class, students are provided with prompt and accurate feedback on their performance at regular intervals throughout the course, plus an explanation as to how their work was graded, and constructive suggestions as to how to improve their standing in the course. In a similar vein, teachers are fair and objective in writing letters of reference for students.

One example of an ethically questionable assessment practice is to grade students on skills that were not part of the announced course objectives and/or were not allocated adequate practice opportunity during the course. If students are expected to demonstrate critical inquiry skills on the final exam, they should have been given the opportunity to develop critical inquiry skills during the course. Another violation of valid assessment occurs when faculty members teaching two different sections of the same course use drastically different assessment procedures or grading standards, such that the same level of student performance earns significantly different final grades in the two sections.

Principle 8   CSTLHE, Valid assessment of students

statements and the following principles show how policy should be developed. However, for current and future development, the stumbling block is always the implementation. In your institution, ask yourself if these 'commonsense' principles are implemented cogently, coherently, and comprehensively – using meta-criteria for indicating quality (Warren Piper, 1984).

In another report on assessment (HEQC, 1997), the role of 'graduateness' is examined and the conclusion reached that much needs to be done to develop assessment expertise. In this regard, there is specific mention of the need for more formal training of staff in assessment techniques. Current and future developments in assessment are predicted:

- Staff should be adequately trained and assessment expertise updated through quality assurance programs as part of university

---

Principles

1.1 Institutions should ensure that assessment rules, regulations and criteria are published in a full and accessible form and made freely available to students, staff and external examiners.

1.2 Assessment practices should be fair, valid, reliable and appropriate to the level of award being offered. Assessment should be undertaken only by appropriately qualified staff, who have been adequately trained and briefed, and given regular opportunities to update and enhance their expertise as assessors.

1.3 Boards of examiners and assessment panels have an important role in overseeing assessment practices and maintaining standards, and institutions should develop policies and procedures governing the structure, operation and timing of their boards/panels.

1.4 Institutions should have in place policies and procedures to deal thoroughly, fairly and expeditiously with problems which arise in the course of assessment of students. These should define the actions to be taken in the event of academic misconduct, and the grounds for student appeals against assessment outcomes.

(HEQC, 1996 p. 48)

Principles

policy for the continuing professional development of all teaching staff.

- There should be national accreditation of such programs (cf. Dearing, 1997 Rec.14).
- External examining can be discounted unless it is put on a professional basis (HEQC, 1996).

A final 'prediction' is provided by the following recommendation:

We recommend that, with immediate effect, all institutions of higher education give high priority to developing and implementing learning and teaching strategies which focus on the promotion of students' learning. (Dearing, 1997 Rec. 8)

The *'bottom line' is assessment – all teaching staff must be professionally capable. This means accountability for the institution and for the individual.*

References

By necessity, by proclivity, and by delight, we all quote. In fact, it is as difficult to appropriate the thoughts of others as it is to invent.

(Ralph Waldo Emerson)

Acker, S and Warren Piper, D (eds) (1984) *Is Higher Education Fair to Women?* SRHE and NFER-Nelson, Guildford, Surrey.

Adderley, K *et al.* (1975) *Project Methods in Higher Education*, Society for Research into Higher Education, University of Surrey.

Allan, J (1996) 'Learning outcomes in higher education', *Studies in Higher Education*, vol. 21, pp. 93–108.

Anastasi, P (1976) *Psychological Testing*, Collier Macmillan, London.

Anderson, AW (1984) *Honours Awards at the University of Western Australia 1978–1982*, The University of Western Australia Research Unit in University Education.

Ashworth, P, Bannister, P and Thorne, P (1997) 'Guilty in whose eyes? University students' perceptions of cheating and plagiarism in academic work and assessment', *Studies in Higher Education*, vol. 22, pp. 187–203.

Australian Vice-Chancellors' Committee (1990) *Report of the Academic Standards Panel: Physics*, AVCC, Canberra.

Australian Vice-Chancellors' Committee (1991) *Report of the Academic Standards Panel: History*, AVCC, Canberra.

Australian Vice-Chancellors' Committee (1992a) *Report of the Academic Standards Panel: Psychology,* AVCC, Canberra.

Australian Vice-Chancellors' Committee (1992b) *Report of the Academic Standards Panel: Economics*, AVCC, Canberra.

Australian Vice-Chancellors' Committee (1995) *Fourth Year Honours Programs: Guidelines for Good Practice*, AVCC, Canberra.

Ausubel, DP (1968) *Educational Psychology: A Cognitive View*, Holt, Rinehart & Winston, New York.

Bailey, DI *et al.* (1987) 'Team design of CAI material', pp. 539–43 in AH Miller and G Sachse-Åkerlind (eds) *Research and Development in Higher*

Education – The Learner in Higher Education: A Forgotten Species? HERDSA, Sydney.

Balla, J and Boyle, P (1994) 'Assessment of student performance: A framework for improving practice', *Assessment and Evaluation in Higher Education*, vol. 19, pp. 17–28.

Bawden, R (1988) 'Assessing the capable agriculturalist', *Assessment and Evaluation in Higher Education*, vol. 13, pp. 151–62.

Beard, RM (1976) *Teaching and Learning in Higher Education* 3rd edn, Penguin, Harmondsworth.

Beard, R and Hartley, J (1984) *Teaching and Learning in Higher Education* 4th edn, Harper & Row, London.

Beard, R, Healey, FG and Holloway, PJ (1974) *Objectives in Higher Education* 2nd edn, Society for Research into Higher Education, London.

Becker, H, Geer, B and Hughes, EC (1968) *Making the Grade: The Academic Side of College Life*, Wiley, New York.

Bell, C and Harris, D (1990) *Assessment and Evaluation*, World Yearbook of Education, Kogan Page, London and Nichols Publishing, New York.

Benett, Y (1993) 'The validity and reliability of assessments and self assessments of work-based learning', *Assessment and Evaluation in Higher Education*, vol. 18, pp. 83–94.

Benson, MJ, Sporakowski, MJ and Stremmel, AJ (1992) 'Writing reviews of family literature: Guiding students using Bloom's Taxonomy of Cognitive Objectives', *Family Relations*, vol. 41, pp. 65–9.

Biggs, JB (1993) 'From theory to practice: A cognitive systems approach', *Higher Education Research and Development*, vol. 12, pp. 73–85.

Biggs, JB (1996a) 'Assessing learning quality: Reconciling institutional, staff and educational demands', *Assessment and Evaluation in Higher Education*, vol. 21, pp. 5–15.

Biggs, JB (1996b) 'Stages of expatriate involvement in educational development: Colonialism, irrelevance, or what?' *Educational Research Journal, The Hong Kong Educational Research Association*, vol. 11, pp. 157–64.

Biggs, JB and Collis, KF (1982) *Evaluating the Quality of Learning: The SOLO Taxonomy*, Academic Press, New York.

Birney, R (1964) 'The effects of grades on students', *Journal of Higher Education*, vol. 35, pp. 96–8.

Bligh, D, Jacques, D and Warren Piper, D (1981) *Seven Decisions When Teaching Students* 2nd edn, University Teaching Services, Exeter.

Bloch, JA (1977) 'Student evaluation in "individualised" science programs', *Studies in Educational Evaluation*, vol. 3, pp. 95–107.

Bloom, BS (ed.) (1956) *Taxonomy of Educational Objectives. Handbook I: Cognitive Domain*, Longman, London.

Bloom, BS (1976) *Human Characteristics and School Learning*, McGraw-Hill, New York.

Bloom, BS, Hastings, JJ and Madaus, GF (1971) *Handbook on Formative and Summative Evaluation of Student Learning*, McGraw-Hill, New York.

REFERENCES

Boud, D (1985) *Problem-based Learning in Education for the Professions*, Higher Education Research and Development Society of Australasia (HERDSA), Sydney.

Boud, D (1988) 'Assessment in problem-based learning', *Assessment and Evaluation in Higher Education*, vol. 13, pp. 87–91.

Boud, D (1989) 'The role of self-assessment in student grading', *Assessment and Evaluation in Higher Education*, vol. 14, pp. 20–30.

Boud, D (1995) *Enhancing Learning Through Self-assessment*, Kogan Page, London.

Boud, D and Falchikov, N (1989) 'Quantitative studies of student self-assessment in higher education: A critical analysis of findings', *Higher Education*, vol. 18, pp. 529–49.

Boud, D and Feletti, G (1991) *The Challenge of Problem-based Learning*, Kogan Page, London.

Bourner, J and Bourner, T (1985) 'Degrees of success in accounting', *Studies in Higher Education*, vol. 10, pp. 55–68.

Bowden, JA (1984) 'Student approaches to learning: influence of assessment in first year', *The University of Melbourne Gazette*, vol. 40, p. 10.

Bowden, JA, Masters, GN and Ramsden, P (1987) 'Influence of assessment demands on first year students' approaches to learning', pp. 397–407 in AH Miller and G Sachse-Åkerlind (eds) *Research and Development in Higher Education – The Learner in Higher Education: A Forgotten Species?* HERDSA, Sydney.

Bowden, JA and Ramsden, P (1986) *Assessment Practices and Student Learning*, Centre for the Study of Higher Education, Melbourne.

Boyer, E (1990) *Scholarship Reconsidered: Priorities of the Professoriate*, The Carnegie Foundation for the Advancement of Teaching, Princeton University Press, New Jersey.

Britton, J *et al.* (1970) 'Multiple marking of English composition', *Schools Council Examination Bulletin*, vol. 12.

Brown, S and Knight, P (1994) *Assessing Learners in Higher Education*, Teaching and Learning in Higher Education Series, Kogan Page, London.

Bunt, S (1997) Personal Communication, 26 September <smbunt @anhb.uwa.edu.au>

Burns, GR, Imrie, BW and Weatherburn, DC (1979) 'Expectations and experiences of first-year university chemistry students', *Proceedings of the Third International Conference on Chemical Education*, Dublin.

Butterworth, C (1992) 'More than one bite at the APEL', *Journal of Further and Higher Education*, vol. 16, pp. 39–51.

CARLA (1997) 'Computer-adaptive testing (CAT) research', Center for Advanced Research on Language Acquisition, University of Minnesota <http://carla.acad.umn.edu/NLRC-CAT.html>

Carter, R (1985) 'A taxonomy of objectives for professional education', *Studies in Higher Education* 10, pp. 135–49.

CELT (1994) *Avoiding Plagiarism*, English Resources Unit, Centre for the Enhancement of Learning and Teaching, University of the South Pacific.

Chapman, K (1994) 'Variability of degree results in geography in United Kingdom universities 1973–90: Preliminary results and policy implications', *Studies in Higher Education*, vol. 19, pp. 89–102.

Charter, D (1995) 'Student wins review', *The Times Higher Education Supplement*, 4 August.

Chickering, AW and Havighurst, RJ (1981) 'The life cycle', Chapter 1 in AW Chickering and Associates (eds) *The Modern American College*, Jossey-Bass, San Francisco.

CityU (1996) 'How to write a law paper', PGD/MA in Arbitration and Dispute Resolution, *Student Handbook* 1995–96, City University of Hong Kong.

CityU (1997) *Assessment Policy and Guidelines* 3rd edn, Quality Assurance Committee, City University of Hong Kong.

Clift, JC and Imrie, BW (1981) *Assessing Students, Appraising Teaching*, Croom Helm, London.

Clift, JC and Imrie BW (1994) *Assessment: Learning and performance* (floppy disc), The Open Polytechnic of New Zealand, Wellington, NZ.

Coates, H and Wright, J (1991) *Guidelines for Good Practice on the Integration of Work-based Learning with Academic Assessment*, Coventry Polytechnic, England.

Cockburn, B and Ross, A (1977a) *Inside Assessment,* Teaching in Higher Education Series: 7, School of Education, Lancaster.

Cockburn, B and Ross, A (1977b) *Essays*, Teaching in Higher Education Series: 8, School of Education, Lancaster.

Collier, KG (1985) 'Teaching methods in higher education: The changing scene, with special reference to group work', *Higher Education Research and Development*, vol. 4, pp. 3–27.

Collins, W (1983) *The New Collins Concise English Dictionary*, William Collins, Glasgow.

Confucius (1989) *A Collection of Confucius' Sayings*, An English-Chinese Bilingual Textbook, Qi Lu Press, Shandong.

Conway, R *et al.* (1993) 'Peer assessment of an individual's contribution to a group project', *Assessment and Evaluation in Higher Education*, vol. 18, pp. 45–56.

Cox, K (1993) 'Using a spreadsheet to process and analyse student marks', *Assessment and Evaluation in Higher Education*, vol. 18, pp. 115–23.

Crooks, T (1988) *Assessing Student Performance*, Green Guide 8, Higher Education Research and Development Society of Australasia, HERDSA, Sydney.

Croucher, J (1994) 'The complete guide to exam cheating', *New Scientist,* pp. 48–9.

Croucher, J (1995) 'The increasing incidence of special consideration cases at university', *Higher Education Research and Development*, vol. 14, pp. 13–20.

Croucher, JS (1996) *Exam Scams*, Allen & Unwin, St Leonards, NSW.

CSTLHE (1996) Canadian Society for Teaching and Learning in Higher Education (see H Murray *et al.*)

Cullen, DJ (ed.) (1993) *Quality in PhD Education*, Australian National University, Canberra.

Curtin University (1997) 'Computer-managed learning (CML)' <www.curtin.edu.au/curtin/dept/cc/academic/cml>

Daniel, J (1975) 'Learning styles and strategies: The work of Gordon Pask', Chapter 7 in N Entwistle and D Hounsell, *How Students Learn*, University of Lancaster, Lancaster.

Dearing, Sir Ron (1997) Chair of the National Committee of Inquiry into Higher Education, *Higher Education in the Learning Society*, HMSO, London, or available on the Internet at <www.leeds.ac.uk/educol/ncihe/>

Dillon, RF and Schmeck, RR (eds) (1983) *Individual Differences in Cognition, Vol. 1*, Academic Press, New York.

Docking, RA (1987) 'Non–destructive testing of student achievement', pp. 408–16 in AH Miller and G Sachse-Åkerlind (eds) *Research and Development in Higher Education – The Learner in Higher Education: A Forgotten Species?* HERDSA, Sydney.

Doughty, G (1996) e-mail network message, 5 January, <g.doughty@elec.gla.ac.uk>

Dressel, PL (1976) *Handbook of Academic Evaluation*, Jossey-Bass, San Francisco.

Drinan, J *et al.* (1985) 'Introduction of problem-based learning into an agricultural college curriculum', Chapter 20 in D Boud, *Problem-based Learning in Education for the Professions*, Higher Education Research and Development Society of Australasia (HERDSA), Sydney.

DSS (1995) *Fieldwork Handbook* 13th edn, Division of Social Studies, City University of Hong Kong.

Dunstan, M (1959) 'The reliabilty of examiners in marking a Leaving Certificate English examination', *Australian Journal of Education*, 3:3.

Earl, S (1986) 'Staff and peer assessment: Measuring an individual's contribution to group performance', *Assessment and Evaluation in Higher Education*, vol. 11, pp. 60–9.

Ebel, RL (1965, 1972) *Essentials of Educational Measurement* rev. edn, Prentice-Hall, Englewood Cliffs, NJ.

EECAE (1995) *2nd European Electronic Conference on Assessment and Evaluation: Self- and Co-assessment,* European Association for Research on Learning and Instruction <earliae@nic.surfnet.nl>

Elton, LRB and Laurillard, DM (1979) 'Trends in research on student learning', *Studies in Higher Education*, vol. 4, pp. 87–102.

Engel, CE and Clarke, RM (1979) 'Medical education with a difference', *Programmed Learning and Educational Technology*, vol. 16, pp. 70-87.

Entwistle, NJ and Brennan, T (1971) 'The academic performance of students. II – Types of successful students', *British Journal of Educational Psychology*, vol. 41, pp. 268–76.

Entwistle, N, Hanley, M and Hounsell, D (1979) 'Identifying distinctive approaches to studying,' *Higher Education*, vol. 8, pp. 365–80.

Entwistle, N and Hounsell, D (1975) *How Students Learn*, University of Lancaster, Lancaster.

Entwistle, N and Ramsden, P (eds) (1983) *Understanding Student Learning*. Croom Helm, London and Canberra.

EPC (1989) *Quality in Engineering Education*, Engineering Professors' Conference (UK), Occasional Paper No. 1.

EPC (1992) *Assessment Methods in Engineering Degree Courses*, Engineering Professors' Conference (UK), Occasional Paper No. 5.

Erwin, TD (1995) 'Attending to assessment: A process for faculty', Chapter 3 in P Knight (ed.) *Assessment for Learning in Higher Education*, Kogan Page, London.

ESEP (1997) 'Evaluation of the student experience (implementation) project, City University of Hong Kong', Homepage <http://www.cityu.edu.hk/pdqs/esep>

ETS (1963) *Multiple-choice Questions: A Close Look*, Educational Testing Service, Princeton.

ETS (1990) *Content Descriptions – Major Field Achievement Tests*, Educational Testing Service, Princeton.

ETS (1991) *ETS News*, Summer, Educational Testing Service, Princeton.

ETS (1997) http://etsis1.ets.org/

Evans, N (1987) *Assessing Experiential Learning,* Longman for Further Education Unit, London.

Falchikov, N and Boud, D (1989) 'Student self-assessment in higher education: A meta-analysis', *Review of Educational Research*, vol. 59, pp. 395–430.

Ferland, JJ, Dorval, J and Levasseur, L (1987) 'Measuring higher cognitive levels by multiple-choice questions: A myth?' *Medical Education*, vol. 21, pp. 109–13.

Feletti, GI (1980) 'Evaluation of a comprehensive programme for the assessment of medical students', *Higher Education*, vol. 9, pp. 169–78.

Feletti, GI (1993) 'Inquiry-based and problem-based learning: How similar are these approaches to nursing and medical education?' *Higher Education Research and Development*, vol. 12, pp. 143–56.

Fishbein, L (1993) 'Curbing cheating and restoring academic integrity' *The Chronicle of Higher Education*, 1 December.

Forbes, P (1997) Personal Communication, 8 October <pforbes@oac.usyd.edu.au> (see also OAC, 1997a).

Fox, P (1995) *Policy*, Fox Institute of Business; Personal Communication, 16 June <Patrickfox@aol.com>

Franklyn-Stokes, A and Newstead, SE (1995) 'Undergraduate cheating: Who does what and why?' *Studies in Higher Education*, vol. 20, pp. 159–72.

Freeman, M (1995) 'Peer assessment by groups of group work', *Assessment and Evaluation in Higher Education*, vol. 20, pp. 289–300.

Fulton, O, Gordon, A and Williams, G (1980) 'Higher education and manpower planning: A comparison of planned and market economies', *Education Policy Bulletin*, vol. 8, no. 1.

Gardner, D (1995) *PLAGIARISM and How to Avoid It*, University of Hong Kong: School of Research Studies.

Garvin, JW *et al.* (1995) 'Group projects for first-year university students: An evaluation', *Assessment and Evaluation in Higher Education*, vol. 20, pp. 273–88.

Gentle, CR (1995) THESYS (developed for the UK Department of Education) <mec3gentlcr@ntic.ac.uk>

Gibbs, G, Habeshaw, S and Habeshaw, T (1986) *53 Interesting Ways to Assess your Students*, Technical and Educational Services, Bristol.

Gibbs, G (1992) 'Improving the quality of student learning through course design', Chapter 10 in R Barnett (ed.) *Learning to Effect*, SRHE/Open University Press.

Glaser, R (1963) 'Instructional technology and the measurement of learning outcomes: Some questions', *American Psychologist,* vol. 18, pp. 519–21.

Goldfinch, J (1994) 'Further developments in peer assessment of group projects', *Assessment and Evaluation in Higher Education*, vol. 19, pp. 29–34.

Goldfinch, JM and Raeside, R (1990) 'Development of a peer assessment technique for obtaining individual marks on a group project', *Assessment and Evaluation in Higher Education*, vol. 15, pp. 210–25.

Gosschalk, F *et al.* (1966) *Measurement of Writing Ability*, College Examinations Board, New York.

Griffin, T (1995) Northern Illinois University Ombudsman, Personal Communication, 16 June <B40TXG1@wpo.cso.niu.edu>

Gronlund, N (1985) *Measurement and Evaluation in Teaching*, Macmillan, New York.

Hall, K (1995) 'Co-assessment: Participation of students with staff in the assessment process (A report of work in progress)', Invited Paper for EECAE (1995) <hallk@unimelb.insted.edu.au>

Hall, C and Imrie, B (1994) *Assessment of Student Performance*, Modules 1–17, 2nd edn, Victoria University of Wellington, New Zealand and City University of Hong Kong.

Halsey, Liz (1997) Personal Communication, 17 October <liz@mailserv.waikato.ac.nz>

Harris, D and Bell, C (1986) *Evaluating and Assessing for Learning*, Kogan Page, London and Nichols Publishing Company, New York.

Harrow, AA (1972) *A Taxonomy of the Psychomotor Domain*, David Mackay, New York.

Hartley, V (1984) 'The assessment of performance', *Royal Air Force Education Bulletin 22*, pp. 39–46.

Hartog, PJ and Rhodes, EC (1935) *An Examination of Examinations*, Macmillan, London.

Harvey, L (1997) quoted in 'Degrees to Work', *Times Higher Education Supplement*, 7 February, with reference to the report *Graduates Work: Organisational Change and Student Attributes*, Harvey et al., University of Central England in Birmingham.

Havighurst, RJ (1953) *Human Development and Education*, Longman, London.

HEPROC (1995) Higher Education Processes; Personal Communication <heproc-l@listserv.american.edu>

HEQC (1996) *Guidelines on Quality Assurance*, Higher Education Quality Council, London.

HEQC (1997) *Assessment in Higher Education and the Role of 'Graduateness'*, Higher Education Quality Council, London.

Hill, G (1997) Canberra Institute of Technology; Personal Communication.

Hind, D (1989a) *Transferable Personal Skills: A Student Guide*, Business Education Publishers, Sunderland.

Hind, D (1989b) *A Tutor's Guide*, Business Education Publishers, Sunderland.

HKPU (1996) 'Guidance notes on avoiding plagiarism and on bibliographic referencing', *Hong Kong Polytechnic University: Student Handbook, 1995–1996*.

Hohne, H (1975) *Success and Failure in Scientific Faculties of the University of Melbourne*, Australian Council for Educational Research, Melbourne.

Holmes, JL et al. (1992) 'The paperless essay: One way to teach writing and computer skills in medical school', *Medical Teacher* vol. 14, pp. 83–8.

Hort, LK and Hogan, AE (1988) 'Setting objectives and assessing competence in professional legal education', *Assessment and Evaluation in Higher Education*, vol. 13, pp. 92–106.

Hounsell, Dai (1979) 'Learning to learn: Research and development in student learning', *Higher Education*, vol. 8, pp. 453–69.

Imrie, BW (1981) 'Facts, factors and fallacies when marks are combined to determine student performance', *UTRC Teaching and Learning Newsletter* No. 5, Victoria University of Wellington, New Zealand.

Imrie, BW (1982) 'Evaluation of the final examination – for the professional judgement of both teacher and student performance', *Assessment and Evaluation in Higher Education*, vol. 7, pp. 85–9.

Imrie, BW (1984) 'In search of academic excellence: Samples of experience', *Proceedings of the Tenth International Conference on Improving University Experience*, Maryland, pp. 160–83.

Imrie, BW (1993) 'Hardgrind revisited', *Assessment and Evaluation in Higher Education*, vol. 18, pp. 149–53.

Imrie, BW (1995) 'Assessment for learning: Quality and taxonomies', *Assessment and Evaluation in Higher Education*, vol. 20, pp. 171–89.

IUPUI (1997) 'Introduction to computerized adaptive testing' (CAT) for placement testing, Indiana University – Purdue University Indianapolis <http://www.assessment.iupui.edu/ MTF/Cat.html>

Jackson, J and McConnell, CR (1980) *Economics – Australian Edition* McGraw-Hill, Sydney.

Jones, J and Grant, B (1991) *Writing, Setting and Marking Essays* 2nd edn, Higher Education Research Office, University of Auckland.

Keeton, WT, Dabney, MW and Zollinhofer, RE (1968) *Laboratory Guide for Biological Science*, WW Norton, New York.

Keller, FS and Sherman, JG (1974) *The Keller Plan Handbook*, Benjamin, New York.

Keyes, ME (1995) Personal Communication, 16 June <Keyesme @McMail.CIS.McMaster.ca>

Kibler, WL and Kibler, PV (1993) 'When students resort to cheating', *The Chronicle of Higher Education*, 14 July.

Kings, CB (1987) 'Improving assessment in higher education', pp. 417–22 in AH Miller and Gerlese Sachse-Åkerlind (eds) *Research and Development in Higher Education – The Learner in Higher Education: A Forgotten Species?* HERDSA, Sydney.

Knapper, CK and Cropley, AJ (1985) *Lifelong Learning and Higher Education*, Croom Helm, London.

Knight, P (ed.) (1995) *Assessment for Learning in Higher Education*, The Staff and Educational Development Series, Kogan Page, London.

Kniveton, BH (1996) 'Student perception of assessment methods', *Assessment and Evaluation in Higher Education*, vol. 21, pp. 229–37.

Kogan, M, Moses, I and El-Khawas, E (1994) *Staffing Higher Education: Meeting New Challenges*, Jessica Kingsley, OECD.

Koh-Kwok, WY (1997) Personal Communication, 2 October <wanyee@tp.ac.sg>

Krathwohl, DR, Bloom, BS and Masia, BB (1964) *Taxonomy of Educational Objectives. Handbook II: Affective Domain*, McKay, New York.

Kuisma, R (1997) Personal Communication <rskuisma@polyu.edu.hk>

Lacey, C and Lawton, D (1983) *Issues in Evaluation and Assessment*, Methuen, London.

Landbeck, R (1995) Personal Communication, 15 June <landbeck_r@ usp.ac.fj> (*no longer at USP*).

Laurillard, D (1979) 'The processes of student learning', *Higher Education*, vol. 8, pp. 395–409.

Lejk, M (1994) 'Team assessment, win or lose', *The New Academic*, Summer, pp. 10–11.

Lewis, B M (1972) 'Course production at the Open University IV: The problem of assessment', *British Journal of Educational Technology*, vol. 2, pp. 108–28.

Lindquist, E F (1953) *Design and Analysis of Experiments in Psychology and Education*, Houghton Mifflin, Boston.

Loacker, G and Jensen, P (1988) 'The power of performance in developing problem-solving and self-assessment abilities', *Assessment and Evaluation in Higher Education*, vol. 13, pp. 128–50.

Lockwood, F (1992) 'Generating assessment material', pp. 243–7 of MS Parer (ed.) *Research and Development in Education – Vol. 15 – Academia under Pressure*, HERDSA, Sydney.

Lynch, R (1990) 'Making access meaningful: Assessing the quality of developmental programs in New Jersey', *Proceedings of the Second International Conference on Assessing Quality in Higher Education*, Center for Assessment Research and Development, University of New Jersey, Knoxville, pp. 333–42.

Macadam, B (1985) 'Introducing problem-based learning into a curriculum: The Hawkesbury experience', Chapter 19 in D Boud *Enhancing Learning Through Self-assessment*, Kogan Page, London.

McDonald, R and Sansom, D (1979) 'Use of assignment attachments in assessment', *Assessment in Higher Education*, vol. 5, pp. 45–55.

McKeachie, WJ (1975) 'The decline and fall of the laws of learning', in NJ Entwistle and DJ Hounsell, *How Students Learn*, University of Lancaster, Lancaster.

McNaughton, W (1995) *Student Handbook on Writing Research Papers*, Department of Chinese, Translation and Linguistics, City University of Hong Kong.

Mager, RF (1975) *Preparing Instructional Objectives* 2nd edn, Fearon-Pitman, Belmont, California.

Mager, RF (1991) *Preparing Instructional Objectives* 2nd rev. edn, Kogan Page, London.

Maramark, S and Maline, MB (1993) *Academic Dishonesty among College Students,* Office of Research, US Department of Education, August.

Mark MJ (1995) 'Teaching academic integrity', *The Chronicle of Higher Education*, 24 November.

Marks, S (1995) *Plagiarism*, Internal paper for Board of Studies, BSc Computer Information Systems Design, Kingston University; Personal Communication, 7 June <marks@kingston.ac.uk>

Marton, F (1981) 'Phenomenography: Describing conceptions of the world around us', *Instructional Science*, vol. 10, pp. 177–200.

Marton, F and Booth, SA (1997) *Learning and Awareness*, Lawrence Erlbaum Associates, Hillsdale, NJ.

Marton, F, Hounsell, D and Entwistle, N (eds) (1984) *The Experience of Learning,* Scottish Academic Press, Edinburgh.

Marton, F and Säljö, R (1976a) 'On qualitative differences in learning. I. Outcome and process', *British Journal of Educational Psychology*, vol. 46, pp. 4–11.

Marton, F and Säljö, R (1976b) 'On qualitative differences in learning. II. Outcome as a function of the learner's conception of the task', *British Journal of Educational Psychology*, vol. 46, pp. 115–27.

Mathews, J (1977) *The Use of Objective Tests. Teaching in Higher Education Series:* 9, School of Education, Lancaster.

Miller, AH (1984) 'The evaluation of university courses', *Studies in Higher Education*, vol 9, pp. 1–15.

Miller, AH (1987) *Course Design for University Lecturers*, Kogan Page, London and Nichols Publishing Company, New York.

Miller, AH and Sachse-Åkerlind, G (eds) (1987) *Research and Development in Higher Education – The Learner in Higher Education: A Forgotten Species?* HERDSA, Sydney.

Miller, CML and Parlett, M (1974) *Up to the Mark: A Study of the Examination Game*, SRHE, London.

Moreira, WA (1980) 'A non-traditional approach to the evaluation of laboratory instruction in general physics courses', *European Journal of Science Education*, vol. 2, pp. 441–8.

Morgan, A, Gibbs, G and Taylor, E (1980) *Students' Approaches to Studying the Social Science and Technology Foundation Courses: Preliminary Studies*, Study Methods Group Report No. 4, Institute of Educational Technology, Open University.

Mortlock, RS and Storer, RJ (1973) 'Progressive assessment with first-year classes of 500', presented at 45th ANZAAS Congress, Perth, Western Australia.

Moses, I (1984) 'Supervision of higher degree students: Problem areas and possible solutions', *Higher Education Research and Development*, vol. 3, pp. 153–65.

Moses, I (1985) *Supervising Postgraduates*, HERDSA Green Guide No. 3, Sydney.

Murray, H *et al.* (1996) *Ethical Principles in University Teaching*, Society for Teaching and Learning in Higher Education, Ontario.

Nelson, GE, Robinson, GG, and Boolootian, RA (1967) *Fundamental Concepts of Biology*, John Wiley & Sons, New York.

Newble, DI and Jaeger, K (1983) 'The effect of assessment and examinations on the learning of medical students', *Medical Education*, vol. 17, pp. 25–31.

Nicol, DJ (1994) Comments on draft chapter; Personal Communication.

Nightingale, P (1984) 'Examination of research theses', *Higher Education Research and Development*, vol. 3, pp. 137–50.

Nightingale, P *et al.* (1996) *Assessing Learning in Universities*, University of New South Wales, Sydney.

Nisbet, JA (1971) 'Innovations and necessary developments in assessment in higher education', in CF Page and H Greenway (eds) *Innovation in*

Higher Education, Society for Research into Higher Education, London.

Nisbet, J and Shucksmith, J (1984) *The Seventh Sense: Reflections on Learning to Learn*, Scottish Council for Research in Education, Edinburgh.

Nott, M (1997) Personal Communication, 29 September <m.nott @science.unimelb.edu.au>

Nulty, DD and Warren Piper, D (1993) 'Degree standards in Australian universities', pp. 501–4 in AR Viskovic (ed.) *Research and Development in Higher Education, Vol. 14*, HERDSA, Wellington, NZ.

OAC (1997a) *Progression Documents used in the Diploma of Agribusiness*, Orange Agricultural College of the University of Sydney, available on Internet at http://www. sls. wau. nl/vlk/pef/pd/ pd02pref. html

OAC (1997b) *Development Document A – A Course Requirement* for Bachelor of Business (Agricultural Commerce) Orange Agricultural College of the University of Sydney, outline provided by ANG Smith.

OAC (1997c) *Development Document B – Course Requirement – Third Year* for Bachelor of Business (Agricultural Commerce) Orange Agricultural College of the University of Sydney, outline provided by ANG Smith.

Otter, S (1992) *Learning Outcomes in Higher Education*, Department for Education, London.

Page, CF and Greenway, H (eds) (1971) *Innovation in Higher Education*, Society for Research into Higher Education, London.

Page, TG and Thomas, JB with Marshall, AR (1979) *International Dictionary of Education*, Kogan Page, London.

Parer, MS (ed.) (1992) *Research and Development in Education – Vol. 15 – Academia under Pressure*, HERDSA, Sydney.

Partington, J (1994) 'Double-marking students' work', *Assessment and Evaluation in Higher Education*, vol. 19, pp. 57–60.

Pask, G (1976) 'Styles and strategies of learning', *British Journal of Educational Psychology*, vol. 46, pp. 128–48.

Pask, G and Scott, BCE (1972) 'Learning strategies and individual competence', *International Journal of Man-Machine Studies*, vol. 4, pp. 217–53.

Paul, J (1994) 'Improving education through computer-based alternative assessment methods', *People and Computers*, vol. 9, pp. 81–90, Cambridge University Press.

Penny, AJ and Grover, C (1996) 'An analysis of student grade expectations and marker consistency', *Assessment and Evaluation in Higher Education*, vol. 21, pp. 173–83.

Perry, WG (1970) *Forms of Intellectual and Ethical Development in the College Years*, Holt, Rinehart & Winston, New York.

Perry, WG (1981) 'Cognitive and ethical growth: The making of meaning', Chapter 3 in AW Chickering and Associates (eds) *The Modern American College*, Jossey-Bass, San Francisco.

Petter, A (1982) 'A closet within a house: Learning objectives and the law school curriculum', Chapter 5 in A Petter, *Essays in Legal Education*, Butterworth, Ontario, Canada.

Pettigrove, M and Pearson, M (1996) *Research and Development in Higher Education, Vol. 17* (Proceedings of the 20th annual conference held in July, 1994), HERDSA, Canberra.

Phillips, E (1993) 'The concept of quality in the PhD', Chapter 1 in DJ Cullen (ed.) *Quality in PhD Education*, Australian National University, Canberra.

Piaget, J and Inhelder, B (1969) *The Psychology of the Child*, Routledge & Kegan Paul, London.

Pole, C (1993) *Assessing and Recording Achievement*, Open University Press, Milton Keynes.

Pollard, G (1989) 'Further scoring systems to remove guessing in multiple-choice examinations', *Mathematics Competitions*, vol. 2, pp. 27–42.

PS News (1996) *PS News: A Sharing of Ideas About Problem Solving*, D Woods, (ed.), Department of Chemical Engineering, McMaster University, July/August.

Pudlowski, Z and Rados, M (1987) 'The computer testing of student aptitude for electrical engineering', pp. 545–53 in AH Miller and G Sachse-Åkerlind (eds) *Research and Development in Higher Education – The Learner in Higher Education: A Forgotten Species?* HERDSA, Sydney.

Rafiq, Y and Fullerton, H (1996) 'Peer assessment of group projects in civil engineering', *Assessment and Evaluation in Higher Education*, vol. 21, pp. 69–81.

Ramsden, P (1979) 'Student learning and perceptions in the academic environment', *Higher Education*, vol. 8, pp. 411–27.

Ramsden, P (1982) 'How academic departments influence students' learning', *HERDSA News*, vol. 4, pp. 3–5.

Ramsden, P (1984) 'The context of learning', in F Marton, D Hounsell and N Entwistle (eds) *The Experience of Learning*, Scottish Academic Press, Edinburgh.

Ramsden, P (1986) 'Students and quality', in GC Moodie (ed.) *Standards and Criteria in Higher Education*, SRHE and NFER-Nelson, Guildford, Surrey.

Ramsden, P (1992) *Learning to Teach in Higher Education*, Routledge, London.

Ramsden, P and Entwistle, N (1981) 'Effects of academic departments on students' approaches to learning', *British Journal of Educational Psychology*, vol. 51, pp. 368–83.

Reeves, MF (1990) 'An application of Bloom's Taxonomy to the teaching of business ethics', *Journal of Business Ethics*, vol. 9, pp. 609–16.

Reid, S (1995) Personal Communication, 21 June, Dept of English, University of Wyoming, <sreid@uwyo.edu>

Richards, O (1995) Personal Communication <owenr@admin.sussex.ac.uk>

Roizen, J and Jepson, M (1985) *Degrees for Jobs: Employer Expectations of Higher Education*, SRHE and NFER-Nelson, Guildford, Surrey.

Rowntree, Derek (1987) *Assessing Students – How Shall We Know Them?* 2nd edn, Harper & Row, London.

Royer, JM, Cisero, CA and Carlo, MS (1993) 'Techniques and procedures for assessing cognitive skills', *Review of Educational Research*, vol. 63, pp. 201–43.

Säljö, R (1982) *Learning and Understanding*, ACTA Universitatis Gothoburgensis, Gothenburg.

Schmeck, RR (1983) 'Learning styles of college students', Chapter 8 in RF Dillon and RR Schmeck (eds) *Individual Differences in Cognition, Vol. 1*, Academic Press, New York.

Science and Engineering Research Council of Great Britain (1983) *Research Student and Supervisor: An Approach to Good Supervisory Practice*, SERC, London.

Scouller, KM and Prosser, M (1994) 'Students' experiences in studying for multiple-choice question examinations', *Studies in Higher Education*, vol. 19, pp. 267–79.

Simpson, EJ (1966) 'The classification of educational objectives, psychomotor domain', *Illinois Teacher of Home Economics*, vol. 10, pp. 110–44.

Singer, R (1990) 'Technology in Chinese educational development', in C Bell and D Harris, *Assessment and Evaluation*, World Yearbook of Education, Kogan Page, London and Nichols Publishing, New York.

Smith, ANG (1997) Personal Communication, 25 October <tsmith@oac.usyd.edu.au>

Smith, K (1995) Personal Communication, 20 June <smith@ext.missouri. edu>

SMTU (1997) *Science Multimedia Teaching Unit*, University of Melbourne http://www.science.unimelb.edu.au/SMTU/

Snyder, BR (1971) *The Hidden Curriculum*, Knopf, New York.

SRHE (1980) *Research Into Higher Education Abstracts*, vol. 13, p. 387.

Sparkes, JJ (1994) 'Defining quality is easy, achieving it is the problem', paper presented to the 20th International Conference on Improving University Teaching, University of Maryland University College.

Steinaker, NW and Bell, MR (1979) *The Experiential Taxonomy*, Academic Press, New York.

Svensson, L (1977) 'On qualitative differences in learning. III. Study skill and learning', *British Journal of Educational Psychology*, vol. 47, pp. 233–43.

Swinnerton-Dyer, P (1982) (Advisory Board for Research Councils), *Report of the Working Party on Postgraduate Education*, HMSO, London (cited in Moses, 1985).

Sykes, JB (ed.) (1982) *The Concise Oxford Dictionary* 7th edn, Clarendon Press, Oxford.

Tang, C (1997) Personal Communication <etcktang@polyu.edu.hk>

Tang, C and Biggs, J (1997) 'Assessment by portfolio', ESP Conference Report, *Evaluation of the Student Experience Project*, City University of Hong Kong, p. 26, May.

Terwilliger, JS (1977) 'Assigning grades: Philosophical issues and practical recommendations', *Journal of Research and Development in Education*, vol. 10, pp. 21–39.

Thorndike, R and Hagen, EP (1977) *Measurement and Evaluation in Psychology and Education* 4th edn, John Wiley & Sons, New York.

Toohey, S (1996) 'Implementing student self-assessment: Some guidance from the research literature', in P Nightingale *et al.*, *Assessing Learning in Universities*, University of New South Wales, Sydney.

Trevitt, C and Pettigrove, M (1995) 'Towards autonomous criterion-referenced assessment and self-assessment: A case study', Invited paper for EECAE (1995) <cft652@pophost.anu.edu.au>

Trigwell, K (1987) 'Insight into knowledge boundaries from crib cards', pp. 423–8 in AH Miller and G Sachse-Åkerlind (eds) *Research and Development in Higher Education – The Learner in Higher Education: A Forgotten Species?* HERDSA, Sydney.

Trowler, P (1996) 'Angels in marble? Accrediting prior experiential learning in higher education', *Studies in Higher Education*, vol. 21, pp. 17–30.

Tuckman, BW (1975) *Measuring Educational Outcomes: Fundamentals of Testing*, Harcourt Brace, New York.

UGC (1996) *Higher Education in Hong Kong*, Report by the University Grants Committee, October.

UGC (1997) *TLQPR Seminar Report*, 8 April, City University of Hong Kong.

UNE (1996) 'Thinking of more study? What's new for you', *Afterthoughts*, vol. 4, p. 24, University of New England, Armidale, NSW.

University of Glasgow (1993) *Calendar 1993–94*, The University of Glasgow, Glasgow.

University of London (1976) *Introduction and Guide to the Use of Multiple-choice Questions in University Examinations*, University of London, London.

UPGC (1994) 'Assessment of teaching and learning quality', Consultation Paper, University and Polytechnic Grants Committee, Hong Kong, 28 May.

USP (1994) *Regulations, Statutes, Charter and Ordinances*, pp. 116-17, University of the South Pacific, Suva.

UWA (1997) 'Investigative human biology', http://130. 95. 96. 201

Vassiloglou, M and French, S (1982) 'Arrow's theorem and examination assessment', *British Journal of Mathematical and Statistical Psychology*, vol. 35, pp. 183–92.

Villee, CA (1967) *Biology*, 5th edn, WB Saunders, Philadelphia and London.

Viskovic, AR (ed.) (1993) *Research and Development in Higher Education, Vol. 14*, HERDSA, Wellington, NZ.

Wagner, ZM (1996) 'Assessment in a problem-based design curriculum', Theme No. 16 in M Pettigrove and M Pearson (1996) *Research and Development in Higher Education, Vol. 17* (Proceedings of the 20th annual conference held in July, 1994), HERDSA, Canberra.

Warren Piper, D (1984) 'The question of fairness', in S Acker and D Warren Piper (eds), *Is Higher Education Fair to Women?* SRHE and NFER-Nelson, Guildford, Surrey.

Warren Piper, D, Nulty, DD and O'Grady, G (1995) *Examination Practices and Procedures in Australian Universities*, Unpublished report prepared for the Australian Department of Education, Employment and Training.

Whiteley, JM and Yokota, N (1987) 'Character development in the freshman year', Paper delivered to the 2nd International Conference on the First Year Experience, Southampton University, July.

Whittier (1995) *Policy on Academic Honesty,* Whittier College, California.

Wiggins, G (1989) 'A true test: Toward more authentic and equitable assessment', *Phi Delta Kappan*, vol. 70, pp. 703–13.

Williams, E (1992) 'Student attitudes towards approaches to learning and assessment', *Assessment and Evaluation in Higher Education*, vol. 17, pp. 45–58.

Winer, BJ, Brown, DR, and Michels, KW (1991) *Statistical Principles in Experimental Design*, 3rd edn, McGraw-Hill, New York.

Winter, R (1993) 'Education or grading? Arguments for a non-subdivided honours degree', *Studies in Higher Education*, vol. 18, pp. 363-77.

Winter, R (1994) 'Work-based learning and quality assurance in higher education', *Assessment and Evaluation in Higher Education*, vol. 19, pp. 247–57.

Wisker, G (1997) Personal Communication <gwisker@bridge.anglia.ac.uk>

Woods, DR, Marshall, RR and Hrymak, AN (1988) 'Self-assessment in the context of the McMaster problem-solving programme', *Assessment and Evaluation in Higher Education*, vol. 13, pp. 107–27.

Zuber-Skerritt, O and Knight, N (1986) 'Problem definition and thesis writing workshops for the postgraduate student', *Higher Education*, vol. 15, pp. 89–103.

Index

If you don't find it in the index, look very carefully through the entire catalogue.
(Sears, Roebuck, and Co, Consumer's Guide, 1897)

academic integrity   229, 241–8, 254
adjustment of marks   210–20
administration of assessment   209–10
admission requirements   10, 23, 30–1, 154, 227
analysis of grades   205–24
aptitude tests   29, 141, 156–7, 178
assessment vs evaluation   3
assessment defined   4

capability   10, 12, 165, 258
cheating see also plagiarism   20–1, 103, 116, 159, 241–52
codes of ethics   248, 262
comparison of groups   213–14
competency based learning   27–8, 187, 215
computer adaptive testing   258
computer managed assessment   153–5, 209–10, 234, 255–9
computer managed learning   155–7, 257–8
continuous assessment   34–5, 88–93, 226, 256
contribution of individual marks to final grade 210–14
cooperative learning   159, 169, 189
creative performance   31, 70–1, 191–2, 198–9
credit exchange   188
criterion vs norm referencing   24–30, 110–12, 165–6, 208
critical thinking   43, 48, 56, 185
cue consciousness   145

data entry   222–3
diagnostic tests   30–1
double marking   108–9, 231

educational objectives   21, 25, 27–30, 40, 45–75, 95, 143
Educational Testing Service (ETS)   141–2, 146, 215, 258
employers' expectations   12–13, 16, 22, 189–91, 235, 254
employment experience see learning:work-based
essay questions   21, 31, 32, 51, 52, 55, 87, 92, 95–123
   criteria for grading   59, 81, 108, 110–12, 120–1, 259
   drafts   114–16
   examples   116–20
   key terms   105–7

markers' comments   112–14
marking   108–16, 231
setting   104–8
types   96–104
establishment of standards   25–33, 39–40, 111, 128–34, 176, 182–3, 231, 237, 249
evaluation of assessment   225–40
   by accreditation agencies   240
   by colleagues   238–9
   by departmental reviews   239
   by external examiners   129–32, 138, 238
   by student committees   238
   by student surveys   239
external influences on assessment   231–4

facilities for major examinations   195–7
facilities for practical work   181–2
feedback on performance   89, 112–16, 131, 209, 220–1
field work   175–92
final examinations   90–2, 104–8, 193–201, 226
formative vs summative assessment   32–4, 87–92, 98, 209, 227
framework for achievement
   absolute   25–6
   content   24
   normative   25
functions of assessment   4, 23–40, 206, 226–7
functions of higher education   9–22
   academic   15–16
   basis for lifelong learning   14, 19
   cultural   11–15, 19–22
   functional   11–15, 19–22
   perpetuating   12, 15
   professional   16–19
   social   11–15
   vocational   15–19
future developments   253–64

grade point average   37
grades   20, 26–7, 32–3, 88–91, 109–111, 116, 120–1, 131, 165–6, 171–4, 177, 180, 183, 194, 207–8
graphical representations   214–15
group projects   158–74, 184, 261
guidelines for good practice   129–32, 246–7, 264

honours degrees   34–7, 125–32, 135, 139, 239

281

individual contribution to syndicates 165–7
influence of assessment on learning 35–6, 41–5,
   58, 88, 143, 227–30
institutional responsibility 206–8, 221–4
interactions with clients 185–6
internet, use of 255–8

laboratory work 177–81
learning
   approaches to 41–5, 228
   contracts 187
   deep vs surface 42–5, 58–61, 88, 143, 227, 233
   experiential 17
   for understanding 43–5, 58, 61, 91, 143, 169,
      228
   goals 10, 209
   inquiry-based 184–5
   mastery 27, 97
   outcomes 18, 21, 46, 182–3
   problem-based 17, 80, 182–5
   serialist vs holist 41–2
   styles and strategies 32, 41–5, 71, 91, 143,
      225–31, 238
   work-based 12–15, 186–91
levels of objectives, affective
   characterization 68–9
   organization 67–8
   receiving 66
   responding 66–7
   valuing 67
levels of objectives, cognitive
   analysis 50–2, 107
   application 49–50
   comprehension 48–9
   evaluation 53, 104
   recall 48
   synthesis 52–3

measuring
   achievement 23–8, 33, 35, 37, 88, 157
   potential 23, 33
   research skills 125–40
   teaching quality 38–40
metacognitive skills 62
motivation
   extrinsic 16
   influences on 229
   intrinsic 16

objective tests 141–57
   compare and contrast 151–2
   completion 147–8
   definitions 151
   diagrams 151
   marking of 153–5
   matching 149–50
   multiple completion 148–9
   multiple grid 148
   multiple-choice 31, 49, 142–6, 152, 155
   relationship analysis 150
   review of 152
   true-false 146–7
objectives, domains of 46–7
   affective 54, 58–9, 62, 65–9
   cognitive 41–63, 95, 143, 193
   psychomotor 69–71
   relationships between domains 55, 71–4
open book examinations 199
optical mark reading 154
originality 58, 121, 126, 129, 138, 173

participation in discussion 166
peer-assessment see also self and peer assessment
   169–74
Personalised System of Instruction (PSI) 27
phenomenographic research 137
plagiarism 241–52
portfolios, use in assessment 259–62
practical skills 17, 21, 35–6, 69, 156, 175–92,
   195
prior learning, accreditation of 46, 188–91
professional development 18, 165, 259, 261, 264
professional experience see also field work 13, 15,
   18, 37, 175–7, 185–92, 260
progress files see portfolios, use in assessment
projects 164–5, 258–9, 261
psychomotor skills see taxonomies of objectives –
   psychomotor

qualitative vs quantitative research 136–8
quality assurance 129, 250, 254–5, 262–4
quantity or quality of learning? 228

ranking of grades 210–20
recording students' achievements see also reporting
   on assessment 36–8, 206
redemptive work 115–16
relating assessment to objectives 60–3, 74–5,
   193–4
reliability 108–10, 142, 172, 176, 187, 198, 235
reporting on assessment 205–24
responsibility of supervisors 128–40

self and peer assessment 166–74
self assessment see also self and peer assessment
   167–9, 183
social context 11
special examinations 90, 232, 246
stages in intellectual development 77–83
   commitment 81–2
   dualism 77–9
   multiplicity 79–80
   relativism 80–1
   transitional 82–3
student choice in assessment 91, 100, 101, 108,
   126–7, 197–8
studio work 177–80
supervision of postgraduate research 127–34
syndicates 160–4

taxonomies of objectives
   affective (Krathwohl) 65–9
   cognitive (Bloom) 47–53
   cognitive (Crooks) 56–7
   cognitive (experiential) 58–9
   cognitive (RECAP) 54–5
   experiential 58–9
   professional education 72–4
   psychomotor (Harrow) 69–71
team work 160–4
theses 125–40
timing of assessment 87–93, 194–5
transcripts of results 206–8

university regulations 138, 232, 242, 245–6, 264

validity 142, 152, 177, 187, 198, 233–5, 263

weighting see also adjustment of marks 212
work experience see also professional experience
   13, 37, 235, 260